5.95
dir

CLUES
PR6019 Z52638
CHACE JOYCE: A COLLECTION OF C

||||||||||||||||||||||||||||
☑ **W9-BSP-188**

CM 00 0090249

PR   73—1008
6019   Chace,
09   Joyce.
Z52638
                JUL   2000
            Date Due

		JUN 2004
		JUN JUL 09
		JUL XX 2015

PRINTED IN U.S.A.

TWENTIETH CENTURY VIEWS

The aim of this series is to present the best in contemporary critical opinion on major authors, providing a twentieth century perspective on their changing status in an era of profound revaluation.

Maynard Mack, *Series Editor*
Yale University

Joyce writing a sentence

Drawn by Guy Davenport

JOYCE

A COLLECTION OF CRITICAL ESSAYS

Edited by

William M. Chace

Prentice-Hall, Inc.
A SPECTRUM BOOK
Englewood Cliffs, N.J.

CUMBERLAND COUNTY COLLEGE
LEARNING RESOURCE CENTER
P. O. BOX 517
VINELAND, N. J. 08360

PR
6019
.O9
Z52638

73-1008

Library of Congress Cataloging in Publication Data

CHACE, WILLIAM M. COMP.
   Joyce: a collection of critical essays.

   (Twentieth century views) (A Spectrum Book)
   CONTENTS: Dubliners: Cixous, H. Political ignominy;
"Ivy day." Ellmann, R. The backgrounds of "The dead."—
A portrait of the artist as a young man: Kenner, H.
The portrait in perspective.—Ulysses: Wilson, E.
James Joyce. Goldberg, S. L. Homer and the nightmare
of history. Cronin, A. The advent of Bloom. Ellmann, R.
Why Molly Bloom menstruates. [etc.]

   1. Joyce, James, 1882–1941. I. Title.
PR6019.O9Z52638   823'.9'12   73–18496
ISBN 0–13–511303–2
ISBN 0–13–511295–8 (pbk.)

© 1974 by Prentice-Hall, Inc., Englewood Cliffs, New Jersey. A SPECTRUM BOOK.
All rights reserved. No part of this book may be reproduced in any form or by any
means without permission in writing from the publisher. Printed in the United States
of America.

10   9   8   7   6   5   4   3   2   1

PRENTICE-HALL INTERNATIONAL, INC. (*London*)
PRENTICE-HALL OF AUSTRALIA PTY. LTD. (*Sydney*)
PRENTICE-HALL OF CANADA LTD. (*Toronto*)
PRENTICE-HALL OF INDIA PRIVATE LIMITED (*New Delhi*)
PRENTICE-HALL OF JAPAN, INC. (*Tokyo*)

Acknowledgments

Quotations from the following works of James Joyce are used by kind permission of The Viking Press, Inc., Jonathan Cape Ltd, and The Society of Authors, literary representative of the Estate of James Joyce:

A Portrait of the Artist as a Young Man. Copyright © 1964 by the Estate of James Joyce. All rights reserved.

Dubliners. Copyright © 1967 by the Estate of James Joyce. All rights reserved.

Quotations from *Finnegans Wake* by James Joyce are used by kind permission of The Viking Press, Inc. and The Society of Authors, literary representative of the Estate of James Joyce. Copyright © 1939 by James Joyce; © 1967 by George Joyce and Lucia Joyce.

Quotations from *Ulysses* are used by kind permission of Random House, Inc. and The Bodley Head. Copyright 1914, 1918 by Margaret Caroline Anderson and renewed 1942, 1946 by Nora Joseph Joyce.

Quotations from *Stephen Hero* are used by kind permission of Jonathan Cape Ltd and The Society of Authors, literary representative of the Estate of James Joyce.

The frontispiece is used by the kind permission of Guy Davenport. It originally appeared in *Flaubert, Joyce and Beckett: The Stoic Comedians*, by Hugh Kenner (Boston: Beacon Press, 1963).

Contents

Finnegans Wake

Retrospection

Introduction

In "The Dead," we learn of a horse named Johnny, inured to the steady circular labor of driving a mill in a glue factory. He was brought out one day by his master to review a military parade, and "everything went on beautifully until Johnny came in sight of King Billy's statue: and whether he fell in love with the horse King Billy sits on or whether he thought he was back again in the mill, anyhow he began to walk round the statue." James Joyce, who sometimes pleasured himself by thinking of events in his fictional works as prophetic, might have drawn some enjoyment from today's continuing spectacle of the horse, the mill, and the statue. In the world of Joycean scholarship, the horse forever circles the statue, habituated to its labor; the mill operates ceaselessly.

And Joyce, whose entire writing life was a protracted struggle against time, poverty, emotional crises, semiblindness, and public misunderstanding, might have found something to admire in the steadiness with which the mill grinds on. One of those now harnessed to the labor, his attention loyally fixed to one part of Joycean statuary, has declared of the story "The Boarding House": "If it was written by Joyce, there should be things to explicate." Having in his later years discovered the advantages of collecting about himself a small team of workers to whom questions, errands, and learning projects could be given, Joyce would have found interesting the ways in which his own amateur helpers have by now been supplanted by professional exegetes and commentators (mostly American, a nationality that had never gained his affections) whose efforts are a model of relentlessly systematic investigation. They do, in every aspect of Joyce's achievement, find things to explicate.

Just as their unremitting labors are now a part of the Joycean spectacle, so also are comments akin to mine above. One customarily explores the landscape of Joycean scholarship by first noting how densely crowded it is; one then looks about for a place to deposit one more interpretation. Here, however, the custom will not be observed. No new interpretation can be offered. Instead, a few observations on the statue, the horse, and the mill.

The statue itself, Joyce's achievement, seems to have proved awesome enough over the years to dissuade most critics from doing much more than walking round it with respect, remarking on parts and pieces. Having invited little serious criticism of its ultimate value (save from those, such as publishers and printers, anxious about its alleged obscenity),

Joyce's work has become known to many readers for its prefect integrity in part and whole, the production of an encyclopedic and infallibly disciplined mind. This Joyce serves the explicators well; they may begin with the assumption of absolute control on the part of the author, and then proceed to show how the wizardry manifests itself. Against this kind of reverence few writers have spoken out. The most important of the early iconoclasts was Wyndham Lewis, whose boisterous and overwritten attack on what he thought was the formlessness of Joyce's work is not now much read. Lewis saw Joyce's mind as one more victim of the Bergsonian time-cult, caught in a flux of objects without means of judgment or escape. Joyce was the logical end result of Naturalism, of a fascination with *matter,* of absorption in detail without recourse to the ventilating power of abstraction.

Lewis's pugnacious refusal to be awed by the statue has had two important results for readers today. The first was Stuart Gilbert's pioneering analysis, chapter by chapter, of *Ulysses* (1930). The second has been Hugh Kenner's view of Joyce. Gilbert's book, composed with Joyce's own help and in reaction to Lewis's attack, is a patient elaboration of the minutely organized structural details of the novel. It offers a picture of Joyce as one wholly consumed in organization and pattern: organ, art, color, symbol, and technic are the terms out of which the novel is shown to have grown. Not flux, but mastery and control. Gilbert's book and its famous schema of correspondences have since been central to any classroom reading of Joyce; so central, in fact, that a few readers have transported its vision of Joyce to other of his works than *Ulysses.* Thus, in 1944 two scholars, Richard Levin and Charles Shattuck, brought forth the finding that *Dubliners* is no mere collection of stories somehow connected with the social paralysis of Dublin life, but a work whose organization also issues from a parallel, finely conceived, with Homer. Just as *Ulysses,* with its Telemachiad and Nostos, mirrors the *Odyssey,* so do the fifteen stories, held in tight structural union, from "The Sisters" through to "The Dead."

Although such exegetical performances today seem embarrassing ways to honor the statue, they permit us to see the awe the statue can evoke. So strong is that power that even with one of the first of the sustained critical achievements, unaided by Joyce himself and written with more than exegesis in mind—that by Hugh Kenner (*Dublin's Joyce,* 1956)— the reverence remains almost wholly pure. Kenner, all of whose brilliant encounters with certain great modernists (Pound, Eliot, Lewis, Beckett) are a function of his mimetic adoption of their vocabulary and stance, was able to imagine Joyce from the inside out. As temporary owner of the Joycean mask, Kenner could pontificate that Joyce's books were the work of a master ironist, and although he agreed with Lewis that Joyce was preoccupied with the matter of the universe, that this was no weakness derived from Bergson, but a strength. Joyce's willing absorption in detail,

his fact-ridden Naturalism, his exploitation of the emotional and linguistic clichés of Dublin—all are means to high parody. Dublin is a city
of the paralyzed and dead, Joyce's characters speak lifeless language, spirituality is inert. Behind and above this meaninglessness, the artist reigns
supreme. Having given his absurd characters a world evacuated of sense in
which to bang about, he suffuses them with irony. Thus Bloom, a mere
"sentimental Jew," is amorphous and pathetic; his wife Molly is smugly
given over to the body, and her famous "Yes" is one that "kills the soul"
and "has darkened the intellect and blunted the moral sense of all Dublin." Stephen, in both *Ulysses* and *A Portrait of the Artist as a Young
Man,* is an "indigestibly Byronic hero," and he shows what happens when
idealistic Romanticism runs free. When we read the later book, we are
asked by Kenner to see what an insufferable prig Stephen is in *A Portrait*.
The earlier novel is to be read, in fact, as the tale of one who becomes
no artist, but only an esthete, and whose final vision of freedom is "mur-
derously lambasted" in *Ulysses*. Only when Kenner admits that his reading of *A Portrait* renders the last forty pages of that novel very heavy
going—"an intolerable strain on the reader"—and when he warns that
A Portrait cannot truly be appreciated without *Ulysses* on the reading
table beside it, does his gaze at the statue seem to flicker.

The care, however, with which he disentangles the many elements of
A Portrait and *Ulysses,* and the intellectual sophistication that he brings
to the novels, make his approach a turning point in the critical history.
His animadversions about the unsatisfactory end of *A Portrait* have
called forth many answers and "solutions"—none wholly satisfactory.[1]
His assumption that Joyce must be taken primarily as an ironist is a
provocation to which every reader will find himself again and again
returning.

Much of the criticism before Kenner's book, some of it gathered in
Seon Given's *James Joyce: Two Decades of Criticism* (1948), reflects the
need felt by earlier writers to legitimize Joyce, to transcend the legal
controversy surrounding him, to separate him from Dadaism, Surrealism,
and Expressionism, to insist on the order manifest in his achievements.
T. S. Eliot saw him in 1923 as a "classicist" who, in pursuing an ancient
myth within modern circumstances, was helping to give shape to "the
immense panorama of futility and anarchy which is contemporary history." [2] He was also, by peculiar coincidence, combining past and present
in ways similar to Eliot's own. Ezra Pound, who had done much to get
Joyce into print, saw *Ulysses* in the year of its publication, 1922, as a con-

---

[1] But for two particularly admirable efforts, see Wayne Booth, "The Problem of
Distance in *A Portrait of the Artist as a Young Man,*" in his *The Rhetoric of Fiction*
(Chicago: The University of Chicago Press, 1961), pp. 323–36; and F. Parvin Sharpless,
"Irony in Joyce's *Portrait:* The Stasis of Pity," *James Joyce Quarterly* (Summer 1967),
pp. 320–30.

[2] "Ulysses, Order and Myth," *Dial* LXXV, 5 (November 1923), 480–83.

tinuation of the art of writing "where Flaubert left it." [3] Eliot rather thought the novel as a possible art form to have passed into obsolescence before Joyce got to it; Pound thought Joyce had moved it a quantum jump ahead. But both, as early watchers of the statue, were willing to let the term "novel" stand for what Joyce had done.

With Gilbert's Homeric reading available as a semiofficial pronouncement, however, other terms were set by which many readers could approach *Ulysses*: not as a novel, but as a compendium of symbols, esoteric knowledge, labyrinthine connections. The work as mosaic, the reader as initiate, the artist as lord of his creation; such things early became staples of Joycean study. Cutting against the mystique was the analysis presented by Edmund Wilson (in *Axel's Castle*, 1931). Determined to read *A Portrait*, *Ulysses*, and even *Finnegans Wake* as novels, even while praising their symbolic richness, Wilson offered an approach to Joyce still eminently solid today: an approach emphasizing the accessibility of the works once certain rules are understood, but not succumbed to. Wilson sets forth many of the most compelling Homeric parallels, but urges us to see that Joyce was not enclosed by them. Seeing Joyce's world, particularly that of *Ulysses*, as informed by both the omnivorous grasp of Naturalism and the special interior density of Symbolism, he treats Joyce's mind as that of a poet, "playing a rôle absolutely impersonal and always imposing upon itself all the Naturalistic reactions in regard to the story it is telling at the same time that it allows itself to exercise all the Symbolistic privileges in regard to the way it tells it." While thus preserving for Joyce his standing as a poet (something Joyce's own poems fall short of doing), Wilson also gives us a way to appreciate his much-acclaimed technical virtuosity—not as an end in itself but as a new means to enlarge our apprehension of the psychological life all around us. As Wilson moved beyond mere praise of Joyce's ability with words ("I have discovered I can do anything I want with language," Joyce once grandiosely said), he pointed out a step that every serious reader of the novelist one day takes.

Wilson's essay not only represents a departure in the steady movement round the statue; it is unusual for quite another kind of reason. That is, Wilson criticizes Joyce. Negative criticism had hitherto largely been the preserve of weekly reviewers (". . . inartistic, incoherent, unquotably nasty—a book that one would think could only emanate from a criminal lunatic asylum," wrote one of *Ulysses*) and certain other notable writers of the period—like Virginia Woolf, E. M. Forster, and G. B. Shaw—all of whom, while politely respecting Joyce's abilities, were disgusted by the irregular uses to which he put them. Wilson's criticism, by contrast, is concerned not with irregularity of any sort but with prodigality. He sees Joyce's work as suffering from the "excess of design" brought

[3] "Paris Letter," *Dial*, LXXII, 6 (June 1922), 623–29.

to bear on it. Joyce, possessing no solicitude for his reader, simply gave him too much to absorb. Therefore, while Gilbert's authorized *vade mecum* shows us how much is there to be dug out, it also reveals how much we are inevitably missing. Joyce has overwhelmed us, and he has done so because, as a novelist, he lacks the ability to move things ahead dramatically, as a novelist should. He responds to dramatic opportunity with verbal resourcefulness. His fiction suffers from being static.

Wilson's criticism has been echoed in various ways by, among others, Harry Levin and, more lately, S. L. Goldberg. Levin's compact study (1941), which is still the very best of all the introductory books, also points to the essential stasis of Joyce's picture of that one extraordinary and un-exceptional Dublin day, June 16, 1904. Levin locates, moreover, the appropriate aesthetic principle governing not only the stasis of *Ulysses* but, by implication, the paralysis of *Dubliners,* the circularity of *Finnegans Wake.* "Characterization in Joyce," says Levin, "is finally reducible to a few stylized gestures and simplified attitudes." He argues that Joyce's works are limited in their psychological insight to the degree that they are rich in technical brilliance because Joyce remained true to the rules of art enunciated first in *A Portrait:* "Aristotle has not defined pity and terror. I have. . . . Pity is the feeling which arrests the mind in the presence of whatsoever is grave and constant in human sufferings and unites it with the human sufferer. Terror is the feeling which arrests the mind in the presence of whatsoever is grave and constant in human sufferings and unites it with the secret cause. . . . You see, I use the word *arrest* . . . the esthetic emotion . . . is therefore static." These words, evoked by virtually all Joyce's commentators and evaluated with greatest care and thoroughness in 1946 by Irene H. Chayes[4]—who also provides a detailed analysis of the importance of the Joycean epiphany—are crucial to Levin because they explain why so little happens in Joyce, and why such negligibility is stuffed with such tumultuous linguistic energy.

The vexing question of Joyce's success or failure as a dramatic novelist is given its most complex and satisfying treatment in S. L. Goldberg's extraordinarily good book on *Ulysses* (*The Classical Temper,* 1961). Its excellence stems in part from Goldberg's recognition that Joyce calls for criticism as much as explication, and that Wilson was wise indeed in refusing to treat *Ulysses* or any of Joyce's works as sacred books of the arts. Goldberg sustains for the length of his book one central thesis: the meaning of the novel lies in the ways its human experience is realized and ordered. Joyce is not primarily a parodist, a philosopher, a linguist, or a maker of myths. He is a novelist, faced with the same obligation as any novelist—to give imaginative illumination to the moral experience of certain human beings. Goldberg, who owes much of his own critical sensi-

---

[4] See her essay "Joyce's Epiphanies" in Seon Givens, ed., *James Joyce: Two Decades of Criticism* (New York: Vanguard Press, 1948), pp. 27–46. The essay appeared originally in *The Sewanee Review,* LIV, 3 (July–September 1946), 449–67.

bility to F. R. Leavis, responds to the criticism offered by Wilson and by
Levin by simply treating the acclaimed technical virtuosity of Joyce's
method as trivial compared to the dramatic situation posed by the exist-
ences, within *Ulysses,* of Molly and Leopold Bloom and of Stephen
Dedalus. Joyce, in coming to terms with the opportunities they presented,
achieved the temper by which dogma, explicit belief, metaphysics, and
abstractions are repulsed. That temper is open instead to what is cen-
trally human; Goldberg opens himself to the lives of the three central
characters as the meanings of those lives are enacted.

In bringing the criticism of *Ulysses,* and thereby of Joyce in his other
works, to a new level of intelligence and sophistication, Goldberg's book
does not terminate the critical discussion. Rather, in true Joycean terms,
such ends mean only new beginnings, new revolutions in the progress
round the statue. Thus, two of the most interesting readings of Joyce
since Goldberg, those by Anthony Cronin and Richard Ellmann, return
to the employment of critical techniques acclaimed in early years, then
later discarded as obsolete. Cronin will have nothing to do with the idea
that *Ulysses* is to be read for its plot, for its dramatic sequences. Joyce
has liberated the novel from such artificialities and, in directing the
reader to the "profane joy" of living, dispenses with the many corrupt
falsehoods of traditional novels while infusing his work with ephiphanies,
with the power of words themselves, with poetry. The result is a novel
of comic joy, of tolerance and liberation. Moreover, in lifting from the
world of Dublin the heavy hand of societal judgment, Joyce resolved for
himself the painfully deep tensions of love and hate he had held for many
years toward his fatherland. And in settling upon Leopold Bloom as his
chief character, Joyce accepted the sordid, fallible, comic, and absurd
father he had once, as the proud esthete Stephen, held at arm's length.
Incorporating and redeeming what is most embarrassing and most noble
in humanity, Joyce showed at last what a Stephen grown into artistic
maturity could do, and what such a man as Leopold Bloom could be.

Ellmann's book, *Ulysses on the Liffey* (1972), returns, by "commodious
vicus of recirculation," to the world of Joyce as it had been charted out
some forty years before by Gilbert. The return, however, is illuminated
by a brilliance and a sympathy unachieved by Gilbert. In joining the
circle back to Gilbert, Ellmann also advances beyond the kind of purely
biographical criticism within whose limits he had so brilliantly written
his essay on "The Dead." He is in his way also fascinated by Homeric
parallels, and he too makes available a schema of correspondences. His
schema, that originally sent by Joyce to his friend Carlo Linati in 1920,
antedates Gilbert's by one year. The differences between Gilbert and Ellmann consist, however, of rather more than this. Where Gilbert's authorized version of *Ulysses* can quickly prove mechanical—can prove,
in fact, a burden, for all its knowledge—Ellmann's version is elegant,
witty, and profoundly responsive to the Joyce who would see the oceanic

forces of nature overcoming the denying forces of man-made power, the Joyce who would marry the real to the ideal in order that each might have its splendor, the Joyce who would praise the affirmative power of art. As Leopold and Stephen close the distance between them, bringing forth a harmony from such apparent discord in character, and as Stephen learns to unite the sordid and the rarefied in his own life, so the novel is everywhere founded on syntheses between unlikely partners. Many years ago, Frank O'Connor drew attention to the way Joyce could evoke the beautiful while keeping his eyes glued to a Dublin city directory. Later students have suffered to learn that Joyce, at ease as well with Blake as with Defoe, constructed his most sublime story, "The Dead," partly out of literary materials left behind by Bret Harte.[5] One recent writer, Hélène Cixous, has found it quite difficult to exhaust Joyce's sense of polarity, contradiction, and irony. Her tangled and fascinating book, *The Exile of James Joyce,* as long as *Ulysses* itself but not as nicely ordered, is given over to rich meditations on tensions within Joyce's life and work. Her essay on "Ivy Day in the Committee Room" indicates how well Joyce had learned to explore and refine those tensions.

Ellmann shows us that as that day in 1904 comes to an end, we are left with a strange trinity, balanced so precariously and beautifully, assembled at 7 Eccles Street: a cuckolded advertising canvasser who, having masturbated that day, now represents love; a semi-inebriated and homeless intellectual of sorts who has come into possession of a vision of love "as the basic act of art"; and a somnolent bleeding woman, no better than she should be, representing love as "the final penetration by the wisdom of the body of the wisdom of the mind." None of the three is complete in himself; together they "sum up what is affirmable." By fusions and reconciliations intricately brought into being by Joyce and subtly exposed by Ellmann, *Ulysses* is formed by a geometry that balances each thing against itself, each balance then posed against a synthesis elsewhere in force. Behind the complex structure, moreover, grows a figure manlike in form. Each episode of *Ulysses,* keyed to a part of the body, contributes to his creation. He is more than Bloom, more than Molly and Stephen: "The androgynous man who stands within and behind and beyond might be called Hibernion. One day he will be Finnegan."

Of *Finnegans Wake,* where Joyce at last lodged that figure, almost anything might be, and has been, said by the critics. The extremes have by now been struck. S. L. Goldberg: "I do not believe *Finnegans Wake* is worth detailed exegesis." To such a critic, so responsive to *Ulysses,* *Finnegans Wake* is no novel, and no drama, but only a disastrous experiment. But to Robert Martin Adams, ". . . in the near future it is *Finne-*

---

[5] See Gerhard Friedrich, "Bret Harte as a Source for James Joyce's 'The Dead,'" *Philological Quarterly,* XXXIII (October 1954), 442–44.

gans Wake on which the major reputation of Joyce will depend. . . .
It carries to their logical conclusion the modalities of visionary insight
and multiple imitation which we have learned to admire in *Ulysses* and
The Portait; it is an immense mine of verbal invention, from which artists will be quarrying for years to come."

Between such contrariety, so appropriate to Joyce's sense of opposi-
tions, lies *Wake* scholarship. Its history is not unlike that of the circular
path of Joycean criticism in general. At first, awe before the mystery,
and admiration conditioned by the belief that Joyce could do no wrong.
Thus the early volume, evangelical in spirit, published while the *Wake*
was still being written: *Our Exagmination Round his Factification for
Incamination of "Work in Progress."* Then, Edmund Wilson with another sober propaedeutic approach.[6] Both had received some help from
Joyce himself, who once again was faced with a largely uncomprehending,
and even hostile, world of readers. Then, in the year of Joyce's death,
Harry Levin's book, containing as useful and as encouraging a reading of
the *Wake* as has been written. Afterwards, virtual silence from those who
would offer a general analysis of the book; rather, the steady movement
of explication, positivistic and sensible in the face of all that must be
known for the book to be understood, but Swiftian in the way certain
questions of value are tabled while the work proceeds. Thus Joseph
Campbell and Henry Morton Robinson's *A Skeleton Key to Finnegans
Wake*, Adaline Glasheen's *A Census of Finnegans Wake: An Index of
the Characters and Their Roles* (particularly the first edition), and,
among many other noteworthy efforts, the *Wake Newslitter*. As Gilbert's
book has proved of greatest classroom serviceability for *Ulysses*, so the
Skeleton Key and William York Tindall's *Reader's Guide to Finnegans
Wake* are most often consulted for the later work. They introduce the
well-known mythological patterns, the Viconian cycles, the emphasis on
mankind's Fall and Resurrection, the rituals and repetitions by which
man knows and makes himself known. Glasheen indexes and cross-references the specific elements and characters so that a base for general analysis will be at the ready. That such analysis, at once critical in the freest
sense, and well informed in the widest sense, is not yet forthcoming is
evident from the pages of the *Wake Newslitter*. There, as in the *James
Joyce Quarterly*, the struggle for first principles is constantly bogged
down by preoccupation with textual detail, linguistic reference, and
previous error on the part of other professionals. It is probably correct to
argue, as a number of Joyce scholars do, that *Finnegans Wake* will not
be known until a great deal of spadework has been done. That argument, most happily formulated after setting aside the consideration that
life is short, is in fact now in the ascendant among Joyce scholars. One

---

[6] Contained in two essays, one in *Axel's Castle* (New York: Charles Scribner's Sons,
1931), pp. 225–36; the other in *The Wound and the Bow* (New York: Oxford University
Press, 1947), pp. 243–71.

of them, Clive Hart, has written well of Joyce, and brilliantly of the structure of the *Wake*, even after confessing that "whether the riches are sufficient to repay the considerable labour which must be expended" is a question sure to bother him, and us, for as long as we turn our attention to Joyce's last work.

But, as Mr. Hart surmounts his own doubts, so also do scholars such as James S. Atherton, in his *The Books at the Wake*, and David Hayman, in his *A First Draft Version of Finnegans Wake*. The result is a tough, hard-edged scholarship, long on fact and short on subjective treatment. Hart shows that the text of the *Wake*, so difficult even after renewed attacks upon it, its themes apparently so inaccessible, is in fact given order and some accessibility by Joyce's use of certain motifs. These motifs had to be substantial in length because they had to serve as conspicuous fixed points in a work saturated by verbal flux. One such motif was lifted by Joyce from Edgar Quinet's *Introduction à la philosophie de l'histoire de l'humanité*. The spirit of Quinet's paragraph, so congenial to Joyce's own temper, serves to remind us of permanence amid change, of the circularity of history, of the vanity of man. Joyce, fleeing from the nightmare of Irish politics and history, sought to organize his own emotional and intellectual life so that contemporary folly or tyranny could be seen as merely local—and therefore ephemeral—instances of perennial human weaknesses. The same device that allowed him to put distance between himself and his own troubled historical circumstances was used to provide structural order to his last, and most troubled, artistic achievement.

Joyce's preoccupation with the folly of man, with the ways in which his loudly proclaimed journeys arrive at only their starting point, with the repetitions of life that provide the illusion of meaning, was nonetheless a loving preoccupation. Joyce was absorbed by the vanities and the repetitions; he was also compelled to see through them. He did not seek a hasty reduction of life, or an art that would cruelly puncture its noble silliness. His, as Lionel Trilling implies, was a skepticism that fully embraced. It moved, as Trilling says, "through the fullest realization of the human, the all-too-human, to that which transcends and denies the human." Its ultimate station is something other than the *stasis* the young writer had sought; it is the full acceptance of *nullity*. That acceptance is governed by gigantic curiosity and industry; it slights nothing on its way to denying everything. Trilling also implies, I think, that to challenge Joyce's denial is possible only for those who have made a preliminary acceptance as large as Joyce's. To quarrel with Joyce, we must embrace that bewildering profusion of life mirrored in *Ulysses* and *Finnegans Wake*. No smart, easy negativism is possible. In this way, Joyce's arrogant claim that he expected his readers to spend as much time in understanding *Finnegans Wake* as he spent in writing it loses some of its arrogance. Joyce, we come again and again to see, is a writer great enough to be an imposition. That is a distinction not easily gained. As

Adams points out, it is an imposition to which we as readers have responded now in one way, now in another. To see him as lord supreme over his perfectly integrated and ordered work is one way to respond to the imposition. To see him as a cosmic ironist is another. To see him, as Adams decides to do, as the great modern humorist is yet another. That we feel constrained to make such responses is a measure of the gravity, or the greatness, of the imposition. To that imposition we will continue to respond imperfectly in our progress round the statue.

Political Ignominy—"Ivy Day"

by Hélène Cixous

This was Joyce's favourite of his own novellas; if "Cyclops" satirises the disproportionately vast ambition of Irish nationalism, then inversely "Ivy Day," written in 1905, satirises the Irish political situation, which derived its meaning and relative proportion from the presence of an invisible giant, present and alive in people's minds. This, it could be said, is the Lilliputian method of satire at work, reducing everything by reference to a superior, larger being. On this 6 October, a group of Dubliners from various social strata assemble in Wicklow Street to make their preparations for a municipal election, and the day is the anniversary of Parnell's death. Some of the agents, assembling at the end of a rainy day, have remembered this and wear an ivy leaf behind their lapel. The ivy is perennially green, but memory is less lasting; this 6 October soon appears as a day of forgetfulness, of shame, or of inconvenient recollections. The agents discuss local politics, and their conversation bears witness to the disintegration of political and moral values that has come about since the Leader's death. The rain matches both the mourning of the past and the sadness of the present, while the imagery that lights up the darker corners of this evening and its events only accentuates the shadows.

In the small bare room, the ancient caretaker fans a fire which is in danger of being choked by ashes; and the commemoration begins under the auspices of a dying fire, guarded by a weeping old man. The Phoenix would find it difficult to arise from these ashes, and despite the direct allusion to resurrection in the poem recited at the end ("They had their way: they laid him low./ But Erin, list, his spirit may/ Rise, like the Phoenix from the flames,/ When breaks the dawning of the day"), it is clear that there is no faith now, and that no one really wishes to revive the spirit of Parnell, for he would be too intransigent and too honest to suit anyone in this new generation, except perhaps (this is the Triestine, socialist Joyce speaking) the workers. But the workers would have very little chance in competition with the two parties capable of financing election campaigns, the Nationalist party in whose favour the Conservative candidate has stood down, and the unnamed party of Mr. Tierney, for which

"Political Ignominy—'Ivy Day.'" From Hélène Cixous, *The Exile of James Joyce*, pp. 266–72. Copyright © 1972 by Hélène Cixous. Reprinted by permission of David Lewis, Inc.

the O'Conners, Croftons, Henchys, and Lyons are working. It is Joe Hynes who speaks up for the working classes, in Marxist terms which suggest that all the virtues have taken refuge among the proletariat:

> —The working-man, said Mr. Hynes, gets all kicks and no halfpence. But it's labour produces everything. The working-man is not looking for fat jobs for his sons and nephews and cousins. The working-man is not going to drag the honour of Dublin in the mud to please a German monarch.
> —How's that? said the old man.
> —Don't you know they want to present an address of welcome to Edward Rex if he comes here next year? What do we want kowtowing to a foreign king?

We shall see that Joe Hynes, "a tall, slender young man with a light brown moustache," who looks like Joyce, is a "loyalist"; as his friend O'Connor says, "poor Joe is a decent skin." He clearly has a sense of humour, a certain firmness, and real loyalty to Parnell and to the Socialist creed. If Parnell were alive, say Hynes, O'Connor, and old Jack, things would be different now; and old Jack says, "Musha, God be with them times! There was some life in it then." And this is true; then, Parnell was God. But the door opens and a little man bustles in, hurries to the fire, "rubbing his hands as if he intended to produce a spark from them," and Mr. Henchy has arrived. It can be seen that he does not like Hynes, or the working class, or the "hillsiders and fenians" whom he confuses together and insults in a most conventional fashion: "Some of these hillsiders and fenians are a bit too clever if you ask me, said Mr. Henchy. Do you know what my private and candid opinion is about some of those little jokers? I believe half of them are in the pay of the Castle" (that is, of the English government).

In the half-light there come and go various representatives of the alienation from which Dublin suffers, the most typical being the indefinable person, "resembling a poor clergyman or a poor actor," whose face has "the appearance of damp yellow cheese," and whose voice is "discreet, indulgent, velvety." It eventually turns out that he is a poor, unbeneficed priest, "travelling on his own account." Everything rings false in this devalued world, except the elementary desires: Everyone is thirsty and impatiently awaits the arrival of the promised bottles of stout. Here can be observed the beginnings of that downgrading technique Joyce was to use so freely in *Ulysses*; just as the princess Nausicaa is replaced by a lame schoolgirl, the times of Parnell and his glory are cheapened by the succeeding age. The ambitions of Ireland are limited to the consumption of alcohol, and Mr. Henchy, the most active and unscrupulous of the Dubliners present, burlesques the rise of a citizen to the highest bourgeois honours thus: "You must owe the City Fathers money nowadays if you want to be made Lord Mayor. . . . Would I do for the job? . . . Driving out of the Mansion House, in all my vermin, with Jack here standing up behind me in a powdered wig, eh? . . . And I'll make Father Keon my private chaplain. We'll have a family party."

Henchy has a sense of humour that springs from his awareness of the country's degradation. This is not a source of grief to him, however; on the contrary, he exploits it. He knows how to make use of circumstances as best he can, for purely selfish ends. He is the anti-idealist, who sees politics as nothing more than a business proposition. The well-told joke may make his audience forget the date of this day which for Henchy has been profitably employed; but pettiness is apparent in all his jokes and actions. Everything that is done or said is appallingly trivial, even when it is not a matter of vulgar sentiments or cowardice; the assembled agents carry out their campaign, not for a beloved or trusted leader, but for "Tricky Dicky," who is known for his untrustworthiness, and who "only wants to get some job or other." The agents are not deceived by him, because there is no question of politics in the business for them; they have simply taken temporary jobs as agents, in order to pay some urgent debt, and all that counts is that they should be paid. As they wait, because the trickster "with those little pig's eyes" for whom they work is in no hurry to honour his debts, they fall back upon the drink, which they have also been awaiting with growing impatience.

The scene is indeed far from the majesty of Ireland's "uncrowned King." The imaginary presence of Parnell embarrasses them, and the behaviour of these men who live with the times expresses their embarrassment or their excessive joviality. This meeting is quite a close parody of an "heroic" political gathering; but these Dubliners have assembled at a time when politics is the exact opposite of heroism; Mr. Henchy pretends to act energetically, bustling about, talking loudly, calling for more light and warmth. There can be little honesty and less dignity when the deified leader is replaced by a mean little man whose father was a money-lender and pawnbroker. Worst of all, this downfall is accompanied by a renewal of treachery; there is no longer such a thing as individual honour, and soon there will be no national honour left either. The only subject which evokes any reaction from the agents' guilty consciences is the possibility of King Edward's projected visit to Ireland.

The tone changes abruptly from the sordid to the slanderous. The comedy acts as a disguise for unscrupulousness; for Henchy, for example, the king is not a symbolic figure and his visit ought not to be treated sentimentally, but accepted for what it is, an opportunity to revive the Irish economy. "The King's coming here will mean an influx of money into this country. The citizens of Dublin will benefit by it." We are no longer concerned with freedom, but with profit; "It's capital we want." Mr. Henchy takes no account of any sense of honour, for, after all, "Parnell is dead." This is of course true, but here it sounds like a repetition of the treachery, a denial of all he stood for. "Look at all the money there is in the country if we only worked the old industries, the mills, the shipbuilding yards and factories." Mr. Henchy knows where his interests lie, and Ireland needs money. The citizens, the ratepayers, everyone concerned would benefit, if this "jolly fine, decent fellow," Edward VII, came to Dublin.

Some of those present feel that they must, rather inconveniently, raise objections; Mr. Lyons points out that "King Edward's life, you know, is not the very . . ." But Henchy will not have any moralising in political matters, and judiciously recommends that they "let bygones be bygones"; he reminds them that Edward is a human being, which is true, and that he likes his amusements like the rest of them—"he's just an ordinary knockabout like you and me." Basically, what can they find in him to complain about? He is a "man of the world," [1] and if he were not English, he would have all the qualities of a good Irishman: "He's fond of his glass of grog and he's a bit of a rake, perhaps, and he's a good sportsman. Damn it, can't we Irish play fair?" This is a good example of the impeccable logic of treachery. Mr. Lyons is not fully convinced by the argument, though: "That's all very fine. . . . But look at the case of Parnell now," he says.

But Mr. Henchy replies, "Where's the analogy between the two cases?" In the name of what does Mr. Lyons claim that one can compare Edward with Parnell? But there is no answer; Henchy pretends not to understand "the connection," and with the skill of all those who practise the political trade, he changes the subject, ignoring the contradictions of the doubtful morality involved and acting the part of the generous, forgiving man who reconciles opposing views. Everything falls back into the chaos of degeneracy and lies again. "Don't let us stir up any bad blood," says Mr. O'Connor with subtle hypocrisy, quietening his own conscience by this act of reconciliation. "We all respect him now that he's dead and gone," he adds, meaning that Parnell no longer frightens us, though while he was alive his frankness and honesty hindered and embarrassed us because we were cowards. This is what Bloom thought also, in the cabmen's shelter. Even the conservatives forgive the adulterer, now that he is dead, and respect him "because he was a gentleman." Parnell, of course, as gentleman is not of the same species as Edward, "a man of the world" and "a jolly, fine, decent fellow, and no damn nonsense about him."

"Parnell is dead," and nothing need hinder Ireland from welcoming the English king. And so, who *is* worthy to revive the flame, and who is not unworthy to wear the ivy leaf? Not the younger generation, to judge by old Jack's son, who is at the worst stages of degeneracy; if he is forced to get himself a job, "he drinks it all." Another proof is offered by the boy who brings the bottles of stout; Mr. Henchy offers him a drink, much against old Jack's will, and as Jack gives the boy a bottle, he asks him how old he is, as though trying to recall him to sense and health before it is too

---

[1] Like the Jesuits in "Grace," who are "men of the world like ourselves."

late. But the lad already knows whom to heed and whom to respect, not the distressed old father but the tempter Henchy; "That's the way it begins," says the old man, but in fact that is how it ends. They suddenly remember that today is the anniversary of Parnell's death, and feel slightly embarrassed by this. Parnell exists so little that when the need to communicate is felt, they do not know quite what to do, not having thought of preparing any ceremony. Hynes, who had vanished during the discussion, as though Joyce had obscurely wished to keep him from being a witness to this deadly wake, now returns, and the vague Parnell wake that takes place has this in common with the wake for Finnegan the mason: that if the shade of Parnell has made even a timid appearance in people's minds, they have hastened to reduce it again to its customary impotence, and similarly the guests at the wake persuade Tim Finnegan, whom the scent of whiskey has recalled to life, to lie down again. Parnell, however, resembles Hamlet's father much more than he resembles Finnegan; and whatever they do to exorcise him, he remains firmly ensconced in the individual conscience.

At the end, Joyce's intention is to evoke more concretely the death of the Leader, because the presence of their eternally absent king is so strongly felt by all the characters, *as it was felt by Joyce himself,* as a perpetual reproach and remorse for their decadent state. Through a paradox which represents the highest achievement of his deceptively realistic art in *Dubliners,* Joyce is, in the writing of "Ivy Day," doubly present; he is every Irishman, and thereby guilty of the murder of Parnell, and he also *is* Parnell, invisible but present behind every line and every word, to such an extent that one can sense his irony informing everything that is said. It is all written down in the characters' uneasy consciences. Mr. Henchy shamelessly invites Joe Hynes to recite "that thing you wrote," as though to demonstrate that the break between living present and dead past is complete, and that Parnell henceforth belongs to literature rather than to history.

The poem is ambiguous; what the metaphor actually alludes to and what it makes manifest can be interpreted on many levels, some of them liable to become mutually contradictory, and we must examine all of these levels and not just the apparently literary one which is the first to be perceived. The thematic tension thus established acts upon the reader's mind, making him sensitive to the smallest variations in tone; and "The Death of Parnell" is seen to be a poem of several different degrees of irony. To begin with, there is the literal irony of reciting a poem of grief and indignation to an audience that remains completely cold and unmoved. Then, by its relationship with this audience, the poem acquires an aggressive tone, because Parnell died betrayed by people whose description ("modern hypocrites," "coward hounds") identifies them with the audience, who are complacently listening to the poem; they behave as though they were not the people being criticised in the poem, as though they had nothing

to do with it, and applaud their own condemnation. Next, the irony becomes historical too; the contrast is established between the message of
hope which the poet cries prayerfully towards the future and the reality
of this future, made concrete as the moment in which the poem is being
read—and the hope is seen to be both vain and ridiculous.

> "His spirit may/ Rise, like the Phoenix from the flames,/ When breaks
> the dawning of the day," cries the poet, and on this echo of the Psalms,
> the fire in the grate goes out. Erin is compared to an Eastern queen who
> sees all the hopes of her life perish on the pyre where her dead king is
> burned:—"He lies slain by the coward hounds/ He raised to glory from
> the mire;/ And Erin's hopes and Erin's dreams/ Perish upon her monarch's
> pyre.// In palace, cabin, or in cot/ The Irish heart where'er it be/ Is
> bowed with woe—for he is gone/ Who would have wrought her destiny./
> He would have had his Erin famed,/ The green flag gloriously unfurled,/
> Her statesmen, bards, and warriors raised/ Before the nations of the
> world./ He dreamed (alas, 'twas but a dream!)/ Of Liberty: but as he
> strove/ To clutch that idol, treachery/ Sundered him from the thing he
> loved."

Yet in reality Erin had taken great delight in raising that pyre and in
burning her "hopes and dreams," for fear that they might come true.

Insensibly the distance grows, between Parnell's death, theatrically
deplored as a great loss, and the real indifference of his so-called follow-
ers; between the tragedy of the hero's death and the meanness of the chorus
who bewail it; between the swollen rhetoric of the lamentations that are
recited and the actual paucity of the Dubliners' vocabulary; between the
dead dream and the living nightmare; and as it grows, the irony is further
modified. Read before an innocent audience it would simply be an expression of some puerile optimism; but, to a guilty audience, it denounces
their crimes clearly and candidly. Hynes reciting "The Death of Parnell"
is like the actors in *Hamlet* acting out the murder of a king before the
king's murderer; the whole tragedy is in Claudius' silence. Similarly,
when Hynes finishes his poem, there is a silence, lasting for a moment
while everyone hastens to adjust his mind to the consciousness of guilt
and to decide on the appropriate behaviour to adopt; this moment of
mutual admission of guilt is broken by their applause, for the guilty have
found their line of defence, and their reply to the indirect accusation.
They choose the role of spectators, excusing themselves thus from any
responsibility, and they congratulate the poet on his mastery of the art.

Yet there was that moment in which Parnell almost began to exist
again, that silence which he occupied so fully that he almost returned to
them; and in that silence, that moment, was produced their awareness of
the discord between the last verse and its echo in time present, in actuality
as they knew it. It was not the silence of shamefaced reluctance to speak,
but the silence in which the dishonourable Dubliner was faced with the

image of the honourable man who was to exist when Parnell returned, when freedom ruled, in the psalmist's ideal future.

"And on that day may Erin well/ Pledge in the cup she lifts to Joy/ One grief—the memory of Parnell." Each knows that the memory of Parnell is only a form of remorse, and each lifts the bitter drink of guilty conscience to his lips, but no toast is drunk to freedom, because they are soon to drink to King Edward. All the themes which could have led to tragedy have been turned aside into farce.

The Backgrounds of "The Dead"

by Richard Ellmann

The silent cock shall crow at last. The west shall shake the east awake.
Walk while ye have the night for morn, lightbreakfastbringer. . . .
                                        —*Finnegans Wake* (473)

The stay in Rome had seemed purposeless, but during it Joyce became aware of the change in his attitude toward Ireland and so toward
the world. He embodied his new perceptions in "The Dead." The story,
which was the culmination of a long waiting history, began to take shape
in Rome, but was not set down until he left the city. The pressure of
hints, sudden insights, and old memories rose in his mind until, like King
Midas's barber, he was compelled to speech.

Although the story dealt mainly with three generations of his family in
Dublin, it drew also upon an incident in Galway in 1903. There Michael
("Sonny") Bodkin courted Nora Barnacle; but he contracted tuberculosis
and had to be confined to bed. Shortly afterwards Nora resolved to go to
Dublin, and Bodkin stole out of his sickroom, in spite of the rainy
weather, to sing to her under an apple tree and bid her goodbye. In Dublin Nora soon learned that Bodkin was dead, and when she met Joyce she
was first attracted to him, as she told a sister, because he resembled Sonny
Bodkin.[1]

Joyce's habit of ferreting out details had made him conduct minute in-
terrogations of Nora even before their departure from Dublin. He was
disconcerted by the fact that young men before him had interested her.
He did not much like to know that her heart was still moved, even in
pity, by the recollection of the boy who had loved her. The notion of
being in some sense in rivalry with a dead man buried in the little cemetery at Oughterard was one that came easily, and gallingly, to a man of
Joyce's jealous disposition. It was one source of his complaint to his Aunt
Josephine Murray that Nora persisted in regarding him as quite similar
to other men she had known.[2]

"The Backgrounds of 'The Dead.'" From Richard Ellmann, *James Joyce* (New York:
Oxford University Press, 1959), pp. 252–63. Copyright © 1959 by Richard Ellmann.
Reprinted by permission of Oxford University Press, Inc.

[1] Letter to me from Mrs. Kathleen Barnacle Griffin.
[2] See p. 222 [of *James Joyce* by Ellmann].

18

A few months after expressing this annoyance, while Joyce and Nora Barnacle were living in Trieste in 1905, Joyce received another impulsion toward "The Dead." In a letter Stanislaus happened to mention attending a concert of Plunket Greene, the Irish baritone, which included one of Thomas Moore's *Irish Melodies* called 'O, Ye Dead!'[3] The song, a dialogue of living and dead, was eerie enough, but what impressed Stanislaus was that Greene rendered the second stanza, in which the dead answer the living, as if they were whimpering for the bodied existence they could no longer enjoy:

> It is true, it is true, we are shadows cold and wan;
> And the fair and the brave whom we loved on earth are gone;
> > But still thus ev'n in death,
> > So sweet the living breath
> Of the fields and the flow'rs in our youth we wandered o'er,
> > That ere, condemn'd, we go
> > To freeze, 'mid Hecla's snow,
> We would taste it awhile, and think we live once more!

James was interested and asked Stanislaus to send the words, which he learned to sing himself. His feelings about his wife's dead lover found a dramatic counterpart in the jealousy of the dead for the living in Moore's song: It would seem that the living and the dead are jealous of each other. Another aspect of the rivalry is suggested in *Ulysses,* where Stephen cries out to his mother's ghost, whose "glazing eyes, staring out of death, to shake and bend my soul, . . . to strike me down," he cannot put out of mind: "No, mother. Let me be and let me live."[4] That the dead do not stay buried is, in fact, a theme of Joyce from the beginning to the end of his work; Finnegan is not the only corpse to be resurrected.

In Rome the obtrusiveness of the dead affected what he thought of Dublin, the equally Catholic city he had abandoned, a city as prehensile of its ruins, visible and invisible. His head was filled with a sense of the too-successful encroachment of the dead upon the living city; there was a disrupting parallel in the way that Dublin, buried behind him, was haunting his thoughts. In *Ulysses* the theme was to be reconstituted, in more horrid form, in the mind of Stephen, who sees corpses rising from their graves like vampires to deprive the living of joy. The bridebed, the childbed, and the bed of death are bound together, and death "comes, pale vampire, through storm his eyes, his bat sails bloodying the sea, mouth to her mouth's kiss."[5] We can be at the same time in death as well as in life.[6]

---

[3] S. Joyce, "The Background to 'Dubliners,'" *Listener,* **LI** (March 25, 1954), 526–7.
[4] *Ulysses* (New York: Vintage Books, 1961), p. 10.
[5] *Ibid.,* p. 48.
[6] The converse of this theme appears in *Ulysses* (113 [107]), when Bloom, walking in

By February 11, 1907, after six months in Rome, Joyce knew in general what story he must write. Some of his difficulty in beginning it was due, as he said himself,[7] to the riot in Dublin over *The Playboy of the Western World.* Synge had followed the advice of Yeats that Joyce had rejected, to find his inspiration in the Irish folk, and had gone to the Aran Islands. This old issue finds small echoes in the story. The nationalistic Miss Ivors tries to persuade Gabriel to go to Aran (where Synge's *Riders to the Sea* is set), and when he refuses, twits him for his lack of patriotic feeling. Though Gabriel thinks of defending the autonomy of art and its indifference to politics, he knows such a defense would be pretentious, and only musters up the remark that he is sick of his own country. But the issue is far from settled for him.

"The Dead" begins with a party and ends with a corpse, so entwining "funferal" and "funeral" as in the wake of Finnegan. That he began with a party was due, at least in part, to Joyce's feeling that the rest of the stories in *Dubliners* had not completed his picture of the city. In a letter of September 25, 1906,[8] he had written his brother from Rome to say that some elements of Dublin had been left out of his stories: "I have not reproduced its ingenuous insularity and its hospitality, the latter 'virtue' so far as I can see does not exist elsewhere in Europe." He allowed a little of this warmth to enter "The Dead." In his speech at the Christmas party, Gabriel Conroy explicitly commends Ireland for this very virtue of hospitality, though his expression of the idea is distinctly after-dinner: "I feel more strongly with every recurring year that our country has no tradition which does it so much honour and which it should guard so jealously as that of its hospitality. It is a tradition that is unique as far as my experience goes (and I have visited not a few places abroad) among the modern nations." This was Joyce's oblique way, in language that mocked his own, of beginning the task of making amends.

The selection of details for "The Dead" shows Joyce making those choices which, while masterly, suggest the preoccupations that mastered him. Once he had determined to represent an Irish party, the choice of the Misses Morkans' as its location was easy enough. He had already reserved for *Stephen Hero* a Christmas party at his own house, a party which was also to be clouded by a discussion of a dead man. The other festive occasions of his childhood were associated with his hospitable great-aunts Mrs. Callanan and Mrs. Lyons, and Mrs. Callanan's daughter Mary Ellen, at their house at 15 Usher's Island, which was also known as the "Misses Flynn school."[9] There, every year the Joyces who were old enough would go, and John Joyce carved the goose and made the speech.

Glasnevin, thinks, "They are not going to get me this innings. Warm beds: warm fullblooded life."

[7] See p. 248 [of *James Joyce* by Richard Ellmann].

[8] See p. 239 [of *James Joyce* by Richard Ellmann].

[9] Interview with Mrs. May Joyce Monaghan, 1953.

Stanislaus Joyce says that the speech of Gabriel Conroy in "The Dead" is a good imitation of his father's oratorical style.[10]

In Joyce's story, Mrs. Callanan and Mrs. Lyons, the Misses Flynn, become the spinster ladies, the Misses Morkan; and Mary Ellen Callanan becomes Mary Jane. Most of the other party guests were also reconstituted from Joyce's recollections. Mrs. Lyons had a son Freddy, who kept a Christmas card shop in Grafton Street.[11] Joyce introduces him as Freddy Malins, and situates his shop in the less fashionable Henry Street, perhaps to make him need that sovereign Gabriel lent him. Another relative of Joyce's mother, a first cousin, married a Protestant named Mervyn Archdale Browne, who combined the profession of music teacher with that of agent for a burglary insurance company. Joyce keeps him in "The Dead" under his own name. Bartell d'Arcy, the hoarse singer in the story, was based upon Barton M'Guckin, the leading tenor in the Carl Rosa Opera Company. There were other tenors, such as John McCormack, whom Joyce might have used, but he needed one who was unsuccessful and uneasy about himself; and his father's often-told anecdote about M'Guckin's lack of confidence furnished him with just such a singer as he intended Bartell d'Arcy to be.

The making of his hero, Gabriel Conroy, was more complicated. The root situation, of jealousy for his wife's dead lover, was of course Joyce's. The man who is murdered, D. H. Lawrence has one of his characters say, desires to be murdered,[12] some temperaments demand the feeling that their friends and sweethearts will deceive them. Joyce's conversation often returned to the word "betrayal," [13] and the entangled innocents whom he uses for his heroes are all aspects of his conception of himself. Though Gabriel is less impressive than Joyce's other heroes, Stephen, Bloom, Richard Rowan, or Earwicker, he belongs to their distinguished, put-upon company.

There are several specific points at which Joyce attributes his own experiences to Gabriel. The letter which Gabriel remembers having written to Gretta Conroy early in their courtship is one of these; from it Gabriel quotes to himself the sentiment, "Why is it that words like these seem to me so dull and cold? Is it because there is no word tender enough to be your name?" These sentences are taken almost directly from a letter Joyce wrote to Nora in 1904.[14] It was also Joyce, of course, who wrote book reviews, just as Gabriel Conroy does, for the *Daily Express*. Since the *Daily Express* was pro-English, he had probably been teased for writing for it during his frequent visits to the house of David Sheehy, M. P. One of the Sheehy daughters, Kathleen, may well have been the model for Miss Ivors,

[10] He excepts the quotation from Browning, but even this was quite within the scope of the man who could quote Vergil when lending money to his son.

[11] Interview with Mrs. Monaghan.

[12] Birkin, in *Women in Love*.

[13] Information from Professor Joseph Prescott.

[14] At Cornell [the Joyce Collection of the Cornell University Library].

for she wore that austere bodice and sported the same patriotic pin.[15] In
Gretta's old sweetheart, in Gabriel's letter, in the book reviews and the
discussion of them, as well as in the physical image of Gabriel with hair
parted in the middle and ... glasses, Joyce drew directly upon his own life.

His father was also deeply involved in the story. Stanislaus Joyce recalls that when the Joyce children were too young to bring along to the
Misses Flynn's party, their father and mother sometimes left them with
a governess and stayed at a Dublin hotel overnight instead of returning
to their house in Bray.[16] Gabriel and Gretta do this too. Gabriel's quarrels
with his mother also suggest John Joyce's quarrels with his mother, who
never accepted her son's marriage to a woman of lower station.[17] But
John Joyce's personality was not like Gabriel's; he had no doubts of himself, in the midst of many failures he was full of self-esteem. He had the
same unshakable confidence as his son James. For Gabriel's personality,
there is among Joyce's friends another model.[18] This was Constantine
Curran, sometimes nicknamed "Cautious Con." He is a more distinguished man than Joyce allows, but Joyce was building upon, and no
doubt distorting, his memories of Curran as a very young man. That he
has Curran partly in mind is suggested by the fact that he calls Gabriel's
brother by Curran's first name, Constantine, and makes Gabriel's brother,
like Curran's, a priest.[19] Curran has the same high color and nervous,
disquieted manner as Gabriel, and like Gabriel he has traveled to the
continent and has cultivated cosmopolitan interests. Curran, like Conroy,
married a woman who was not a Dubliner, though she came from only as
far west as Limerick. In other respects he is quite different. Gabriel was
made mostly out of Curran, Joyce's father, and Joyce himself. Probably
Joyce knew there was a publican on Howth named Gabriel Conroy; or,
as Gerhard Friedrich has proposed,[20] he may have borrowed the name
from the title of a Bret Harte novel. But the character, if not the name,
was of his own compounding.[21]

Joyce now had his people, his party, and something of its development.
In the festive setting, upon which the snow keeps offering a different perspective until, as W. Y. Tindall suggests,[22] the snow itself changes, he

[15] Interview with Mrs. Mary Sheehy Kettle, 1953.

[16] *My Brother's Keeper* (New York: The Viking Press, 1958), p. 38.

[17] See p. 17 [of *James Joyce* by Richard Ellmann].

[18] Interview with S. Joyce, 1953.

[19] Suggested to me by Professor Vivian Mercier.

[20] Gerhard Friedrich, "Bret Harte as a Source for James Joyce's 'The Dead,'"
Philological Quarterly, XXXIII (October 1954), 442–44.

[21] The name of Conroy's wife Gretta was borrowed from another friend, Gretta
(actually Margaret) Cousins, the wife of James H. Cousins. Since Joyce mentioned in
a letter, at the same time that he was meditating "The Dead," the danger of becoming
"a patient Cousins," this family was evidently on his mind.

[22] W. Y. Tindall, *The Literary Symbol* (New York: Columbia University Press, 1955),
p. 227.

develops Gabriel's private tremors, his sense of inadequacy, his uncomfortable insistence on his small pretensions. From the beginning he is vulnerable; his well-meant and even generous overtures are regularly checked. The servant girl punctures his blithe assumption that everyone is happily in love and on the way to the altar. He is not sure enough of himself to put out of his head the slurs he has received long ago; so in spite of his uxorious attitude towards Gretta, he is a little ashamed of her having come from the west of Ireland. He cannot bear to think of his dead mother's remark that Gretta was "country cute," and when Miss Ivors says of Gretta, "She's from Connacht, isn't she?" Gabriel answers shortly, "Her people are." He has rescued her from that bog. Miss Ivors's suggestion, a true Gaelic Leaguer's, that he spend his holiday in the Irish-speaking Aran Islands (in the west) upsets him; it is the element in his wife's past that he wishes to forget. During most of the story, the west of Ireland is connected in Gabriel's mind with a dark and rather painful primitivism, an aspect of his country which he has steadily abjured by going off to the continent. The west is savagery; to the east and south, lie people who drink wine and wear galoshes.

Gabriel has been made uneasy about this attitude, but he clings to it defiantly until the ending. Unknown to him, it is being challenged by the song, "The Lass of Aughrim." Aughrim is a little village in the west, not far from Galway. The song has a special relevance; in it a woman who has been seduced and abandoned by Lord Gregory comes with her baby in the rain to beg for admission to his house. It brings together the peasant mother and the civilized seducer, but Gabriel does not listen to the words; he only watches his wife listening. Joyce had heard this ballad from Nora; perhaps he considered also using Tom Moore's "O, Ye Dead" in the story, but if so he must have seen that "The Lass of Aughrim" would connect more subtly with the west and with Michael Furey's visit in the rain to Gretta. But the notion of using a song at all may well have come to him as the result of the excitement generated in him by Moore's song.

And now Gabriel and Gretta go to the Hotel Gresham, Gabriel fired by his living wife and Gretta drained by the memory of her dead lover. He learns for the first time of the young man in Galway, whose name Joyce has deftly altered from Sonny or Michael Bodkin to Michael Furey. The new name implies, like the contrast of the militant Michael and the amiable Gabriel, that violent passion is in her Galway past, not in her Dublin present. Gabriel tries to cut Michael Furey down. "What was he?" he asks, confident that his own profession of language teacher (which of course he shared with Joyce) is superior; but she replies, "He was in the gasworks," as if this profession was as good as any other. Then Gabriel tries again, "And what did he die of so young, Gretta? Consumption, was it?" He hopes to register the usual expressions of pity, but Gretta silences

and terrifies him by her answer, "I think he died for me." [23] Since Joyce
has already made clear that Michael Furey was tubercular, this answer of
Gretta has a fine ambiguity. It asserts the egoism of passion, and unconsciously defies Gabriel's reasonable question.

Now Gabriel begins to succumb to his wife's dead lover, and becomes
a pilgrim to emotional intensities outside of his own experience. From
a biographical point of view, these final pages compose one of Joyce's
several tributes to his wife's artless integrity. Nora Barnacle, in spite of
her defects of education, was independent, unselfconscious, instinctively
right. Gabriel acknowledges the same coherence in his own wife, and he
recognizes in the west of Ireland, in Michael Furey, a passion he has himself always lacked. "Better pass boldly into that other world, in the full
glory of some passion, than fade and wither dismally with age," Joyce
makes Gabriel think. Then comes that strange sentence in the final paragraph: "The time had come for him to set out on his journey westward."
The cliché runs that journeys westward are towards death, but the west
has taken on a special meaning in the story. Gretta Conroy's west is the
place where life had been lived simply and passionately. The context and
phrasing of the sentence suggest that Gabriel is on the edge of sleep, and
half-consciously accepts what he has hitherto scorned, the possibility of
an actual trip to Connaught. What the sentence affirms, at last, on the
level of feeling, is the west, the primitive, untutored, impulsive country
from which Gabriel had felt himself alienated before; in the story, the
west is paradoxically linked also with the past and the dead. It is like
Aunt Julia Morkan who, though ignorant, old, grey-skinned, and stupe-
fied, seizes in her song at the party "the excitement of swift and secure
flight."

The tone of the sentence, "The time had come for him to set out on
his journey westward," is somewhat resigned. It suggests a concession, a
relinquishment, and Gabriel is conceding and relinquishing a good deal
—his sense of the importance of civilized thinking, of continental tastes,
of all those tepid but nice distinctions on which he has prided himself.
The bubble of his self-possession is pricked; he no longer possesses himself, and not to possess oneself is in a way a kind of death. It is a self-
abandonment not unlike Furey's, and through Gabriel's mind runs the
imagery of Calvary. He imagines the snow on the cemetery at Oughterard,
lying "thickly drifted on the crooked crosses and headstones, on the spears
of the little gate, on the barren thorns." He thinks of Michael Furey who,
Gretta has said, died for her, and envies him his sacrifice for another kind
of love than Christ's. To some extent, Gabriel too is dying for her, in giving up what he has most valued in himself, all that holds him apart from

---

[23] Adaline Glasheen has discovered here an echo of Yeats's nationalistic play, *Cathleen
ni Houlihan* (1902), where the old woman who symbolizes Ireland sings a song of
"yellow-haired Donough that was hanged in Galway." When she is asked, "What was
it brought him to his death?" she replies, "He died for love of me; many a man has
died for love of me." I am indebted to Mrs. Glasheen for pointing this out to me.

the simpler people at the party. He feels close to Gretta through sympathy if not through love; now they are both past youth, beauty, and passion; he feels close also to her dead lover, another lamb burnt on her altar, though she too is burnt now; he feels no resentment, only pity. In his own sacrifice of himself, he is conscious of a melancholy unity between the living and the dead.

Gabriel, who has been sick of his own country, finds himself drawn inevitably into a silent tribute to it of much more consequence than his spoken tribute to the party. He has had illusions of the rightness of a way of life that should be outside of Ireland; but through this experience with his wife he grants a kind of bondage, of acceptance, even of admiration to a part of the country and a way of life that are most Irish. Ireland is shown to be stronger, more intense than he. At the end of *A Portrait of the Artist*, too, Stephen Dedalus, who has been so resolutely opposed to nationalism, makes a similar concession when he interprets his departure from Ireland as an attempt to forge a conscience for his race.

Joyce did not invent the incidents that conclude his story, the second honeymoon of Gabriel and Gretta which ends so badly. His method of composition was very like T. S. Eliot's, the imaginative absorption of stray material. The method did not please Joyce very much because he considered it not imaginative enough, but it was the only way he could work. He borrowed the ending for "The Dead" from another book. In that book a bridal couple receive, on their wedding night, a message that a young woman whom the husband jilted has just committed suicide. The news holds them apart, she asks him not to kiss her, and both are tormented by remorse. The wife, her marriage unconsummated, falls off at last to sleep, and her husband goes to the window and looks out at "the melancholy greyness of the dawn." For the first time he recognizes, with the force of a revelation, that his life is a failure, and that his wife lacks the passion of the girl who has killed herself. He resolves that, since he is not worthy of any more momentous career, he will try at least to make her happy. Here surely is the situation that Joyce so adroitly recomposed. The dead lover who comes between the lovers, the sense of the husband's failure, the acceptance of mediocrity, the resolve to be at all events sympathetic, all come from the other book. But Joyce transforms them. For example, he allows Gretta to kiss her husband, but without desire, and rarefies the situation by having it arise not from a suicide but from a memory of young love. The book Joyce was borrowing from was one that nobody reads any more, George Moore's *Vain Fortune*; but Joyce read it,[24] and in his youthful essay, "The Day of the Rabblement," overpraised it as "fine, original work." [25]

---

[24] He evidently refreshed his memory of it when writing "The Dead," for his copy of *Vain Fortune*, now at Yale, bears the date "March 1907."

[25] *The Critical Writings of James Joyce*, ed. Ellsworth Mason and Richard Ellmann (New York: Viking, 1959), p. 71.

Moore said nothing about snow, however. No one can know how Joyce conceived the joining of Gabriel's final experience with the snow. But his fondness for a background of this kind is also illustrated by his use of the fireplace in "Ivy Day," of the streetlamps in "Two Gallants," and of the river in *Finnegans Wake*. It does not seem that the snow can be death, as so many have said, for it falls on living and dead alike, and for death to fall on the dead is a simple redundancy of which Joyce would not have been guilty. For snow to be "general all over Ireland" is of course unusual in that country. The fine description, "It was falling on every part of the dark central plain, on the treeless hills, falling softly upon the Bog of Allen and, farther westward, softly falling into the dark mutinous Shannon waves," is probably borrowed by Joyce from a famous simile in the twelfth book of the Iliad, which Thoreau translates:[26] "The snowflakes fall thick and fast on a winter's day. The winds are lulled, and the snow falls incessant, covering the tops of the mountains, and the hills, and the plains where the lotus-tree grows, and the cultivated fields, and they are falling by the inlets and shores of the foaming sea, but are silently dissolved by the waves." But Homer was simply describing the thickness of the arrows in the battle of the Greeks and Trojans; and while Joyce seems to copy his topographical details, he uses the image here chiefly for a similar sense of crowding and quiet pressure. Where Homer speaks of the waves silently dissolving the snow, Joyce adds the final detail of "the mutinous Shannon waves" which suggests the "Furey" quality of the west. The snow that falls upon Gabriel, Gretta, and Michael Furey, upon the Misses Morkan, upon the dead singers and the living, is mutuality, a sense of their connection with each other, a sense that none has his being alone. The partygoers prefer dead singers to living ones, the wife prefers a dead lover to a live lover.

The snow does not stand alone in the story. It is part of the complex imagery that includes heat and cold air, fire, and rain, as well as snow. The relations of these are not simple. During the party, the living people, their festivities, and all human society seem contrasted with the cold outside, as in the warmth of Gabriel's hand on the cold pane. But this warmth is felt by Gabriel as stuffy and confining, and the cold outside is repeatedly connected with what is fragrant and fresh. The cold, in this sense of piercing intensity, culminates in the picture of Michael Furey in the rain and darkness of the Galway night.

Another warmth is involved in "The Dead." In Gabriel's memory of his own love for Gretta, he recalls incidents in his love's history as stars, burning with pure and distant intensity, and recalls moments of his passion for her as having the fire of stars. The irony of this image is that the sharp and beautiful experience was, though he has not known it until

---

[26] Professor Walter B. Rideout kindly called my attention to the similarity of these passages.

this night, incomplete. There is a telling metaphor: He remembers a moment of happiness, standing with Gretta in the cold, looking in through a window at a man making bottles in a roaring furnace, and suddenly calling out to the man, "Is the fire hot?" The question sums up his naïve deprivation; if the man at the furnace had heard the question, his answer, thinks Gabriel, might have been rude; so the revelation on this night is rude to Gabriel's whole being. On this night he acknowledges that love must be a feeling which he has never fully had.

Gabriel is not utterly deprived. Throughout the story there is affection for this man who, without the sharpest, most passionate perceptions, is yet generous and considerate. The intense and the moderate can meet; intensity bursts out and declines, and the moderated can admire and pity it, and share the fate that moves both types of mankind towards age and death. The furthest point of love of which Gabriel is capable is past. Furey's passion is past because of his sudden death. Gretta is perhaps the most pitiful, in that knowing Furey's passion, and being of his kind, she does not die but lives to wane in Gabriel's way; on this night she too is fatigued, not beautiful, her clothes lie crumpled beside her. The snow seems to share in this decline; viewed from inside at the party, it is desirable, unattainable, just as at his first knowledge of Michael Furey, Gabriel envies him. At the end as the partygoers walk to the cab, the snow is slushy and in patches, and then, seen from the window of the hotel room, it belongs to all men, it is general, mutual. Under its canopy, all human beings, whatever their degrees of intensity, fall into union. The mutuality is that all men feel and lose feeling, all interact, all warrant the sympathy that Gabriel now extends to Furey, to Gretta, to himself, even to old Aunt Julia.

In its lyrical, melancholy acceptance of all that life and death offer, "The Dead" is a linchpin in Joyce's work. There is that basic situation of cuckoldry, real or putative, which is to be found throughout. There is the special Joycean collation of specific detail raised to rhythmical intensity. The final purport of the story, the mutual dependency of living and dead, is something that he meditated a good deal from his early youth. He had expressed it first in his essay on Mangan in 1902, when he spoke already of the union in the great memory of death along with life;[27] even then he had begun to learn like Gabriel that we are all Romes, our new edifices reared beside, and even joined with, ancient monuments. In *Dubliners* he developed this idea. The interrelationship of dead and living is the theme of the first story in *Dubliners* as well as of the last; it is also the theme of "A Painful Case," but an even closer parallel to "The Dead" is the story, "Ivy Day in the Committee Room." This was in one sense an answer to his university friends who mocked his remark that death is the most beautiful form of life by saying that absence is the

[27] *The Critical Writings*, p. 83.

highest form of presence. Joyce did not think either idea absurd. What binds "Ivy Day" to "The Dead" is that in both stories the central agitation derives from a character who never appears, who is dead, absent. Joyce wrote Stanislaus that Anatole France had given him the idea for both stories.[28] There may be other sources in France's works, but a possible one is "The Procurator of Judaea." In it Pontius Pilate reminisces with a friend about the days when he was procurator in Judaea, and describes the events of his time with Roman reason, calm, and elegance. Never once does he, or his friend, mention the person we expect him to discuss, the founder of Christianity, until at the end the friend asks if Pontius Pilate happens to remember someone of the name of Jesus, from Nazareth, and the veteran administrator replies, "Jesus? Jesus of Nazareth? I cannot call him to mind." The story is overshadowed by the person whom Pilate does not recall; without him the story would not exist. Joyce uses a similar method in "Ivy Day" with Parnell and in "The Dead" with Michael Furey.

In *Ulysses* the climactic episode, *Circe,* whirls to a sepulchral close in the same juxtaposition of living and dead, the ghost of his mother confronting Stephen, and the ghost of his son confronting Bloom. But Joyce's greatest triumph in asserting the intimacy of living and dead was to be the close of *Finnegans Wake.* Here Anna Livia Plurabelle, the river of life, flows toward the sea, which is death; the fresh water passes into the salt, a bitter ending. Yet it is also a return to her father, the sea, that produces the cloud which makes the river, and her father is also her husband, to whom she gives herself as a bride to her groom. Anna Livia is going back to her father, as Gabriel journeys westward in feeling to the roots of his fatherland; like him, she is sad and weary. To him the Shannon waves are dark and mutinous, and to her the sea is cold and mad. In *Finnegans Wake* Anna Livia's union is not only with love but with death; like Gabriel she seems to swoon away.

That Joyce at the age of twenty-five and -six should have written this story ought not to seem odd. Young writers reach their greatest eloquence in dwelling upon the horrors of middle age and what follows it. But beyond this proclivity which he shared with others, Joyce had a special reason for writing the story of "The Dead" in 1906 and 1907. In his own mind he had thoroughly justified his flight from Ireland, but he had not decided the question of where he would fly *to.* In Trieste and Rome he had learned what he had unlearned in Dublin, to be a Dubliner. As he had written his brother from Rome with some astonishment, he felt humiliated when anyone attacked his "impoverished country." [29] "The Dead" is his first song of exile.

[28] Letter to S. Joyce, February 11, 1907.
[29] Letter to S. Joyce, September 25, 1906.

The *Portrait* in Perspective

by Hugh Kenner

From wrong to wrong the exasperated spirit
Proceeds, unless restored by that refining fire
Where you must move in measure, like a dancer.

T. S. Eliot

Faites votre destin, âmes désordonnées,
Et fuyez l'infini que vous portez en vous!

Baudelaire

And yet he felt that, however he might revile and mock her
image, his anger was also a form of homage.

Portrait (P259/251)

A Portrait of the Artist as a Young Man, which in its definitive form
initiates the second cycle, was some ten years in the writing. A 1,000-page
first draft was written around 1904–1906, about the same time as the
bulk of *Dubliners.* This was scrapped and a more compressed version undertaken in 1908; the third and final text was being composed in 1911,
and was finished early in 1914.[1] About one-third of the first draft (the
Stephen Hero fragment) survives to show us what was going on during the
gestation of this book, the only one which it cost Joyce far more
trouble to focus than to execute.

Joyce first conceived the story of Stephen Dedalus in a picaresque mode.
The original title was meant to incorporate the ballad of Turpin Hero,
a reference to which still survives in the final text. Turpin spends most

---

"The *Portrait* in Perspective." From Hugh Kenner, *Dublin's Joyce* (Bloomington,
Ind.: Indiana University Press, 1956), pp. 109–33. Reprinted by permission of Indiana
University Press and A D Peters and Company.

[1] [Herbert Gorman, *James Joyce* (New York: Rinehart & Co., 1939; rev. ed., 1948), pp.
142–45, 190–97, 202–9, 220–23.] See also Theodore Spencer's introduction to *Stephen
Hero* [(New York: New Directions Publishing Corporation, 1963), pp. 7–18.]

of the ballad achieving gestes at the expense of a gallery of middle-class dummies, beginning with a lawyer:

> . . . As they rode down by the powder mill,
> Turpin commands him to stand still;
> Said he, your cape I must cut off,
> For my mare she wants her saddle cloth.
> > O rare Turpin Hero,
> > O rare Turpin O.
> This caus'd the lawyer much to fret,
> To think he was so fairly bit;
> And Turpin robb'd him of his store,
> Because he knew he'd lie for more.
> > O rare Turpin Hero,
> > O rare Turpin O.

The lawyer's mistake was to admit the plausible stranger to his intimacy. Stephen in the same way achieves a series of dialectical triumphs over priests, parents, and schoolfellows. The typical dialogue commences amid courtesies:

> Stephen raised his cap and said "Good evening, sir." The President answered with the smile which a pretty girl gives when she receives some compliment which puzzles her—a "winning" smile:
> —What can I do for you? he asked in a rich deep calculated voice. . . .

But cut-and-thrust soon follows:

> —May I ask you if you have read much of [Ibsen's] writing? asked Stephen.
> —Well, no . . . I must say . . .
> —May I ask you if you have read even a single line?
> —Well, no . . . I must admit . . .

Stephen always relieves the interlocutor of his complacence:

> —I should not care for anyone to identify the ideas in your essay with the teaching in our college. We receive this college in trust. . . .
> —If I were to publish tomorrow a very revolutionary pamphlet on the means of avoiding potato-blight would you consider yourself responsible for my theory?
> —No, no, of course not . . . but then this is not a school of agriculture.
> —Neither is it a school of dramaturgy, answered Stephen.

The ballad ends with Turpin in jail condemned to the gallows; *Stephen Hero* was presumably to end, as the *Portrait* does, with Stephen Protomartyr on the brink of continental exile, acknowledged enemy of the Dublin people. This Stephen is an engaging fellow with an explosive laugh, an image of the young Joyce whom Yeats compared to William

Morris "for the joyous vitality one felt in him," or of the student Joyce who emerges from his brother's *Memoir*:

> Uncompromising in all that concerned his artistic integrity, Joyce was, for the rest, of a sociable and amiable disposition. Around his tall, agile figure there hovered a certain air of youthful grace and, despite the squalors of his home, a sense of happiness, as of one who feels within himself a joyous courage, a resolute confidence in life and in his own powers. . . . Joyce's laugh was characteristic . . . of that pure hilarity which does not contort the mouth.[2]

When Stephen's uncompromising side occasionally becomes absurd, Joyce the recorder is always at hand to supply a distancing phrase: "the fiery-hearted revolutionary"; "this heaven-ascending essayist"; "he was foolish enough to regret having yielded to the impulse for sympathy from a friend." Toward the end of the existing fragment we find more and more of these excusing clauses: "No young man can contemplate the fact of death with extreme satisfaction and no young man, specialised by fate or her stepsister chance for an organ of sensitiveness and intellectiveness, can contemplate the network of falsities and trivialities which make up the funeral of a dead burgher without extreme disgust." This clumsy sentence, its tone slithering between detachment, irony, and anger, is typical of the bad writing which recurs in the *Stephen Hero* fragment to signal Joyce's periodic uncertainty of Stephen's convincingness.

The book ran down unfinished in 1906, stalled partly by its own inner contradictions, partly by the far maturer achievement of *Dubliners.* It had never, Joyce saw, had a theme; it was neither a novel, nor an autobiography, nor a spiritual or social meditation. It contained three sorts of materials that would not fuse: documentation from the past, transcribed from the Dublin notebooks; Joyce's memories of his earlier self, transmuted by a mythopoeic process only partly controlled; and his present complex attitude to what he thought that self to have been.

Fortunately, the catalytic theme was not long in coming. In the late fall of 1906, he wrote from Rome to his brother about a new story for *Dubliners,* "Ulysses." On February 6, 1907, he admitted that it "never got any forrarder than the title." It coalesced, instead, with the autobiographical theme, and both subjects were returned to the smithy. A novel, *Ulysses,* as Joyce told a Zurich student ten years later, began to be planned as sequel to a rewritten *Portrait.* In 1908 *Stephen Hero* was discarded for good, and the job of lining up the two works began. And once the final balance of motifs for the *Portrait* had been at last struck and the writing of the definitive text completed, the last exorcism, *Exiles,* took only three spring months. *Ulysses* and *Finnegans Wake* took seven and seventeen years, but their recalcitrance was technical merely. The *Portrait* includes

[2] Stanislaus Joyce, "James Joyce: A Memoir," *Hudson Review,* II. 4, [(Winter 1950)] 496.

their scenario: first "the earth that had borne him" and "the vast indifferent dome" (Penelope, Ithaca), then sleep and a plunge into "some new
world, fantastic, dim, uncertain as under sea, traversed by cloudy shapes
and beings." These are lyric anticipations of the dense epic and dramatic
works to come; the actual writing of those works went forward during the
next quarter-century with scarcely a false step.

Linking Themes

In the reconceived *Portrait,* Joyce abandoned the original intention of
writing the account of his own escape from Dublin. One cannot escape
one's Dublin. He recast Stephen Dedalus as a figure who could not even
detach himself from Dublin because he had formed himself on a denial of
Dublin's values. He is the egocentric rebel become an ultimate. There is
no question whatever of his regeneration. "Stephen no longer interests
me to the same extent [as Bloom]," said Joyce to Frank Budgen one day.
"He has a shape that can't be changed." [3] His shape is that of aesthete.
The Stephen of the first chapter of *Ulysses* who "walks wearily," constantly "leans" on everything in sight, invariably sits down before he has
gone three paces, speaks "gloomily," "quietly," "with bitterness," and
"coldly," and "suffers" his handkerchief to be pulled from his pocket by
the exuberant Mulligan, is precisely the priggish, humourless Stephen of
the last chapter of the *Portrait* who cannot remember what day of the
week it is, sentimentalizes like Charles Lamb over the "human pages" of
a second-hand Latin book, conducts the inhumanly pedantic dialogue
with Cranly on mother-love, writes Frenchified verses in bed in an erotic
swoon, and is epiphanized at full length, like Shem the Penman beneath
the bedclothes, shrinking from the "common noises" of daylight:

> Shrinking from that life he turned towards the wall, making a cowl [!]
> of the blanket and staring at the great overblown scarlet flowers of the
> tattered wall-paper. He tried to warm his perishing joy in their scarlet
> glow, imaging a roseway from where he lay upwards to heaven all strewn
> with scarlet flowers. Weary! Weary! He too was weary of ardent ways.
> [*Portrait,* 221–222.]

This new primrose path is a private Jacob's ladder let down to his bed
now that he is too weary to do anything but go to heaven.

To make epic and drama emerge naturally from the intrinsic stresses
and distortions of the lyric material meant completely new lyric techniques for a constatation exact beyond irony. The *Portrait* concentrates
on stating themes, arranging apparently transparent words into configura-
tions of the utmost symbolic density. Here is the director proposing that
Stephen enter the priesthood:

[3] Budgen, 107. [Frank Budgen, *James Joyce and the Making of "Ulysses" and Other
Writings* (London: Oxford University Press, 1972), p. 107.—Ed.]

The director stood in the embrasure of the window, his back to the light, leaning an elbow on the brown crossblind, and, as he spoke and smiled, slowly dangling and looping the cord of the other blind, Stephen stood before him, following for a moment with his eyes the waning of the long summer daylight above the roofs or the slow deft movements of the priestly fingers. The priest's face was in total shadow, but the waning daylight from behind him touched the deeply grooved temples and the curves of the skull.   [*Portrait,* 153–154.]

The looped cord, the shadow, the skull, none of these is accidental. The "waning daylight," twice emphasized, conveys that denial of nature which the priest's office represented for Stephen; "his back to the light" co-operates toward a similar effect. So "crossblind": "blind to the cross"; "blinded by the cross." "The curves of the skull" introduces another death-image; the "deathbone" from Lévy-Bruhl's Australia, pointed by Shaun in *Finnegans Wake,* is the dramatic version of an identical symbol. But the central image, the epiphany of the interview, is contained in the movement of the priest's fingers: "slowly dangling and looping the cord of the other blind." That is to say, coolly proffering a noose. This is the lyric mode of *Ulysses'* epical hangman, "The lord of things as they are whom the most Roman of Catholics call *dio boia,* hangman god."

The Contrapuntal Opening

According to the practice inaugurated by Joyce when he rewrote "The Sisters" in 1906, the *Portrait,* like the two books to follow, opens amid elaborate counterpoint. The first two pages, terminating in a row of asterisks, enact the entire action in microcosm. An Aristotelian catalogue of senses, faculties, and mental activities is played against the unfolding of the infant conscience.

> Once upon a time and a very good time it was there was a moocow coming down along the road and this moocow that was down along the road met a nicens little boy named baby tuckoo. . . .
> His father told him that story: his father looked at him through a glass: he had a hairy face.
> He was baby tuckoo. The moocow came down along the road where Betty Byrne lived: she sold lemon platt.
> > *O, the wild rose blossoms*
> > *On the little green place.*
> He sang that song. That was his song.
> > *O, the green wothe botheth.*
> When you wet the bed, first it is warm then it gets cold. His mother put on the oilsheet. That had the queer smell.

This evocation of holes in oblivion is conducted in the mode of each of the five senses in turn; hearing (the story of the moocow), sight (his father's face), taste (lemon platt), touch (warm and cold), smell (the oil-

sheet). The audible soothes: the visible disturbs. Throughout Joyce's
work, the senses are symbolically disposed. Smell is the means of discriminating empirical realities ("His mother had a nicer smell than his father"
is the next sentence), sight corresponds to the phantasms of oppression,
hearing to the imaginative life. Touch and taste together are the modes
of sex. Hearing, here, comes first, via a piece of imaginative literature.
But as we can see from the vantage-point of *Finnegans Wake,* the whole
book is about the encounter of baby tuckoo with the moocow: the Gripes
with the Mookse.[4] The father with the hairy face is the first Mookse-
avatar, the Freudian infantile analogue of God the Father.

In the *Wake,*

> Derzherr, live wire, fired Benjermine Funkling outa th'Empyre, sin right
> hand son.

Der Erzherr (arch-lord), here a Teutonic Junker, is the God who visited
his wrath on Lucifer; the hairy attribute comes through via the music-hall
refrain, "There's hair, like wire, coming out of the Empire."

Dawning consciousness of his own identity ("He was baby tuckoo")
leads to artistic performance ("He sang that song. That was his song.")
This is hugely expanded in chapter IV:

> Now, as never before, his strange name seemed to him a prophecy . . .
> of the end he had been born to serve and had been following through the
> mists of childhood and boyhood, a symbol of the artist forging anew in
> his workshop out of the sluggish matter of the earth a new soaring im-
> palpable imperishable being.   [*Portrait,* 168–169.]

By changing the red rose to a green and dislocating the spelling, he makes
the song his own ("But you could not have a green rose. But perhaps
somewhere in the world you could.")

> His mother had a nicer smell than his father. She played on the piano
> the sailor's hornpipe for him to dance. He danced:

> > *Tralala lala,*
> > *Tralala tralaladdy,*
> > *Tralala lala,*
> > *Tralala lala.*   [*Portrait,* 7.]

Between this innocence and its Rimbaudian recapture through the purga-
tion of the *Wake* there is to intervene the hallucination in Circe's sty:

> The Mother. (*With the subtle smile of death's madness.*) I was once the
> beautiful May Goulding. I am dead. . . .

---

[4] Compare the . . . sentence: "Eins within a space and a wearywide space it wast ere
wohned a Mookse." . . . Mookse is moocow plus fox plus mock turtle. The German
"Eins" evokes Einstein, who presides over the interchanging of space and time; space
is the Mookse's "spatialty."

Stephen. (*Eagerly.*) Tell me the word, mother, if you know it now. The word
  known to all men. . . .
The Mother. (*With smouldering eyes.*) Repent! O, the fire of hell!
                                                                    [*Ulysses,* 580–581.]

This is foreshadowed as the overture to the *Portrait* closes:

He hid under the table. His mother said:
—O, Stephen will apologise.
Dante said:
—O, if not, the eagles will come and pull out his eyes.—

>   Pull out his eyes,
>   Apologise,
>   Apologise,
>   Pull out his eyes.
>
>   Apologise,
>   Pull out his eyes,
>   Pull out his eyes,
>   Apologise.   [*Portrait,* 8.]

The eagles, eagles of Rome, are emissaries of the God with the hairy face:
the punisher. They evoke Prometheus and gnawing guilt: again-bite. So
the overture ends with Stephen hiding under the table awaiting the
eagles. He is hiding under something most of the time: bedclothes, "the
enigma of a manner," an indurated rhetoric, or some other carapace of
his private world.

Theme Words

It is through their names that things have power over Stephen.

—The language in which we are speaking is his before it is mine. How
different are the words *home, Christ, ale, master,* on his lips and on mine!
I cannot speak or write these words without unrest of spirit. His language,
so familiar and so foreign, will always be for me an acquired speech. I
have not made or accepted its words. My voice holds them at bay. My
soul frets in the shadow of his language.   [*Portrait,* 189.]

Not only is the Dean's English a conqueror's tongue; since the loss of
Adam's words which perfectly mirrored things, all language has con-
quered the mind and imposed its own order, askew from the order of
creation. Words, like the physical world, are imposed on Stephen from
without, and it is in their canted mirrors that he glimpses a physical and
moral world already dyed the colour of his own mind since absorbed,
with language, into his personality.

> Words which he did not understand he said over and over to himself
> till he had learnt them by heart; and through them he had glimpses of
> the real world about him.   [*Portrait*, 62.]

Language is a Trojan horse by which the universe gets into the mind.
The first sentence in the book isn't something Stephen sees but a story he
is told, and the overture climaxes in an insistent brainless rhyme, its jingle
corrosively fascinating to the will. It has power to terrify a child who
knows nothing of eagles, or of Prometheus, or of how his own grownup
failure to apologise will blend with gathering blindness.

It typifies the peculiar achievement of the *Portrait* that Joyce can cause
patterns of words to make up the very moral texture of Stephen's mind:

> Suck was a queer word. The fellow called Simon Moonan that name be-
> cause Simon Moonan used to tie the prefect's false sleeves behind his
> back and the prefect used to let on to be angry. But the sound was ugly.
> Once he had washed his hands in the lavatory of the Wicklow hotel and
> his father pulled the stopper up by the chain after and the dirty water
> went down through the hole in the basin. And when it had all gone down
> slowly the hole in the basin had made a sound like that: suck. Only louder.
> To remember that and the white look of the lavatory made him feel
> cold and then hot. There were two cocks that you turned and the water
> came out: cold and hot. He felt cold and then a little hot: and he could
> see the names printed on the cocks. That was a very queer thing.
> [*Portrait*, 11.]

"Suck" joins two contexts in Stephen's mind: a playful sinner toying with
his indulgent superior, and the disappearance of dirty water. The force
of the conjunction is felt only after Stephen has lost his sense of the reality of the forgiveness of sins in the confessional. The habitually orthodox
penitent tangles with a God who pretends to be angry; after a reconciliation the process is repeated. And the mark of that kind of play is disgrace-
ful servility. Each time the sin disappears, the sinner is mocked by an impersonal voice out of nature: "Suck!"

This attitude to unreal good and evil furnishes a context for the next
conjunction: whiteness and coldness. Stephen finds himself, like Simon
Moonan,[5] engaged in the rhythm of obedience to irrational authority,
bending his mind to a meaningless act, the arithmetic contest. He is being
obediently "good." And the appropriate colour is adduced: "He thought
his face must be white because it felt so cool."

The pallor of lunar obedient goodness is next associated with damp re-
pulsiveness: the limpness of a wet blanket and of a servant's apron:

> He sat looking at the two prints of butter on his plate but could not
> eat the damp bread. The table-cloth was damp and limp. But he drank

---

[5] Joyce's names should always be scrutinized. Simon Moonan: moon: the heatless
(white) satellite reflecting virtue borrowed from Simon Peter. Simony, too, is an activity naturally derived from this casually businesslike attitude to priestly authority.

off the hot weak tea which the clumsy scullion, girt with a white apron,
poured into his cup. He wondered whether the scullion's apron was damp
too or whether all white things were cold and damp.   [*Portrait*, 12–13.]

Throughout the first chapter an intrinsic linkage, white-cold-damp-
obedient, insinuates itself repeatedly. Stephen after saying his prayers,
"his shoulders shaking," "so that he might not go to hell when he died,"
"curled himself together under the cold white sheets, shaking and trem-
bling. But he would not go to hell when he died, and the shaking would
stop." The sea, mysterious as the terrible power of God, "was cold day and
night, but it was colder at night"; we are reminded of Anna Livia's gesture of submission: "my cold father, my cold mad father, my cold mad
feary father." "There was a cold night smell in the chapel. But it was
a holy smell." Stephen is puzzled by the phrase in the Litany of the
Blessed Virgin: Tower of Ivory. "How could a woman be a tower of
ivory or a house of gold?" He ponders until the revelation comes:

> Eileen had long white hands. One evening when playing tig she had
> put her hands over his eyes: long and white and thin and cold and soft.
> That was ivory: a cold white thing. That was the meaning of *Tower of
> Ivory*.   [*Portrait*, 36.]

This instant of insight depends on a sudden reshuffling of associations,
a sudden conviction that the Mother of God, and the symbols appropriate
to her, belong with the cold, the white, and the unpleasant in a blindfold
morality of obedience. Contemplation focussed on language is repaid:

> *Tower of Ivory. House of Gold.* By thinking of things you could under-
> stand them.   [*Portrait*, 43.]

The white-damp-obedient association reappears when Stephen is about
to make his confession after the celebrated retreat; its patterns provide
the language in which he thinks. Sin has been associated with fire, while
the prayers of the penitents are epiphanized as "soft whispering cloudlets,
soft whispering vapour, whispering and vanishing." And having been
absolved:

> White pudding and eggs and sausages and cups of tea. How simple and
> beautiful was life after all! And life lay all before him. . . .
> The boys were all there, kneeling in their places. He knelt among
> them, happy and shy. The altar was heaped with fragrant masses of white
> flowers: and in the morning light the pale flames of the candles among
> the white flowers were clear and silent as his own soul.   [*Portrait*, 146.]

We cannot read *Finnegans Wake* until we have realized the significance
of the way the mind of Stephen Dedalus is bound in by language. He is
not only an artist: He is a Dubliner.

The Portrait As Lyric

The "instant of emotion," of which this 300-page lyric is the "simplest verbal vesture," is the exalted instant, emerging at the end of the book, of freedom, of vocation, of Stephen's destiny, winging his way above the waters at the side of the hawklike man: the instant of promise on which the crushing ironies of *Ulysses* are to fall. The epic of the sea of matter is preceded by the lyric image of a growing dream: a dream that like Richard Rowan's in *Exiles* disregards the fall of man; a dream nourished by a sensitive youth of flying above the sea into an uncreated heaven:

> The spell of arms and voices: the white arms of roads, their promise of close embraces and the black arms of tall ships that stand against the moon, their tale of distant nations. They are held out to say: We are alone—come. And the voices say with them: We are your kinsmen. And the air is thick with their company as they call to me, their kinsman, making ready to go, shaking the wings of their exultant and terrible youth.   [*Portrait*, 252.]

The emotional quality of this is continuous with that of the *Count of Monte Cristo*, that fantasy of the exile returned for vengeance (the plot of the *Odyssey*) which kindled so many of Stephen's boyhood dreams:

> The figure of that dark avenger stood forth in his mind for whatever he had heard or divined in childhood of the strange and terrible. At night he built up on the parlour table an image of the wonderful island cave out of transfers and paper flowers and strips of the silver and golden paper in which chocolate is wrapped. When he had broken up this scenery, weary of its tinsel, there would come to his mind the bright picture of Marseilles, of sunny trellises and of Mercedes.   [*Portrait*, 62.]

The prose surrounding Stephen's flight is empurpled with transfers and paper flowers too. It is not immature prose, as we might suppose by comparison with *Ulysses*. The prose of "The Dead" is mature prose, and "The Dead" was written in 1908. Rather, it is a meticulous pastiche of immaturity. Joyce has his eye constantly on the epic sequel.

> He wanted to meet in the real world the unsubstantial image which his soul so constantly beheld. He did not know where to seek it or how, but a premonition which led him on told him that this image would, without any overt act of his, encounter him. They would meet quietly as if they had known each other and had made their tryst, perhaps at one of the gates or in some more secret place. They would be alone, surrounded by darkness and silence: and in that moment of supreme tenderness he would be transfigured.   [*Portrait*, 65.]

As the vaginal imagery of gates, secret places, and darkness implies, this is the dream that reaches temporary fulfilment in the plunge into profane love. But the ultimate "secret place" is to be Mabbot Street, outside Bella

Cohen's brothel; the unsubstantial image of his quest, that of Leopold Bloom, advertisement canvasser—Monte Cristo, returned avenger, Ulysses; and the transfiguration, into the phantasmal dead son of a sentimental Jew:

> *Against the dark wall a figure appears slowly, a fairy boy of eleven, a*
> *changeling, kidnapped, dressed in an Eton suit with glass shoes and a*
> *little bronze helmet, holding a book in his hand. He reads from right to*
> *left inaudibly, smiling, kissing the page.*   [*Ulysses,* 609.]

That Dedalus the artificer did violence to nature is the point of the epigraph from Ovid, *Et ignotas animum dimittit in artes;* the Icarian fall is inevitable.

> In tedious exile now too long detain'd
> Dedalus languish'd for his native land.
> The sea foreclos'd his flight; yet thus he said,
> Though earth and water in subjection laid,
> O cruel Minos, thy dominion be,
> We'll go through air; for sure the air is free.
> *Then to new arts his cunning thought applies,*
> *And to improve the work of nature tries.*

Stephen does not, as the careless reader may suppose, become an artist by rejecting church and country. Stephen does not become an artist at all. Country, church, and mission are an inextricable unity, and in rejecting the two that seem to hamper him, he rejects also the one on which he has set his heart. Improving the work of nature is his obvious ambition ("But you could not have a green rose. But perhaps somewhere in the world you could"), and it logically follows from the aesthetic he expounds to Lynch. It is a Neoplatonic aesthetic; the crucial principle of epiphanization has been withdrawn. He imagines that "the loveliness that has not yet come into the world" is to be found in his own soul. The earth is gross, and what it brings forth is cowdung; sound and shape and colour are "the prison gates of our soul"; and beauty is something mysteriously gestated within. The genuine artist reads signatures, the fake artist forges them, a process adumbrated in the obsession of Shem the Penman (from *Jim the Penman,* a forgotten drama about a forger) with "Macfearsome's Ossean," the most famous of literary forgeries, studying "how cutely to copy all their various styles of signature so as one day to utter an epical forged cheque on the public for his own private profit."

One can sense all this in the first four chapters of the *Portrait,* and *Ulysses* is unequivocal:

> Fabulous artificer, the hawklike man. You flew. Whereto? Newhaven-
> Dieppe, steerage passenger. Paris and back.   [*Ulysses,* 210.]

The Stephen of the end of the fourth chapter, however, is still unstable; he had to be brought into a final balance, and shown at some length as a

being whose development was virtually ended. Unfortunately, the last
chapter makes the book a peculiarly difficult one for the reader to focus,
because Joyce had to close it on a suspended chord. As a lyric, it is finished
in its own terms; but the themes of the last forty pages, though they give
the illusion of focussing, don't really focus until we have read well into
Ulysses. The final chapter, which in respect to the juggernaut of *Ulysses*
must be a vulnerable flank, in respect to what has gone before must be a
conclusion. This problem Joyce didn't wholly solve; there remains a
moral ambiguity (how seriously are we to take Stephen?) which makes
the last forty pages painful reading.

Not that Stephen would stand indefinitely if *Ulysses* didn't topple him
over; his equilibrium in Chapter V, though good enough to give him a
sense of unusual integrity in University College, is precarious unless he
can manage, in the manner of so many permanent undergraduates, to pro-
long the college context for the rest of his life. Each of the preceding chapters, in fact, works toward an equilibrium which is dashed when in the
next chapter Stephen's world becomes larger and the frame of reference
more complex. The terms of equilibrium are always stated with dis-
quieting accuracy; at the end of Chapter I we find:

> He was alone. He was happy and free: but he would not be anyway proud
> with Father Dolan. He would be very quiet and obedient: and he wished
> that he could do something kind for him to show him that he was not
> proud.   [*Portrait*, 59.]

And at the end of Chapter III:

> He sat by the fire in the kitchen, not daring to speak for happiness.
> Till that moment he had not known how beautiful and peaceful life
> could be. The green square of paper pinned round the lamp cast down a
> tender shade. On the dresser was a plate of sausages and white pudding
> and on the shelf there were eggs. They would be for the breakfast in the
> morning after the communion in the college chapel. White pudding and
> eggs and sausages and cups of tea. How simple and beautiful was life
> after all! And life lay all before him.   [*Portrait*, 146.]

Not "irony" but simply the truth: the good life conceived in terms of
white pudding and sausages is unstable enough to need no underlining.

The even-numbered chapters make a sequence of a different sort. The
ending of IV, Stephen's panting submission to an artistic vocation:

> Evening had fallen when he woke and the sand and arid grasses of his
> bed glowed no longer. He rose slowly and, recalling the rapture of his sleep,
> sighed at its joy. . . .   [*Portrait*, 173.]

—hasn't quite the finality often read into it when the explicit parallel
with the ending of II is perceived:

> . . . He closed his eyes, surrendering himself to her, body and mind,
> conscious of nothing in the world but the dark pressure of her softly

parting lips. They pressed upon his brain as upon his lips as though they were the vehicle of a vague speech; and between them he felt an unknown and timid pressure, darker than the swoon of sin, softer than sound or odour. [*Portrait,* 101.]

When we link these passages with the fact that the one piece of literary composition Stephen actually achieves in the book comes out of a wet dream ("Towards dawn he awoke. O what sweet music! His soul was all dewy wet"), we are in a position to see that the concluding "Welcome, O life!" has an air of finality and balance only because the diary form of the last seven pages disarms us with an illusion of auctorial impartiality.

Controlling Images: Clongowes and Belvedere

Ego *vs.* authority is the theme of the three odd-numbered chapters, Dublin *vs.* the dream that of the two even-numbered ones. The generic Joyce plot, the encounter with the alter ego, is consummated when Stephen at the end of the book identifies himself with the sanctified Stephen who was stoned by the Jews after reporting a vision (Acts VII, 56) and claims sonship with the classical Daedalus who evaded the ruler of land and sea by turning his soul to obscure arts. The episodes are built about adumbrations of this encounter: with Father Conmee, with Monte Cristo, with the whores, with the broad-shouldered moustached student who cut the word "Foetus" in a desk, with the weary mild confessor, with the birdgirl. Through this repeated plot intertwine controlling emotions and controlling images that mount in complexity as the book proceeds.

In Chapter I the controlling emotion is fear, and the dominant image Father Dolan and his pandybat; this, associated with the hangman-god and the priestly denial of the senses, was to become one of Joyce's standard images for Irish clericalism—hence the jack-in-the-box appearance of Father Dolan in Circe's nightmare imbroglio, his pandybat cracking twice like thunder. Stephen's comment, in the mode of Blake's repudiation of the God who slaughtered Jesus, emphasizes the inclusiveness of the image: "I never could read His handwriting except His criminal thumbprint on the haddock."

Chapter II opens with a triple image of Dublin's prepossessions: music, sport, religion. The first is exhibited via Uncle Charles singing sentimental ballads in the outhouse; the second via Stephen's ritual run around the park under the eye of a superannuated trainer, which his uncle enjoins on him as the whole duty of a Dubliner; the third via the clumsy piety of Uncle Charles, kneeling on a red handkerchief and reading above his breath "from a thumb-blackened prayerbook wherein catchwords were printed at the foot of every page." This trinity of themes is unwound and entwined throughout the chapter, like a net woven round Stephen; it underlies the central incident, the Whitsuntide play in the Belvedere chapel (religion), which opens with a display by the dumb-bell

team (sport) preluded by sentimental waltzes from the soldier's band
(music).

While he is waiting to play his part, Stephen is taunted by fellow students, who rally him on a fancied love affair and smiting his calf with a
cane bid him recite the *Confiteor*. His mind goes back to an analogous incident, when a similar punishment had been visited on his refusal to "admit that Byron was no good." The further analogy with Father Dolan is
obvious; love, art, and personal independence are thus united in an ideo-
gram of the prepossessions Stephen is determined to cultivate in the teeth
of persecution.

The dream-world Stephen nourishes within himself is played against
manifestations of music, sport, and religion throughout the chapter. The
constant ironic clash of Dublin *vs.* the Dream animates Chapter II, as the
clash of the ego *vs.* authority did Chapter I. All these themes come to
focus during Stephen's visit with his father to Cork. The dream of rebellion he has silently cultivated is externalized by the discovery of the word
Foetus carved in a desk by a forgotten medical student:

> It shocked him to find in the outer world a trace of what he had deemed
> till then a brutish and individual malady of his own mind. His monstrous
> reveries came thronging into his memory. They too had sprung up before
> him, suddenly and furiously, out of mere words. . . .   [*Portrait*, 90.]

The possibility of shame gaining the upper hand is dashed, however,
by the sudden banal intrusion of his father's conversation ("When you
kick out for yourself, Stephen, as I daresay you will one of these days,
remember, whatever you do, to mix with gentlemen. . . ."). Against the
standards of Dublin his monstrous reveries acquire a Satanic glamour,
and the trauma is slowly diverted into a resolution to rebel. After his
father has expressed a resolve to "leave him to his Maker" (religion), and
offered to "sing a tenor song against him" (music) or "vault a fivebarred
gate against him" (sport), Stephen muses, watching his father and two
cronies drinking to the memory of their past:

> An abyss of fortune or of temperament sundered him from them. His
> mind seemed older than theirs: it shone coldly on their strifes and happi-
> ness and regrets like a moon upon a younger earth. No life or youth
> stirred in him as it had stirred in them. He had known neither the pleasure
> of companionship with others nor the vigour of rude male health nor
> filial piety. Nothing stirred within his soul but a cold and cruel and love-
> less lust.   [*Portrait*, 95–96.]

After one final effort to compromise with Dublin on Dublin's terms has
collapsed into futility ("The pot of pink enamel paint gave out and the
wainscot of his bedroom remained with its unfinished and illplastered
coat"), he fiercely cultivates his rebellious thoughts, and moving by day
and night "among distorted images of the outer world," plunges at last
into the arms of whores. "The holy encounter he had then imagined at

which weakness and timidity and inexperience were to fall from him"
finally arrives in inversion of Father Dolan's and Uncle Charles' religion:
his descent into night-town is accompanied by lurid evocations of a Black
Mass:

> The yellow gasflames arose before his troubled vision against the vapoury
> sky, burning as if before an altar. Before the doors and in the lighted
> halls groups were gathered arrayed as for some rite. He was in another
> world: he had awakened from a slumber of centuries.   [*Portrait*, 100.]

Controlling Images: Sin and Repentance

Each chapter in the *Portrait* gathers up the thematic material of the preceding ones and entwines them with a dominant theme of its own. In
Chapter III the fear-pandybat motif is present in Father Arnall's crudely
materialistic hell, of which even the thickness of the walls is specified;
and the Dublin-*vs.*-dream motif has ironic inflections in Stephen's terror-
stricken broodings, when the dream has been twisted into a dream of
holiness, and even Dublin appears transfigured:

> How beautiful must be a soul in the state of grace when God looked
> upon it with love!
> Frowsy girls sat along the curbstones before their baskets. Their dank
> hair trailed over their brows. They were not beautiful to see as they
> crouched in the mire. But their souls were seen by God; and if their
> souls were in a state of grace they were radiant to see; and God loved
> them, seeing them.   [*Portrait*, 140.]

A *rapprochement* in these terms between the outer world and Stephen's
desires is too inadequate to need commentary; and it makes vivid as nothing else could the hopeless inversion of his attempted self-sufficiency. It
underlines, in yet another way, his persistent sin: and the dominant
theme of Chapter III is Sin. A fugue-like opening plays upon the Seven
Deadly Sins in turn; gluttony is in the first paragraph ("Stuff it into you,
his belly counselled him"), followed by lust, then sloth ("A cold lucid indifference reigned in his soul"), pride ("His pride in his own sin, his love-
less awe of God, told him that his offence was too grievous to be atoned
for"), anger ("The blundering answer stirred the embers of his contempt
for his fellows"); finally, a recapitulation fixes each term of the mortal
catalogue in a phrase, enumerating how "from the evil seed of lust all the
other deadly sins had sprung forth."

Priest and punisher inhabit Stephen himself as well as Dublin: When
he is deepest in sin he is most thoroughly a theologian. A paragraph of
gloomy introspection is juxtaposed with a list of theological questions
that puzzle Stephen's mind as he awaits the preacher:

> . . . Is baptism with mineral water valid? How comes it that while the
> first beatitude promises the kingdom of heaven to the poor of heart, the

second beatitude promises also to the meek that they shall possess the
land? . . . If the wine change into vinegar and the host crumble into
corruption after they have been consecrated, is Jesus Christ still present
under their species as God and as man?
    —Here he is! Here he is!
    A boy from his post at the window had seen the rector come from the
house. All the catechisms were opened and all heads bent upon them
silently.   [*Portrait,* 106–107.]

Wine changed into vinegar and the host crumbled into corruption fits
exactly the Irish clergy of "a church which was the scullery-maid of
Christendom." The excited "Here he is! Here he is!" following hard on
the mention of Jesus Christ and signalling nothing more portentous
than the rector makes the point as dramatically as anything in the book,
and the clinching sentence, with the students suddenly bending over
their catechisms, places the rector as the vehicle of pandybat morality.

The last of the theological questions is the telling question. Stephen
never expresses doubt of the existence of God nor of the essential validity
of the priestly office—his *Non serviam* is not a *non credo*, and he talks of
a "malevolent reality" behind these appearances—but the wine and bread
that were offered for his veneration were changed into vinegar and
crumbled into corruption. And it was the knowledge of that underlying
validity clashing with his refusal to do homage to vinegar and rot that
evoked his ambivalent poise of egocentric despair. The hell of Father
Arnall's sermon, so emotionally overwhelming, so picayune beside the
horrors that Stephen's imagination can generate, had no more ontological
content for Stephen than had "an eternity of bliss in the company of the
dean of studies."

The conflict of this central chapter is again between the phantasmal
and the real. What is real—psychologically real, because realized—is
Stephen's anguish and remorse, and its context in the life of the flesh.
What is phantasmal is the "heaven" of the Church and the "good life"
of the priest. It is only fear that makes him clutch after the latter at all;
his reaching out after orthodox salvation is, as we have come to expect,
presented in terms that judge it:

The wind blew over him and passed on to the myriads and myriads of
other souls, on whom God's favour shone now more and now less, stars
now brighter and now dimmer, sustained and failing. And the glimmer-
ing souls passed away, sustained and failing, merged in a moving breath.
One soul was lost; a tiny soul; his. It flickered once and went out, forgotten, lost. The end: black cold void waste.
    Consciousness of place came ebbing back to him slowly over a vast tract
of time unlit, unfelt, unlived. The squalid scene composed itself around
him; the common accents, the burning gasjets in the shops, odours of
fish and spirits and wet sawdust, moving men and women. An old woman
was about to cross the street, an oilcan in her hand. He bent down and
asked her was there a chapel near.   [*Portrait,* 140–141.]

That wan waste world of flickering stars is the best Stephen has been able
to do towards an imaginative grasp of the communion of Saints sustained
by God; "unlit, unfelt, unlived" explains succinctly why it had so little
hold on him, once fear had relaxed. Equally pertinent is the vision of
human temporal occupations the sermon evokes:

> What did it profit a man to gain the whole world if he lost his soul?
> At last he had understood: and human life lay around him, a plain of
> peace whereon antlike men laboured in brotherhood, their dead sleeping
> under quiet mounds.   [*Portrait,* 126.]

To maintain the life of grace in the midst of nature, sustained by so
cramped a vision of the life of nature, would mean maintaining an intolerable tension. Stephen's unrelenting philosophic bias, his determination
to understand what he is about, precludes his adopting the double standard of the Dubliners; to live both the life of nature and the life of grace,
he must enjoy an imaginative grasp of their relationship which stunts
neither. "No one doth well against his will," writes Saint Augustine, "even
though what he doth, be well"; and Stephen's will is firmly harnessed to
his understanding. And there is no one in Dublin to help him achieve
understanding. Father Arnall's sermon precludes rather than secures a
desirable outcome, for it follows the modes of pandybat morality and
Dublin materiality. Its only possible effect on Stephen is to lash his dor-
mant conscience into a frenzy. The description of Hell as "a strait and
dark and foul smelling prison, an abode of demons and lost souls, filled
with fire and smoke," with walls four thousand miles thick, its damned
packed in so tightly that "they are not even able to remove from the eye
the worm that gnaws it," is childishly grotesque beneath its sweeping
eloquence; and the hair-splitting catalogues of pains—pain of loss, pain
of conscience (divided into three heads), pain of extension, pain of intensity, pain of eternity—is cast in a brainlessly analytic mode that effec-
tively prevents any corresponding Heaven from possessing any reality at
all.

Stephen's unstable pact with the Church, and its dissolution, follows
the pattern of composition and dissipation established by his other
dreams: the dream for example of the tryst with "Mercedes," which found
ironic reality among harlots. It parallels exactly his earlier attempt to
"build a breakwater of order and elegance against the sordid tide of life
without him," whose failure, with the exhaustion of his money, was
epiphanized in the running-dry of a pot of pink enamel paint. His regi-
men at that time:

> He bought presents for everyone, overhauled his rooms, wrote out reso-
> lutions, marshalled his books up and down their shelves, pored over all
> kinds of price lists . . .   [*Portrait,* 97–98.]

is mirrored by his searching after spiritual improvement:

His daily life was laid out in devotional areas. By means of ejaculations and prayers he stored up ungrudgingly for the souls in purgatory centuries of days and quarantines and years. . . . He offered up each of his three daily chaplets that his soul might grow strong in each of the three theological virtues. . . . On each of the seven days of the week he further prayed that one of the seven gifts of the Holy Ghost might descend upon his soul.   [*Portrait*, 147–148.]

The "loan bank" he had opened for the family, out of which he had pressed loans on willing borrowers "that he might have the pleasure of making out receipts and reckoning the interests on sums lent" finds its counterpart in the benefits he stored up for souls in purgatory that he might enjoy the spiritual triumph of "achieving with ease so many fabulous ages of canonical penances." Both projects are parodies on the doctrine of economy of grace; both are attempts, corrupted by motivating self-interest, to make peace with Dublin on Dublin's own terms; and both are short-lived.

As this precise analogical structure suggests, the action of each of the five chapters is really the same action. Each chapter closes with a synthesis of triumph which the next destroys. The triumph of the appeal to Father Conmee from lower authority, of the appeal to the harlots from Dublin, of the appeal to the Church from sin, of the appeal to art from the priesthood (the bird-girl instead of the Virgin) is always the same triumph raised to a more comprehensive level. It is an attempt to find new parents; new fathers in the odd chapters, new objects of love in the even. The last version of Father Conmee is the "priest of the eternal imagination"; the last version of Mercedes is the "lure of the fallen seraphim." But the last version of the mother who said, "O, Stephen will apologise" is the mother who prays on the last page "that I may learn in my own life and away from home and friends what the heart is and what it feels." The mother remains.

The Double Female

As in *Dubliners* and *Exiles*, the female role in the *Portrait* is less to arouse than to elucidate masculine desires. Hence the complex function in the book of physical love: The physical is the analogue of the spiritual, as St. Augustine insisted in his *Confessions* (which, with Ibsen's *Brand,* is the chief archetype of Joyce's book). The poles between which this affection moves are those of St. Augustine and St. John: the Whore of Babylon and the Bride of Christ. The relation between the two is far from simple, and Stephen moves in a constant tension between them.

His desire, figured in the visions of Monte Cristo's Mercedes, "to meet in the real world the unsubstantial image which his soul so constantly beheld" draws him toward the prostitute ("In her arms he felt that he had suddenly become strong and fearless and sure of himself") and simultaneously toward the vaguely spiritual satisfaction represented with equal vagueness by the wraithlike E— C—, to whom he twice writes verses. The Emma Clery of *Stephen Hero,* with her loud forced manners and her body compact of pleasure, was refined into a wraith with a pair of initials to parallel an intangible Church. She is continually assimilated to the image of the Blessed Virgin and of the heavenly Bride. The torture she costs him is the torture his apostasy costs him. His flirtation with her is his flirtation with Christ. His profane villanelle draws its imagery from religion—the incense, the eucharistic hymn, the chalice—and her heart, following Dante's image, is a rose, and in her praise "the earth was like a swinging swaying censer, a ball of incense."

The woman is the Church. His vision of greeting Mercedes with "a sadly proud gesture of refusal":

> —Madam, I never eat muscatel grapes.   [*Portrait,* 63.]

is fulfilled when he refuses his Easter communion. Emma's eyes, in their one explicit encounter, speak to him from beneath a cowl. "The glories of Mary held his soul captive," and a temporary reconciliation of his lust and his spiritual thirst is achieved as he reads the Lesson out of the Song of Solomon. In the midst of his repentance she functions as imagined mediator: "The image of Emma appeared before him," and, repenting, "he imagined that he stood near Emma in a wide land, and, humbly and in tears, bent and kissed the elbow of her sleeve." Like Dante's Beatrice, she manifests in his earthly experience the Church Triumphant of his spiritual dream. And when he rejects her because she seems to be flirting with Father Moran, his anger is couched in the anti-clerical terms of his apostasy: "He had done well to leave her to flirt with her priest, to toy with a church which was the scullery-maid of Christendom."

That Kathleen ni Houlihan can flirt with priests is the unforgivable sin underlying Stephen's rejection of Ireland. But he makes a clear distinction between the stupid clericalism which makes intellectual and communal life impossible, and his long-nourished vision of an artist's Church Triumphant upon earth. He rejects the actual for daring to fall short of his vision.

The Final Balance

The climax of the book is of course Stephen's ecstatic discovery of his vocation at the end of Chapter IV. The prose rises in nervous excitement to beat again and again the tambours of a fin-de-siècle ecstasy:

> His heart trembled; his breath came faster and a wild spirit passed over his limbs as though he were soaring sunward. His heart trembled in an ecstasy of fear and his soul was in flight. His soul was soaring in an air beyond the world and the body he knew was purified in a breath and delivered of incertitude and made radiant and commingled with the

element of the spirit. An ecstasy of flight made radiant his eyes and wild
his breath and tremulous and wild and radiant his wind-swept limbs.

> —One! Two! . . . Look out!—
> —O, Cripes, I'm drownded!—   [*Portrait,* 169.]

The interjecting voices of course are those of bathers, but their ironic appropriateness to Stephen's Icarian "soaring sunward" is not meant to
escape us: divers have their own "ecstasy of flight," and Icarus was
"drownded." The imagery of Stephen's ecstasy is fetched from many
sources; we recognize Shelley's skylark, Icarus, the glorified body of the
Resurrection (cf. "His soul had arisen from the grave of boyhood, spurn-
ing her graveclothes") and a tremulousness from which it is difficult to
dissociate adolescent sexual dreams (which the Freudians tell us are frequently dreams of flying). The entire eight-page passage is cunningly organized with great variety of rhetoric and incident; but we cannot help
noticing the limits set on vocabulary and figures of thought. The empurpled triteness of such a cadence as "radiant his eyes and wild his breath
and tremulous and wild and radiant his wind-swept face" is enforced by
recurrence: "But her long fair hair was girlish: and girlish, and touched
with the wonder of mortal beauty, her face." "Ecstasy" is the keyword,
indeed. This riot of feelings corresponds to no vocation definable in mature terms; the paragraphs come to rest on images of irresponsible motion:

> He turned away from her suddenly and set off across the strand. His
> cheeks were aflame; his body was aglow; his limbs were trembling. On
> and on and on and on he strode, far out over the sands, singing wildly
> to the sea, crying to greet the advent of the life that had cried to him.
>   [*Portrait,* 172.]

What "life" connotes it skills not to ask; the word recurs and recurs. So
does the motion onward and onward and onward:

> A wild angel had appeared to him, the angel of mortal youth and beauty,
> an envoy from the fair courts of life, to throw open before him in an in-
> stant of ecstasy the gates of all the ways of error and glory. On and on
> and on and on!   [*Portrait,* 172.]

It may be well to recall Joyce's account of the romantic temper:

> . . . an insecure, unsatisfied, impatient temper which sees no fit abode
> here for its ideals and chooses therefore to behold them under insensible
> figures. As a result of this choice it comes to disregard certain limitations.
> Its figures are blown to wild adventures, lacking the gravity of solid
> bodies. . . .   [*Stephen Hero.*]

Joyce also called *Prometheus Unbound* "the Schwärmerei of a young
jew."

And it is quite plain from the final chapter of the *Portrait* that we are not to accept the mode of Stephen's "freedom" as the "message" of the book. The "priest of the eternal imagination" turns out to be indigestibly Byronic. Nothing is more obvious than his total lack of humour. The dark intensity of the first four chapters is moving enough, but our impulse on being confronted with the final edition of Stephen Dedalus is to laugh; and laugh at this moment we dare not; he is after all a victim being prepared for a sacrifice. His shape, as Joyce said, can no longer change. The art he has elected is not "the slow elaborative patience of the art of satisfaction." "On and on and on and on" will be its inescapable mode. He does not *see* the girl who symbolizes the full revelation; "she seemed like one whom magic had changed into the likeness of a strange and beautiful seabird," and he confusedly apprehends a sequence of downy and feathery incantations. What, in the last chapter, he does see, he sees only to reject, in favour of an incantatory "loveliness which has not yet come into the world."

The only creative attitude to language exemplified in the book is that of Stephen's father:

> —Is it Christy? he said. There's more cunning in one of those warts on his bald head than in a pack of jack foxes.   [*Portrait,* 28.]

His vitality is established before the book is thirty pages under way. Stephen, however, isn't enchanted at any time by the proximity of such talk. He isn't, as a matter of fact, even interested in it. Without a backward glance, he exchanges this father for a myth.

James Joyce

by Edmund Wilson

Ulysses was published in Paris in 1922. It had originally been conceived as a short story for *Dubliners,* and was to have been called "Mr.
Bloom's Day in Dublin" or something of the sort. But this idea was afterwards combined with the further history of Stephen Dedalus, the hero of
the autobiographical *Portrait of the Artist as a Young Man. Ulysses,*
however, in its final form as a volume of seven-hundred-odd large pages,
took shape as something entirely different from either of Joyce's earlier
books, and it must be approached from a different point of view than as
if it were merely, like the others, a straight work of Naturalistic fiction.

The key to *Ulysses* is in the title—and this key is indispensable if we
are to appreciate the book's real depth and scope. Ulysses, as he figures
in the *Odyssey,* is a sort of type of the average intelligent Greek: among
the heroes, he is distinguished for cunning rather than for exalted wisdom, and for common sense, quickness and nerve rather than for, say,
the passionate bravery of an Achilles or the steadfastness and stoutness
of a Hector. The *Odyssey* exhibits such a man in practically every situation and relation of an ordinary human life—Ulysses, in the course of
his wanderings, runs the whole gauntlet of temptations and ordeals and
through his wits he survives them all to return at last to his home and
family and to reassert himself there as master. The *Odyssey* thus provides
a classical model for a writer attempting a modern epic of the ordinary
man—and a model particularly attractive to a modern writer by reason
of the apparently calculated effectiveness, the apparent sophistication,
of its form. By a device suggestive of some of the novels of Conrad, Homer
has framed the wanderings of Ulysses between an introductory group of
books in which our interest is aroused in the hero before we meet him
by Telemachus's search for his lost father, and a culminating group of
books which present dramatically and on a larger scale the wanderer's
return home.

Now the *Ulysses* of Joyce is a modern *Odyssey,* which follows closely
the classical *Odyssey* in both subject and form; and the significance of
the characters and incidents of its ostensibly Naturalistic narrative can-

---

"James Joyce." Excerpt from *Axel's Castle* by Edmund Wilson is reprinted by permission of Charles Scribner's Sons. Copyright 1931 Charles Scribner's Sons; renewal
copyright © 1959 Edmund Wilson.

not properly be understood without reference to the Homeric original. Joyce's Telemachus of the opening books is Stephen Dedalus—that is, Joyce himself. The Dedaluses, as we have already learned from *A Portrait of the Artist as a Young Man,* are a shabby-genteel family of Dubliners. Stephen's father, Simon Dedalus, has run through a great variety of employments to end up as nothing in particular, a drinker, a decayed sport, an amateur tenor, a well-known character of the bars. But Stephen has been given a good education at a Jesuit college, and we have seen him, at the end of the earlier novel, on the point of leaving for France to study and write. At the beginning of *Ulysses,* he has been back in Dublin a year: he had been summoned home from Paris by a telegram that his mother was dying. And now, a year after her death, the Dedalus family, already reduced to poverty, has become completely demoralized and disintegrated. While Stephen's young sisters and brothers have hardly enough to eat, Simon Dedalus makes the rounds of the pubs. Stephen, who has always resented his father, feels now that in effect he has none. He is more isolated in Dublin than ever. He is Telemachus in search of a Ulysses. His friend, the medical student, Buck Mulligan, with whom he is living in an old tower on the coast and who believes himself to share Stephen's artistic tastes and intellectual interests, really humiliates him by patronizing him and turns to ridicule his abilities and ambitions. He is Antinous, that boldest of Penelope's suitors, who, while Ulysses is away, tries to make himself master of his house and mocks at Telemachus. Stephen has announced at the end of the earlier book that he is going forth "to forge in the smithy of my soul the uncreated conscience of my race"; and now he has returned to Dublin baffled and disinherited— his life with Mulligan is dissolute and unproductive. Yet as Telemachus finds friends and helpers, so Stephen is reminded by the old woman who brings the milk for breakfast in the tower of that Ireland whose uncreated conscience it is still his destiny to forge: "Old and secret . . . maybe a messenger." She is Athene in the guise of Mentor who provides Telemachus with his ship; and the memory of Kevin Egan, an Irish exile in Paris, is the Menelaus who speeds him on his way.

The scene now shifts, as it does in the *Odyssey,* to the lost Ulysses himself. Joyce's Ulysses is a Dublin Jew, an advertisement canvasser named Bloom. Like Stephen, he dwells among aliens: a Jew and the son of a Hungarian father, he is still more or less of a foreigner among the Irish; and a man of something less than mediocre abilities, but of real sensibility and intelligence, he has little in common with the other inhabitants of the lower-middle-class world in which he lives. He has been married for sixteen years to the buxom daughter of an Irish army officer, a professional singer, of prodigious sexual appetite, who has been continually and indiscriminately unfaithful to him. They have had one daughter, who is already growing up and apparently going the way of her mother; and one son, of whom Bloom had hoped that he might resemble, that he might refine upon, himself, but who died eleven days after he was born. Things have never been the same between the Blooms since the death of this son; it is now more than ten years since Bloom has attempted complete intercourse with his wife—it is as if the birth of the sickly Rudy had discouraged him and made him doubt his virility. He is aware that his wife has lovers; but he does not complain or try to interfere—he is even resigned to her accepting money from them. He is a Ulysses with no Telemachus and cut off from his Penelope.

We now follow Bloom's adventures on the day of June 16, 1904 (the whole of *Ulysses* takes place within less than twenty-four hours). Lotoseaters allure him; he is affrighted by Laestrygonians. He assists at the burial of an Elpenor and descends with him in imagination to the underworld; he suffers from the varying favor of an Æolus. He escapes by ruse from the ferocity of a Cyclops and he disengages himself through prudence from the maiden charms of a Nausicaa. And he emerges finally a man again from the brothel of a Circe who had transformed him into a swine.

The comings and goings of Stephen during the day are woven in and out among the wanderings of Bloom: the two encounter each other twice but do not recognize each other. Both men, we become aware, are constantly accompanied and oppressed by ideas which they have tried to dismiss from their minds: the family situation of each really lies back of and explains all that he does that day. In Stephen's case, it is only a few days from the anniversary of his mother's death, and he is haunted by the memory of it: she had begged him on her deathbed to kneel down and pray for her soul and, in rebellion against the Catholic education which had disciplined and maimed his spirit, jealous of the independence he had won and in fear of the past to which he had returned, he had cruelly refused and had allowed her to die without the comfort of believing that he had repented of his apostasy. But now that she is dead, this incident tortures him. He has in the early morning reproached Mulligan—accusing really himself—for something the latter had said about Stephen's mother at the time of her death which Stephen had overheard and resented; and, as he has looked out upon the bright morning sea, the pathos and horror of her life have become suddenly vivid to him—he has been dragged back to relive all that she had suffered. Then, "No, mother!" he has cried out within himself as he thrust her memory down out of his mind, "let me be and let me live!" But through his whole bitter and baffled day, it is his helpless feeling of guilt toward his mother, his hopeless discouragement and disgust with his father, which govern all his thoughts and movements. When he teaches school, he brings the class to a close by a hysterical joke about "the fox burying his grandmother under a hollybush," and in a stupid boy who cannot do his sums he can see now only his own graceless youth which his mother had shielded from the world. After school, he has gone to walk on the beach and has contemplated paying a visit to the family of a maternal uncle whom he despises, as if he could do penance in this fashion for his hardness to his mother and somehow make it up to her now by kindness to her wretched relatives; but again the counter-impulse which had proved too strong on the former occasion comes into play to block his intention: his mind drifts off to other things and he walks beyond where he should have turned. The artist still conflicts with the son—the two are irreconcilable: he sets out to compose a poem, but the poem itself breaks down and he is left gazing at a silent homing ship.—Visiting the library later in the day, he improvises a long, pretentious lecture on the relation of Shakespeare to his father—a lecture which has little to do with Shakespeare, but a good deal to do with Stephen himself.

And as Stephen is ridden by thoughts of his parents, so Bloom is ridden by thoughts of his wife. He has seen Molly at breakfast get a letter which he suspects—and suspects rightly—to be from Blazes Boylan, a flashy buck about town who is managing a concert tour for her and with whom she is having a love affair. All day he has to change the subject when Boylan's name is mentioned—all day he avoids meeting him in the street. In the afternoon, while Bloom is eating at the Ormond Hotel, Boylan comes into the bar, gets a drink and sets off to call on Mrs. Bloom, and when he has gone, Bloom hears the men in the bar talking and laughing about Molly's easy favors. And the conversation, later on in the pub, about Boylan's having won money in a boxing match—in spite of Bloom's gently insistent efforts to induce the company to talk about tennis—is one of the incidents which give rise to an antagonism between Bloom and the rest of the company and eventually to the quarrel between the Cyclops-Citizen and Bloom. At the end of the Nausicaa episode, the voice of the cuckoo-clock from the priest's house tells Bloom that he is now a cuckold.

In the evening, Bloom goes to a maternity hospital to inquire after the wife of a friend, who has been having a hard delivery: there he meets and recognizes Stephen, who is drinking with the medical students. In the *Odyssey*, the final shipwreck of Ulysses and his subsequent misfortunes are the result of the impiety of his companions, who in defiance of all his warnings have killed and eaten the Oxen of the Sun. So Bloom is pained by the impiety of the medical students as they joke obscenely about childbirth and maternity. On the part of Stephen, whose mother died only a year ago, this levity seems especially shocking, but Stephen's very feeling of guilt about her makes him particularly blasphemous and brutal. Yet Bloom has himself in his own way offended against the principle of fertility by his recent prolonged neglect of Molly: the Calypso who has detained him since his shipwreck is the nymph who hangs in his bedroom and whom he makes the object of amorous fantasies. It is this sin against fertility which—at the hour when Mrs. Bloom is entertaining Boylan—has landed Bloom on the Phæacian strand indulging in further

erotic daydreams in connection with little Gerty MacDowell, the Nausicaa of the Dublin beach.

When Mrs. Purefoy's child has finally been born, the party rushes out
to a public house; and, later on—after a drunken altercation between
Dedalus and Buck Mulligan at the tram station, in which Antinous and
Telemachus apparently dispute over the key to the tower and Telemachus
goes away homeless—Stephen, with one of his companions and with
Bloom following some distance behind, proceed to a brothel. Both, by
this time, are pretty drunk—though Bloom, with his invincible prudence,
is not so drunk as Stephen. And in their drunkenness, in the sordid gas-
light and to the tune of the mechanical piano of the brothel, their respective preoccupations emerge fully for the first time since the morning
into their conscious minds: Bloom beholds himself, in a hideous vision,
looking on at Blazes Boylan and Molly, an abject cuckold, the laughing-
stock of the world; and there rises suddenly in Stephen's imagination the
figure of his dead mother come back from the grave to remind him of her
bleak disheartened love and to implore him to pray for her soul. But
again he will not, cannot, acquiesce; in a desperate drunken gesture, in-
tolerably torn by his conflict of impulses, by his emotions which deadlock
each other, he lifts his stick and smashes the chandelier—then rushes out
into the street, where he gets embroiled with two English Tommies and
knocked down. Bloom has followed and, as he bends over Stephen, beholds an apparition of his own dead son, little Rudy, as Bloom would
have had him live to be—learned, cultivated, sensitive, refined: such a
youth, in short, as Stephen Dedalus. Ulysses and Telemachus are united.

Bloom picks Stephen up and takes him first to a coffee-stand, then home
to his own house. He tries to talk to him of the arts and sciences, of the
general ideas which interest him; but Stephen is morose and exhausted
and makes little response. Bloom begs him to spend the night—to come
and live with them, but Stephen declines and presently takes his leave.
Bloom goes up, goes to bed with Molly, describes to her his adventures of
the day, and soon drops off to sleep.

But Bloom's encounter with Stephen is to affect both Stephen's life and
the relations between the Blooms. To have rescued and talked with Stephen has somehow restored Bloom's self-confidence. He has gotten into
the habit in the past of cooking breakfast for Molly in the morning and
bringing it to her in bed—it is the first thing we have seen him doing at
the beginning of the day; but tonight, before he goes to sleep, he gives
her to understand that he expects her to get breakfast next morning herself and to bring it up to him. This amazes and disconcerts Mrs. Bloom,
and the rest of the book is the record of her meditations as she lies awake
thinking over Bloom's homecoming. She has been mystified by his recent
behavior, and her attitude toward him now is at first a mixture of jealousy
and resentment. She congratulates herself upon the fact that, if Bloom
neglects her nowadays, her needs are ably supplied by Blazes Boylan. But

as she begins to ruminate on the possibility of Stephen Dedalus's coming to live with them, the idea of Blazes Boylan's coarseness becomes intolerable to her: the thought of Stephen has made her fastidious, and, rapidly becoming very tender about him, she prefigures a relation between them of an ambiguous but intimate character, half-amorous, half-maternal. Yet it is Bloom himself who has primarily been the cause of this revolution in Molly's mind: in telling her about Stephen, he has imposed upon her again his own values; in staying away from the house all day and coming back very late at night, and in asking for his breakfast in bed, he has reasserted his own will. And she goes back in her mind over her experience of Bloom—their courtship, their married life. She remembers how, when she had promised to marry him, it had been his intelligence and his sympathetic nature, that touch of imagination which distinguished him from other men, which had influenced her in his favor—"because he understood or felt what a woman is and I knew I could always get around him"; and on the day when he had first kissed her, he had called her "a flower of the mountain." It is in the mind of his Penelope that this Ulysses has slain the suitors who have been disputing his place.

As for Stephen, unresponsive as he has seemed to Bloom's interest and cordiality, he has at last, none the less, found in Dublin someone sufficiently sympathetic to himself to give him the clew, to supply him with the subject, which will enable him to enter imaginatively—as an artist—into the common life of his race. It is possible that Molly and Bloom, as a result of Bloom's meeting with Stephen, will resume normal marital relations; but it is certain that Stephen, as a result of this meeting, will go away and write *Ulysses*. Buck Mulligan has told us that the young poet says he is going "to write something in ten years": that was in 1904—*Ulysses* is dated at the end as having been begun in 1914.

II

This is the story of *Ulysses* in the light of its Homeric parallel; but to describe the book in such a way gives no idea of what it is really like—of its psychological and technical discoveries or of its magnificent poetry.

Ulysses is, I suppose, the most completely "written" novel since Flaubert. The example of the great prose poet of Naturalism has profoundly influenced Joyce—in his attitude toward the modern bourgeois world and in the contrast implied by the Homeric parallel of *Ulysses* between our own and the ancient world, as well as in an ideal of rigorous objectivity and of adaptation of style to subject—as the influence of that other great Naturalistic poet, Ibsen, is obvious in Joyce's single play, *Exiles*. But Flaubert had, in general, confined himself to fitting the cadence and the phrase precisely to the mood or object described; and even then it was the phrase rather than the cadence, and the object rather than the mood, with which he was occupied—for mood and cadence in Flaubert do not

really vary much: he never embodies himself in his characters nor identifies his voice with theirs, and as a result, Flaubert's own characteristic
tone of the sombre-pompous-ironic becomes, in the long run, a little mo-
notonous. But Joyce has undertaken in *Ulysses* not merely to render,
with the last accuracy and beauty, the actual sights and sounds among
which his people move, but, showing us the world as his characters perceive it, to find the unique vocabulary and rhythm which will represent
the thoughts of each. If Flaubert taught Maupassant to look for the definitive adjectives which would distinguish a given cab-driver from every
other cab-driver at the Rouen station, so Joyce has set himself the task
of finding the precise dialect which will distinguish the thoughts of a
given Dubliner from those of every other Dubliner. Thus the mind of
Stephen Dedalus is represented by a weaving of bright poetic images and
fragmentary abstractions, of things remembered from books, on a rhythm
sober, melancholy and proud; that of Bloom by a rapid staccato notation,
prosaic but vivid and alert, jetting out in all directions in little ideas
growing out of ideas; the thoughts of Father Conmee, the Rector of the
Jesuit college, by a precise prose, perfectly colorless and orderly; those of
Gerty-Nausicaa by a combination of schoolgirl colloquialisms with the
jargon of cheap romance; and the ruminations of Mrs. Bloom by a long,
unbroken rhythm of brogue, like the swell of some profound sea.

Joyce takes us thus directly into the consciousness of his characters, and
in order to do so, he has availed himself of methods of which Flaubert
never dreamed—of the methods of Symbolism. He has, in *Ulysses*, ex-
ploited together, as no writer had thought to do before, the resources
both of Symbolism and of Naturalism. Proust's novel, masterly as it is,
does perhaps represent a falling over into decadence of psychological fiction: the subjective element is finally allowed to invade and to deteriorate
even those aspects of the story which really ought to be kept strictly objective if one is to believe that it is actually happening. But Joyce's grasp
on his objective world never slips: his work is unshakably established on
Naturalistic foundations. Where *A la Recherche du Temps Perdu* leaves
many things vague—the ages of the characters and sometimes the actual
circumstances of their lives, and—what is worse—whether they may not
be merely bad dreams that the hero has had, *Ulysses* has been logically
thought out and accurately documented to the last detail: everything that
happens is perfectly consistent, and we know precisely what the characters
wore, how much they paid for things, where they were at different times
of the day, what popular songs they sang and what events they read of in
the papers, on June 16, 1904. Yet when we are admitted to the mind of
any one of them, we are in a world as complex and special, a world sometimes as fantastic or obscure, as that of a Symbolist poet—and a world
rendered by similar devices of language. We are more at home in the
minds of Joyce's characters than we are likely to be, except after some
study, in the mind of a Mallarmé or an Eliot, because we know more

about the circumstances in which they find themselves; but we are confronted with the same sort of confusion between emotions, perceptions, and reasonings, and we are likely to be disconcerted by the same sort of hiatuses of thought, when certain links in the association of ideas are dropped down into the unconscious mind so that we are obliged to divine them for ourselves.

But Joyce has carried the methods of Symbolism further than merely to set a Naturalistic scene and then, in that frame, to represent directly the minds of his different characters in Symbolistic monologues like "Mr. Prufrock" or "L'Après-midi d'un Faune." And it is the fact that he has not always stopped here which makes parts of *Ulysses* so puzzling when we read them for the first time. So long as we are dealing with internal monologues in realistic settings, we are dealing with familiar elements merely combined in a novel way—that is, instead of reading, "Bloom said to himself, 'I might manage to write a story to illustrate some proverb or other. I could sign it, Mr. and Mrs. L. M. Bloom,'" we read, "Might manage a sketch. By Mr. and Mrs. L. M. Bloom. Invent a story for some proverb which?" But as we get further along in *Ulysses*, we find the realistic setting oddly distorting itself and deliquescing, and we are astonished at the introduction of voices which seem to belong neither to the characters nor to the author.

The point is that of each of his episodes Joyce has tried to make an independent unit which shall blend the different sets of elements of each —the minds of the characters, the place where they are, the atmosphere about them, the feeling of the time of day. Joyce had already, in *A Portrait of the Artist,* experimented, as Proust had done, in varying the form and style of the different sections to fit the different ages and phases of his hero—from the infantile fragments of childhood impressions, through the ecstatic revelations and the terrifying nightmares of adolescence, to the self-possessed notations of young manhood. But in *A Portrait of the Artist,* Joyce was presenting everything from the point of view of a single particular character, Dedalus; whereas in *Ulysses* he is occupied with a number of different personalities, of whom Dedalus is no longer the centre, and his method, furthermore, of enabling us to live in their world is not always merely a matter of making us shift from the point of view of one to the point of view of another. In order to understand what Joyce is doing here, one must conceive a set of Symbolistic poems, themselves involving characters whose minds are represented Symbolistically, depending not from the sensibility of the poet speaking in his own person, but from the poet's imagination playing a rôle absolutely impersonal and always imposing upon itself all the Naturalistic restrictions in regard to the story it is telling at the same time that it allows itself to exercise all the Symbolistic privileges in regard to the way it tells it. We are not likely to be prepared for this by the early episodes of *Ulysses*: they are as sober and as clear as the morning light of the Irish coast in which they take

place: the characters' perceptions of the external world are usually distinct from their thoughts and feelings about them. But in the newspaper
office, for the first time, a general atmosphere begins to be created, beyond
the specific minds of the characters, by a punctuation of the text with
newspaper heads which announce the incidents in the narrative. And in
the library scene, which takes place in the early afternoon, the setting and
people external to Stephen begin to dissolve in his apprehension of them,
heightened and blurred by some drinks at lunchtime and by the intellectual excitement of the conversation amid the dimness and tameness of
the library—"Eglintoneyes, quick with pleasure, looked up shybrightly.
Gladly glancing, a merry puritan, through the twisted eglantine." Here,
however, we still see all through Stephen's eyes—through the eyes of a
single character; but in the scene in the Ormond Hotel, which takes place
a couple of hours later—our reveries absorb the world about us progres-
sively as daylight fades and as the impressions of the day accumulate—
the sights and sounds and the emotional vibrations and the appetites for
food and drink of the late afternoon, the laughter, the gold-and-bronze
hair of the barmaids, the jingling of Blazes Boylan's car on his way to
visit Molly Bloom, the ringing of the hoofs of the horses of the viceregal
cavalcade clanging in through the open window, the ballad sung by Simon
Dedalus, the sound of the piano accompaniment and the comfortable
supper of Bloom—though they are not all, from beginning to end, perceived by Bloom himself—all mingle quite un-Naturalistically in a harmony of bright sound, ringing color, poignant indistinct feeling and de-
clining light. The scene in the brothel, where it is night and where Dedalus and Bloom are drunk, is like a slowed-up moving picture, in which the
intensified vision of reality is continually lapsing into phantasmagoric
visions; and the let-down after the excitement of this, the lassitude and
staleness of the cabmen's shelter where Bloom takes Stephen to get him
some coffee, is rendered by a prose as flavorless, as weary, and as banal as
the incidents which it reports. Joyce has achieved here, by different methods, a relativism like that of Proust: he is reproducing in literature the
different aspects, the different proportions and textures, which things and
people take on at different times and under different circumstances.

III

I do not think that Joyce has been equally successful with all these
technical devices in *Ulysses*; but before it will be possible to discuss them
further, we must approach the book from another point of view.

It has always been characteristic of Joyce to neglect action, narrative,
drama, of the usual kind, even the direct impact on one another of the
characters as we get it in the ordinary novel, for a sort of psychological
portraiture. There is tremendous vitality in Joyce, but very little movement. Like Proust, he is symphonic rather than narrative. His fiction has

its progressions, its developments, but they are musical rather than dramatic. The most elaborate and interesting piece in *Dubliners*—the story called "The Dead"—is simply a record of the modification brought about during a single evening in the relations of a husband and wife by the man's becoming aware, from the effect produced on the woman by a song which she has heard at a family party, that she has once been loved by another man; *A Portrait of the Artist as a Young Man* is simply a series of pictures of the author at successive stages of his development; the theme of *Exiles* is, like that of "The Dead," the modification in the relations of a husband and wife which follows the reappearance of a man who has been the wife's lover. And *Ulysses,* again, for all its vast scale, is simply the story of another small but significant change in the relations of yet another married couple as a result of the impingement on their household of the personality of an only slightly known young man. Most of these stories cover a period of only a few hours, and they are never carried any further. When Joyce has explored one of these situations, when he has established the small gradual readjustment, he has done all that interests him.

All, that is, from the point of view of ordinary incident. But though Joyce almost entirely lacks appetite for violent conflict or vigorous action, his work is prodigiously rich and alive. His force, instead of following a line, expands itself in every dimension (including that of time) about a single point. The world of *Ulysses* is animated by a complex inexhaustible life: We revisit it as we do a city, where we come more and more to recognize faces, to understand personalities, to grasp relations, currents, and interests. Joyce has exercised considerable technical ingenuity in introducing us to the elements of his story in an order which will enable us to find our bearings: yet I doubt whether any human memory is capable, on a first reading, of meeting the demands of *Ulysses.* And when we reread it, we start in at any point, as if it were indeed something solid like a city which actually existed in space and which could be entered from any direction—as Joyce is said, in composing his books, to work on the different parts simultaneously. More than any other work of fiction, unless perhaps the *Comédie Humaine, Ulysses* creates the illusion of a living social organism. We see it only for twenty hours, yet we know its past as well as its present. We possess Dublin, seen, heard, smelt and felt, brooded over, imagined, remembered.

Joyce's handling of this immense material, his method of giving his book a shape, resembles nothing else in modern fiction. The first critics of *Ulysses* mistook the novel for a "slice of life" and objected that it was too fluid or too chaotic. They did not recognize a plot because they could not recognize a progression; and the title told them nothing. They could not even discover a pattern. It is now apparent, however, that *Ulysses* suffers from an excess of design rather than from a lack of it. Joyce has drawn up an outline of his novel, of which he has allowed certain of his

commentators to avail themselves, but which he has not allowed them
to publish in its entirety (though it is to be presumed that the book on
Ulysses which Mr. Stuart Gilbert has announced will include all the information contained in it); and from this outline it appears that Joyce has
set himself the task of fulfilling the requirements of a most complicated
scheme—a scheme which we could scarcely have divined except in its
more obvious features. For even if we had known about the Homeric
parallel and had identified certain of the correspondences—if we had
had no difficulty in recognizing the Cyclops in the ferocious professional
Fenian, or Circe in the brothel-keeper, or Hades in the cemetery—we
should never have suspected how closely and how subtly the parallel had
been followed—we should never have guessed, for example, that when
Bloom passes through the National Library while Stephen is having his
discussion with the literary men, he is escaping, on the one hand, a Scylla
—that is, Aristotle, the rock of Dogma; and, on the other, a Charybdis—
Plato, the whirlpool of Mysticism; nor that, when Stephen walks on the
seashore, he is reënacting the combat with Proteus—in this case, primal
matter, of whose continual transformations Stephen is reminded by the
objects absorbed or washed up by the sea, but whose forms he is able to
hold and fix, as the Homeric Proteus was held and vanquished, by power
of the words which give him images for them. Nor should we have known
that the series of phrases and onomatopoetic syllables placed at the beginning of the Sirens episode—the singing in the Ormond Hotel—and selected from the narrative which follows, are supposed to be musical
themes and that the episode itself is a fugue; and though we may have
felt the ironic effect of the specimens of inflated Irish journalism introduced at regular intervals in the conversation with the patriot in the pub
—we should hardly have understood that these had been produced by a
deliberate technique of "gigantism"—for, since the Citizen represents the
Cyclops, and since the Cyclops was a giant, he must be rendered formida-
ble by a parade of all the banalities of his patriotic claptrap swollen to
gigantic proportions. We should probably never have guessed all this,
and we should certainly never have guessed at the ingenuity which Joyce
has expended in other ways. Not only, we learn from the outline, is there
an elaborate Homeric parallel in *Ulysses,* but there is also an organ of the
human body and a human science or art featured in every episode. We
look these up, a little incredulously, but there, we find, they all actually
are—buried and disguised beneath the realistic surface, but carefully
planted, unmistakably dwelt upon. And if we are tipped off, we are able
further to discover all sorts of concealed ornaments and emblems: in the
chapter of the Lotos-Eaters, for example, countless references to flowers;
in the Laestrygonians, to eating; in the Sirens, puns on musical terms;
and in Æolus, the newspaper office, not merely many references to wind
but, according to Mr. Gilbert—the art featured in this episode being
Rhetoric—some hundred different figures of speech.

Now the Homeric parallel in *Ulysses* is in general pointedly and charmingly carried out and justifies itself: It does help to give the story a universal significance and it enables Joyce to show us in the actions and the relations of his characters meanings which he perhaps could not easily have indicated in any other way—since the characters themselves must be largely unaware of these meanings and since Joyce has adopted the strict objective method, in which the author must not comment on the action. And we may even accept the arts and sciences and the organs of the human body as making the book complete and comprehensive, if a little laboriously systematic—the whole of man's experience in a day. But when we get all these things together and further complicated by the virtuosity of the technical devices, the result is sometimes baffling or confusing. We become aware, as we examine the outline, that when we went through *Ulysses* for the first time, it was these organs and arts and sciences and Homeric correspondences which sometimes so discouraged our interest. We had been climbing over these obstacles without knowing it, in our attempts to follow Dedalus and Bloom. The trouble was that, beyond the ostensible subject and, as it were, beneath the surface of the narrative, too many other subjects and too many different orders of subjects were being proposed to our attention.

It seems to me difficult, then, not to conclude that Joyce elaborated *Ulysses* too much—that he tried to put too many things into it. What is the value of all the references to flowers in the Lotos-Eaters chapter, for example? They do not create in the Dublin streets an atmosphere of lotus-eating—we are merely puzzled, if we have not been told to look for them, as to why Joyce has chosen to have Bloom think and see certain things, of which the final explanation is that they are pretexts for mentioning flowers. And do not the gigantic interpolations of the Cyclops episode defeat their object by making it impossible for us to follow the narrative? The interpolations are funny in themselves, the incident related is a masterpiece of language and humor, the idea of combining them seems happy, yet the effect is mechanical and annoying: in the end we have to read the whole thing through, skipping the interpolations, in order to find out what has happened. The worst example of the capacities for failure of this too synthetic, too systematic, method seems to me the scene in the maternity hospital. I have described above what actually takes place there as I have worked it out, after several readings and in the light of Joyce's outline. The Oxen of the Sun are "Fertility"—the crime committed against them is "Fraud." But, not content with this, Joyce has been at pains to fill the episode with references to real cattle and to include a long conversation about bulls. As for the special technique, it seems to me in this case not to have any real appropriateness to the situation, but to have been dictated by sheer fantastic pedantry: Joyce describes his method here as "embryonic," in conformity to the subject, maternity, and the chapter is written as a series of parodies of English literary styles from the bad Latin of the early chronicles up through Huxley and Carlyle, the development of the language corresponding to the growth of the child in the womb. Now something important takes place in this episode —the meeting between Dedalus and Bloom—and an important point is being made about it. But we miss the point because it is all we can do to follow what is happening at the drinking party, itself rather a confused affair, through the medium of the language of the Morte d'Arthur, the seventeenth-century diaries, the eighteenth-century novels, and a great many other kinds of literature in which we are not prepared at the moment to be interested. If we pay attention to the parodies, we miss the story; and if we try to follow the story, we are unable to appreciate the parodies. The parodies have spoiled the story; and the necessity of telling the story through them has taken most of the life out of the parodies.

Joyce has as little respect as Proust for the capacities of the reader's attention; and one feels, in Joyce's case as in Proust's, that the *longueurs* which break our backs, the mechanical combinations of elements which fail to coalesce, are partly a result of the effort of a supernormally energetic mind to compensate by piling things up for an inability to make them move.

We have now arrived, in the maternity hospital, at the climactic scenes of the story, and Joyce has bogged us as he has never bogged us before. We shall forget the Oxen of the Sun in the wonderful night-town scene which follows it—but we shall be bogged afterwards worse than ever in the interminable let-down of the cabman's shelter and in the scientific question-and-answer chapter which undertakes to communicate to us through the most opaque and uninviting medium possible Dedalus's conversation with Bloom. The night-town episode itself and Mrs. Bloom's soliloquy, which closes the book, are, of course, among the best things in it—but the relative proportions of the other three latter chapters and the jarring effect of the pastiche style sandwiched in with the straight Naturalistic seem to me artistically absolutely indefensible. One can understand that Joyce may have intended the colorless and tiresome episodes to set off the rich and vivid ones, and also that it is of the essence of his point of view to represent the profoundest changes of our lives as beginning naturally between night and morning without the parties' appreciating their importance at the time; but a hundred and sixty-one more or less deliberately tedious pages are too heavy a dead weight for even the brilliant flights of the other hundred and ninety-nine pages to carry. Furthermore, Joyce has here half-buried his story under the virtuosity of his technical devices. It is almost as if he had elaborated it so much and worked over it so long that he had forgotten, in the amusement of writing parodies, the drama which he had originally intended to stage; or as if he were trying to divert and overwhelm us by irrelevant entertainments and feats in order that we might not be dissatisfied with the flatness—except for the drunken scene—of Dedalus's final meeting with Bloom; or even perhaps as if he did not, after all, quite want us to understand his story, as if he had, not quite conscious of what he was doing, ended by throwing up between us and it a fortification of solemn burlesque prose —as if he were shy and solicitous about it, and wanted to protect it from us.

IV

Yet even these episodes to which I have objected contribute something valuable to *Ulysses*. In the chapter of parodies, for example, Joyce seems to be saying to us: "Here are specimens of the sort of thing that man has written about himself in the past—how naïve or pretentious they seem! I have broken through these assumptions and pretences and shown you how he must recognize himself today." And in the question-and-answer chapter, which is written entirely from the conventional point of view of science and where we are supplied with every possible physical, statistical, biographical, and astronomical fact about Stephen's visit to Bloom: "This is all that the twentieth-century man thinks he knows about himself and his universe. Yet how mechanical and rigid this reasoning seems when we apply it to Molly and Bloom—how inadequate to explain them!"

For one of the most remarkable features of *Ulysses* is its interest as an investigation into the nature of human consciousness and behavior. Its importance from the point of view of psychology has never, it seems to me, been properly appreciated—though its influence on other books and, in consequence, upon our ideas about ourselves, has already been profound. Joyce has attempted in *Ulysses* to render as exhaustively, as precisely, and as directly as it is possible in words to do, what our participation in life is like—or rather, what it seems to us like as from moment to moment we live. In order to make this record complete, he has been obliged to disregard a number of conventions of taste which, especially in English-speaking countries, have in modern times been pretty strictly observed, even by the writers who have aimed to be most scrupulously truthful. Joyce has studied what we are accustomed to consider the dirty, the trivial and the base elements in our lives with the relentlessness of a modern psychologist; and he has also—what the contemporary Naturalist has seldom been poet enough for—done justice to all those elements in our lives which we have been in the habit of describing by such names as love, nobility, truth and beauty. It is curious to reflect that a number of critics—including, curiously enough, Arnold Bennett—should have found Joyce misanthropic. Flaubert is misanthropic, if you like—and in reproducing his technique, Joyce sometimes suggests his acrid tone. But Stephen, Bloom and Mrs. Bloom are certainly not either unamiable or unattractive—and for all their misfortunes and shortcomings, they inspire us with considerable respect. Stephen and Bloom are played off a little against the duller and meaner people about them; but even these people can scarcely be said to be treated with bitterness, even when, as in the case of Buck Mulligan or the elder Dedalus, Stephen's feeling about them is bitter. Joyce is remarkable, rather, for equanimity: in spite of the nervous intensity of *Ulysses,* there is a real serenity and detachment behind it—we are in the presence of a mind which has much in common with that of a certain type of philosopher, who in his effort to understand the causes of things, to interrelate the different elements of the universe, has reached a point where the ordinary values of good and bad, beautiful and ugly, have been lost in the excellence and beauty of transcendent understanding itself.

I believe that the first readers of *Ulysses* were shocked, not merely by Joyce's use of certain words ordinarily excluded today from English literature, but by his way of representing those aspects of human nature which we tend to consider incongruous as intimately, inextricably mingled. Yet the more we read *Ulysses,* the more we are convinced of its psychological truth, and the more we are amazed at Joyce's genius in mastering and in presenting, not through analysis or generalization, but by the complete recreation of life in the process of being lived, the relations of human beings to their environment and to each other; the nature of their perception of what goes on about them and of what goes on within themselves; and the interdependence of their intellectual, their physical, their professional and their emotional lives. To have traced all these interdependencies, to have given each of these elements its value, yet never to have lost sight of the moral through preoccupation with the physical, nor to have forgotten the general in the particular; to have exhibited ordinary humanity without either satirizing it or sentimentalizing it—this would already have been sufficiently remarkable; but to have subdued all this material to the uses of a supremely finished and disciplined work of art is a feat which has hardly been equalled in the literature of our time.

In Stephen's diary in *A Portrait of the Artist,* we find this significant entry apropos of a poem by Yeats: "Michael Robartes remembers forgotten beauty and, when his arms wrap her round, he presses in his arms the loveliness which has long faded from the world. Not this. Not at all. I desire to press in my arms the loveliness which has not yet come into the world."

And with *Ulysses,* Joyce has brought into literature a new and unknown beauty. Some readers have regretted the extinction in the later Joyce of the charming lyric poet of his two little books of poems and the *fin de siècle* prose writer of the *fin de siècle* phases of *A Portrait of the Artist as a Young Man* (both the prose and verse of the early Joyce showed the influence of Yeats). This poet is still present in *Ulysses:* "Kind air defined the coigns of houses in Kildare Street. No birds. Frail from the housetops two plumes of smoke ascended, pluming, and in a flaw of softness softly were blown." But the conventions of the romantic lyric, of "æsthetic" *fin de siècle* prose, even of the æsthetic Naturalism of Flaubert, can no longer, for Joyce, be made to accommodate the reality of experience. The diverse elements of experience are perceived in different relations and they must be differently represented. Joyce has found for this new vision a new language, but a language which, instead of diluting or doing violence to his poetic genius, enables it to assimilate more materials, to readjust itself more completely and successfully than that of perhaps any other poet of our age to the new self-consciousness of the modern world. But in achieving this, Joyce has ceased to write verse. I have suggested, in connection with Valéry and Eliot, that verse itself as a literary medium is coming to be used for fewer and fewer and for more and more special purposes, and that it may be destined to fall into disuse. And it seems to me that Joyce's literary development is a striking corroboration of this view. His prose works have an artistic intensity, a definitive beauty of surface and of form, which make him comparable to the great poets rather than to most of the great novelists.

Joyce is indeed really the great poet of a new phase of the human consciousness. Like Proust's or Whitehead's or Einstein's world, Joyce's world is always changing as it is perceived by different observers and by them at different times. It is an organism made up of "events," which may be taken as infinitely inclusive or infinitely small and each of which involves all the others; and each of these events is unique. Such a world cannot be presented in terms of such artificial abstractions as have been conventional in the past: solid institutions, groups, individuals, which play the parts of distinct durable entities—or even of solid psychological factors: dualisms of good and evil, mind and matter, flesh and spirit, instinct and reason; clear conflicts between passion and duty, between conscience and interest. Not that these conceptions are left out of Joyce's world: they are all there in the minds of the characters; and the realities they represent are there, too. But everything is reduced to terms of "events" like those of modern physics and philosophy—events which make up a "continuum," but which may be taken as infinitely small. Joyce has built out of these events a picture, amazingly lifelike and living, of the everyday world we know—and a picture which seems to allow us to see into it, to follow its variations and intricacies, as we have never been able to do before.

Nor are Joyce's characters merely the sum of the particles into which their experience has been dissociated: we come to imagine them as solidly, to feel their personalities as unmistakably, as we do with any characters in fiction; and we realize finally that they are also symbols. Bloom himself is in one of his aspects the typical modern man: Joyce has made him a Jew, one supposes, partly in order that he may be conceived equally well as an inhabitant of any provincial city of the European or Europeanized world. He makes a living by petty business, he leads the ordinary middle-class life—and he holds the conventional enlightened opinions of the time: he believes in science, social reform and internationalism.

But Bloom is surpassed and illuminated from above by Stephen, who represents the intellect, the creative imagination; and he is upheld by Mrs. Bloom, who represents the body, the earth. Bloom leaves with us in the long run the impression that he is something both better and worse than either of them; for Stephen sins through pride, the sin of the intellect; and Molly is at the mercy of the flesh; but Bloom, though a less powerful personality than either, has the strength of humility. It is difficult to describe the character of Bloom as Joyce finally makes us feel it: it takes precisely the whole of *Ulysses* to put him before us. It is not merely that Bloom is mediocre, that he is clever, that he is commonplace—that he is comic, that he is pathetic—that he is, as Rebecca West says, a figure of abject "squatting" vulgarity, that he is at moments, as Foster Damon says, the Christ—he is all of these, he is all the possibilities of that ordinary humanity which is somehow not so ordinary after all; and it is the proof of Joyce's greatness that, though we recognize Bloom's perfect truth and typical character, we cannot pigeonhole him in any familiar category, racial, social, moral, literary or even—because he does really have, after all, a good deal in common with the Greek Ulysses—historical.

Both Stephen and Molly are more easily describable because they represent extremes. Both are capable of rising to heights which Bloom can never reach. In Stephen's rhapsody on the seashore, when he first realizes his artist's vocation, in *A Portrait of the Artist as a Young Man,* we have had the ecstasy of the creative mind. In the soliloquy of Mrs. Bloom, Joyce has given us another ecstasy of creation, the rhapsody of the flesh. Stephen's dream was conceived in loneliness, by a drawing apart from his fellows. But Mrs. Bloom is like the earth, which gives the same life to all: she feels a maternal kinship with all living creatures. She pities the "poor donkeys slipping half asleep" in the steep street of Gibraltar, as she does "the sentry in front of the governor's house . . . half roasted" in the sun; and she gives herself to the bootblack at the General Post Office as readily as to Professor Goodwin. But, none the less, she will tend to breed from the highest type of life she knows: she turns to Bloom, and, beyond him, toward Stephen. This gross body, the body of humanity, upon which the whole structure of *Ulysses* rests—still throbbing with so strong a rhythm amid obscenity, commonness and squalor—is laboring to throw up some knowledge and beauty by which it may transcend itself.

These two great flights of the mind carry off all the ignominies and trivialities through which Joyce has made us pass: they seem to me—the soaring silver prose of the one, the deep embedded pulse of the other—among the supreme expressions in literature of the creative powers of humanity: they are, respectively, the justifications of the woman and the man.

Homer and the Nightmare of History

by S. L. Goldberg

At the beginning, Stephen's crisis is portrayed in terms of his rejection of Mulligan, or rather of the image of him that Mulligan wishes to impose. Against Mulligan's easy compromises with the material values he affects to despise, and his possessiveness and aesthetic provinciality—both of which are neatly exemplified in *his* naming of the tower in which they live the *omphalos*—Stephen opposes his scorn in return, a scrupulous evasion of commitment, and a contemptuous compliance with Mulligan's desire for the key to the Martello tower. When Mulligan (and the peasant milk-woman whose respect for him identifies the nature of his power) usurp what Stephen regards as his place, he is ready to go. The key is, of course, a symbol of his attachment to a centre; he is willing enough to give it up when he feels the centre (home and country) usurped, but he goes with the burden of bitterness. And as Wyndham Lewis and Mr. Kenner have pointed out, his emotional attitudes do seem rather theatrical. In this first chapter, he gives the impression of posturing—an impression only the more heightened by the contrast with his more private attitudes as they are revealed in the third chapter ("Proteus"): the rigid and somewhat operatic posture largely dissolves once we see him from the inside. Here, in "Telemachus," he is presenting an image of himself to the world; but he is presenting it in deliberate opposition to those Mulligan and others wish him to adopt. His own image may be false and immature; theirs, he feels, would involve a fundamental lie to his true nature and vocation. "To discover the mode of life or of art whereby [his] spirit could express itself in unfettered freedom" (*Portrait*, p. 280): his own youthful image, inadequate as it is already beginning to appear to him, at least offers a negative ideal, and he uses it as a shield. If he cannot be much more positive, he does know what he does not want.[1]

"Homer and the Nightmare of History." Abridged from S. L. Goldberg, *The Classical Temper: A Study of James Joyce's "Ulysses,"* pp. 154–63; 170–80. Copyright © 1961 by S. L. Goldberg. Reprinted by permission of Barnes & Noble Books, Division of Harper & Row, Publishers, Inc. and Chatto and Windus Ltd. Two footnotes have been deleted.

[1] Cf. [Stuart] Gilbert [*James Joyce's "Ulysses"* (New York: Alfred A. Knopf, Inc., 1952),] p. 107, though Mr. Gilbert seems to imply that Stephen is presenting his true personality to Mulligan and Haines.

The waves of his personal crisis spread wider than the immediate struggle with Mulligan, however. For one thing, he is entangled with a kinetic remorse, a sense of guilt arising from his rejection of Roman Catholicism and the fear that his rejection may have contributed to his mother's death. This, it must be said, is an aspect of his character that does seem wholly theatrical, an unpleasant combination of self-accusation, self-pity and pride. He can evidently see through the current "romantic" and pretentious twaddle about Ireland, as his speculations about the milk-woman suggest. But although he savours that sentimentality with a dry irony, it is in fact very like many of his own thoughts about his mother:

> In a dream, silently, she had come to him, her wasted body within its loose graveclothes giving off an odour of wax and rosewood, her breath bent over him with mute secret words, a faint odour of wetted ashes.
> Her glazing eyes, staring out of death, to shake and bend my soul. On me alone. The ghostcandle to light her agony. Ghostly light on the tortured face. Her hoarse loud breath rattling in horror, while all prayed on their knees. Her eyes on me to strike me down. *Liliata rutilantium te confessorum turma circumdet: iubilantium te virginum chorus excipiat.*
>
> [*Ulysses*, 10.]

Yet it is worth noticing that, even despite the self-pity, the unfortunately Gothic horrors, and the overelaborate cadences (which it is hard to be quite sure whether to ascribe to Stephen or to Joyce), the passage does conclude with an instinctive, and significantly direct, cry for freedom and life:

> Ghoul! Chewer of corpses!
> No, mother. Let me be and let me live.

It is hardly a conscious critical response, an appeal to ideals positively held; Stephen is too divided for that. It is still a kinetic reaction, but it is very much in the right direction.

Similarly with the other false images of himself: he regards them, as he had regarded them in the *Portrait,* as nets to be avoided. The Englishman, Haines, comments,

> —After all, I should think you are able to free yourself. You are your own master, it seems to me.
> —I am the servant of two masters, Stephen said, an English and an Italian. . . .
> —And a third, Stephen said, there is who wants me for odd jobs.
>
> [20.]

As Haines replies, "It seems history is to blame." To Stephen the past does seem almost overwhelmingly determinant. He sees tradition not as a liberating force but (with a more intimate knowledge of some traditions than has every *laudator temporis acti*) as constricting and deadening. Yet again, although his freedom seems little more than the minimum of mere escape, he is shown groping towards something more. Carefully placed beside this conversation with Haines is a passage about a man drowned in the bay, which reinforces the point already implicit in Stephen's rejection of possible masters. Throughout *Ulysses* the sea appears as a symbol of the chaotic flux of experience, the element;[2] drowning is defeat, submergence, the death of the spirit in the overwhelming flood of kinetic appetencies. Stephen fears death by water. The drowned man objectifies his fear of suffocation, his need to rise above the waves, to swim in the element—in other words, to achieve a free *stasis* of spirit by understanding and accepting himself, his predicament, and his necessities. He must, as he clearly realizes, launch out. When the chapter ends, he is literally homeless. We do not know where he is going, nor does he.

The second chapter explores the historical aspects of his situation further. It begins by crystallizing our feeling, and Stephen's too, about his "victory" over Mulligan and his other potential masters: it is not enough, not decisive, indeed Pyrrhic. And the main theme of the chapter is Stephen's hostility to, and fear of, the past. Time seems to him only to repeat itself in "the same room and hour, the same wisdom. . . . Three nooses round me here," or in the repeated experience of the Jews:

> Time surely would scatter all. A hoard heaped by the roadside: plundered and passing on. Their eyes knew the years of wandering and, patient, knew the dishonours of their flesh.
> —Who has not? Stephen said.   [34.]

In short, "history was a tale like any other too often heard." The individual seems helplessly bound to the pattern; the "dear might of Him that walked the waves" does not exist for Stephen. He can see as little in the present as he can see in Elizabethan England—"an age of exhausted whoredom groping for its god." The ages, as John Eglinton puts it, seem only to "succeed one another" without change or hope. So conceived, history must seem a nightmare.

> —History, Stephen said, is a nightmare from which I am trying to awake.
> From the playfield the boys raised a shout. A whirring whistle: goal.
> What if that nightmare gave you a back kick?

---

[2] Cf. [William York] Tindall, *James Joyce* [(New York: Charles Scribner's Sons, 1950)], p. 30: "water means reality." Professor Curtius and Mr. Gilbert take the sea as the "primordial element, giver and taker of life" (Gilbert, p. 128). Mr. Kenner [in *Dublin's Joyce* (Bloomington: Indiana University Press, 1956)], on the other hand, takes it as "matter" (p. 211), with the implication, which I think unjustified, of *mere* matter. Of course the sea is a traditional Neo-Platonic symbol for matter or the amorphous substance in which natural forms are embodied, but, as with all such symbols, its meaning in *Ulysses* is what the work *makes* of it. The most thorough discussion of Joyce's related symbols of woman, moon, water and life, together with Stephen's fear of drowning, is Maurice Beebe, "James Joyce: Barnacle Goose and Lapwing," *Publications of the Modern Language Association of America*, LXXI, 1956, pp. 302-20.

—The ways of the Creator are not our ways, Mr Deasy said. All history
moves towards one great goal, the manifestation of God.
    Stephen jerked his thumb towards the window, saying:
    —That is God.
    Hooray! Ay! Whrrwhee!
    —What? Mr Deasy asked.
    —A shout in the street, Stephen answered, shrugging his shoulders.
                                                                        [34.]

Stephen cannot accept that history moves to any supernatural end outside itself. If God exists, He manifests Himself here and now, in all life
however pointless or trivial it may seem. History is not like a detective
story; there are no comforting revelations to follow. When Stephen uses
teleological arguments himself later on, he does so only analogously for
another and very different conclusion.

    His obsessive fear of the past is partly balanced, however, by a differ-
ent strain of thought about history. If past events limit the present and
the future, they also, as acts of will, liberate possibilities into the world
of fact. Stephen ponders this dual aspect of history in Aristotelian terms:

> Had Pyrrhus not fallen by a beldam's hand in Argos or Julius Caesar
> not been knifed to death. They are not to be thought away. Time has
> branded them and fettered they are lodged in the room of the infinite
> possibilities they have ousted. But can those have been possible seeing
> that they never were? Or was that only possible which came to pass?
> Weave, weaver of the wind.   [25.]

And during the schoolboys' reading of *Lycidas*, the grounds of hope occur to him: time is not only a burden, it is also a means to the fruition
and fulfilment of the soul in action. As he tells himself a little later, he
could, if he willed it, break free of his present nooses—and in fact he
does. History involves more than the ossification of life; it is also dy-
namic:

> It must be a movement then, an actuality of the possible as possible.
> Aristotle's phrase formed itself within the gabbled verses and floated out
> into the studious silence of the library of Sainte Geneviève where he had
> read, sheltered from the sin of Paris, night by night. By his elbow a delicate
> Siamese conned a handbook of strategy. Fed and feeding brains about me:
> under glowlamps, impaled, with faintly beating feelers: and in my mind's
> darkness a sloth of the underworld, reluctant, shy of brightness, shifting
> her dragon scaly folds. Thought is the thought of thought. Tranquil bright-
> ness. The soul is in a manner all that is: the soul is the form of forms.
> Tranquillity sudden, vast, candescent: form of forms.   [25–26.]

The relevance of this (even the Siamese student) to his moral problems
as an artist, his desire to mature and freely and creatively to act, requires
no emphasis. Mr. Deasy's ambiguous wisdom confirms the implications

of Stephen's drift: "to learn one must be humble. But life is the great teacher." For Stephen's situation, that cliché is the wisdom of Nestor.

"Proteus" develops these implications still further, both in Stephen's reflections about them and in the dramatic presentation of the way his reflections themselves progress. Joyce's writing here has often been praised for its sensitive delicacy, but it is not always realized how much more it is than that, how finely and firmly the chapter is organized as a poetic, dramatic unit. Generally speaking, the chapter explores the Protean transformations of matter in time—matter, as we should expect from Stephen's aesthetic theory, both as object, the "ineluctable modality of the visible and audible," apprehensible only in the condition of flux,[3] and as subject, Stephen himself. In the one aspect, Stephen is seeking the principles of change and the underlying substance of sensory experience; in the other, he is seeking his self among its temporal manifestations. Consequently, he seems narcissistic, self-conscious, *lisant au livre de lui-même* like Hamlet. Yet, although he is still egocentric and still in uneasy kinetic relationship to his environment and himself, he exhibits in this chapter more of the incipient irony he had displayed at the end of the *Portrait,* a dawning capacity to stand off from himself and criticize what he sees, and concomitantly, to observe external reality with a certain detachment. His potentiality of growth is perhaps here most clearly visible. The humourless and priggish aesthete appears much less certain about his poses; he has after all, we discover, some sense of the ridiculous and some glimmerings of maturer values. "Proteus," in fact, is the crucial chapter for our conception of him. Without it, his other appearances in the book would hardly convince us of his solidity or interest as a protagonist; as it is, they are all enriched and qualified by his presentation here.

The setting on the seashore has an obvious metaphorical significance. Stephen speculates at the edge of life about the meanings in, and beyond, the immediate sensible world—his material as an artist. Bloom, who finds himself on the same shore in the evening, can make nothing of it:

> All these rocks with lines and scars and letters. O, those transparent! Besides they don't know. What is the meaning of that other world. I called you naughty boy because I do not like.
> [He draws with a stick: I. AM. A.]
> No room. Let it go.
> Mr Bloom effaced the letters with his slow boot. Hopeless thing sand. Nothing grows in it. All fades. . . .   [381.]

But Stephen has the intellectual and imaginative capacity to read the "signatures of all things," to penetrate the diaphanous sensible world

---

[3] See Joseph E. Duncan, "The Modality of the Audible in Joyce's *Ulysses*," *Publications of the Modern Language Association of America,* LXXII, 1957, pp. 286–95, for an exposition of the Aristotelian terminology Stephen uses here.

and the ineluctable *nacheinander* and *nebeneinander* placed before the individual consciousness, the world that is "there all the time without you: and ever shall be, world without end."[37.]

His thoughts turn to the permanent patterns of change—in particular, to the pattern of the life-cycle within which the individual's destiny is played out. He scorns theosophical hocus-pocus about the navelcord, but he acknowledges the common bond of continuity it represents. For him —and for Bloom, too—womankind represents the permanent force and pattern of biological history: birth, copulation, family and death. Indeed, when we recall the figure of Molly Bloom, it is true to say that this is one of the constant symbolic values of the book as a whole. Women do not figure in it as people but as biological symbols. And the polarity some of Joyce's critics have observed between Stephen ("intellectual life") and Molly ("biological life") already exists in Stephen's own point of view—especially in the rather abstractly "deep" speculations about Woman in which both he and Bloom sometimes indulge.

The first transformation of "matter" lies in the changing substance of Stephen's thoughts from the life-cycle in general towards his family and its particular life, and equally in his rejection of their "paralysis": "Houses of decay, mine, his and all. . . . Come out of them, Stephen. Beauty is not there." His father, as he says to Bloom later, is "all too Irish," and his criticism here includes the whole "hundred-headed rabble of the cathedral close," the general state of Ireland.

Swift provides the link to the second transformation—Stephen's "temptation" to enter the priesthood, or, more generally, to achieve and exercise magical powers; and, correspondingly, in "subjective" terms, his rejection of the possibility in both its religious and aesthetic aspects:

> Cousin Stephen, you will never be a saint. . . . You were awfully holy, weren't you? . . . On the top of the Howth tram alone crying to the rain: *naked women!* What about that, eh?
> What about what? What else were they invented for?
> . . . You bowed to yourself in the mirror, stepping forward to applaud earnestly, striking face. . . . No-one saw: tell no-one. Books you were going to write with letters for titles. . . . Remember your epiphanies on green oval leaves, deeply deep. . . . Someone was to read them there after a few thousand years, a mahamanvantara. Pico della Mirandola like. Ay, very like a whale. When one reads these strange pages of one long gone one feels that one is at one with one who once . . .   [40.]

The sharp juxtaposition of this mystico-Symbolist nonsense with the "grainy sand" in the following line adds Joyce's endorsement to Stephen's self-criticism; clearly, we are not invited to take the aesthetic attitude Stephen parodies very seriously. Nor, for that matter, are we Stephen's third transformation, which begins with the sight of a "maze of dark cunning nets." He himself punctures the attitude of the *esprit libre* he had adopted on his flight to Paris: "My latin quarter hat. God, we simply must dress the character."

With his latest transformation—failed missionary to Europe, bedraggled Icarus—he is naturally less detached and less critical. He recognizes his failure, but the recognition is qualified by his sense of undefeated pride:

> His feet marched in sudden proud rhythm over the sand furrows, along by the boulders of the south wall. He stared at them proudly, piled stone mammoth skulls. Gold light on sea, on sand, on boulders. The sun is there, the slender trees, the lemon houses. [42.]

Despite the earlier *débâcle,* Paris still represents something of value to him, though he also recognizes the meaning for himself in Kevin Egan, exiled revolutionary in Paris, forgotten, remembering Sion. But all his retrospection leads him finally to a crucial decision which involves a crucial perception:

> He has the key. I will not sleep there when this night comes. . . . Take all, keep all. My soul walks with me, form of forms. [44.]

The decision to leave again is more than a recognition that he has been forced out; it is based on a firmer knowledge of what his nature positively seeks—the discovery of itself in a deeper experience of ordinary life.

His self-identification with the introspectively heroic Hamlet is the last transformation of matter portrayed. The significance of the parallel is mainly suggested and dramatically qualified by Stephen's theory in "Scylla and Charybdis," but it is also partly qualified (and naturally it can only be partly) by his own self-critical reflections here. The significant point emerges from his fear of attack by a dog on the beach: "Respect his liberty. You will not be master of others or their slave." He rejects all violence. The nightmare of history is within him—

> Famine, plague and slaughters. Their blood is in me, their lusts my waves. I moved among them on the frozen Liffey, that I, a changeling, among the spluttering resin fires. I spoke to no-one: none to me. [45.]

As he says at the end of "Circe," it is *within* that he must kill the king and the priest, symbols of spiritual tyranny and slavery. His means to freedom are still silence, exile, and cunning—the evasion of action and violence—but they also seem like cowardice. He wonders if he too is not another "pretender": he fears drowning, he is not a strong swimmer; he hates water; life may well overwhelm him. In short, ironic self-scrutiny has begun to temper his will.

His reflections now turn reflectively upon themselves. He identifies himself with the sniffing dog, "tatters," "poor dogsbody," fox who has buried his mother under a hollybush; he sees himself "vulturing the dead," "looking for something lost in a past life"—

Dogskull, dogsniff, eyes on the ground, moves to one great goal.   [46.]

His search for the self beneath the protean flux of life concludes with such partial knowledge as he is capable of discovering and with a recognition of the nature of his search. The future can be only prefigured: in a symbolic dream ("That man led me, spoke. I was not afraid"); in his adolescent longing for contact with the female tides of life; in his continual effort to find his self in reality yet avoid the sterility of solipsism, to grasp the significance of the sensible world, where subject and object unite by "parallax":

> Hold hard. Coloured on a flat: yes, that's right. Flat I see, then think distance, near, far, flat I see, east, back. Ah, see now. Falls back suddenly, frozen in stereoscope. Click does the trick.   [48.]

The scribbled note for his poem is part of the action of the chapter, a transformation that transcends all those that precede it, an emblem of the "great goal" of his process of self-scrutiny, a symbol in little of *Ulysses* itself. History, understood, moves towards the goal of art, but art is itself a symbol of the wider spiritual life it ideally embodies. The phrase from Yeats that Stephen quotes—"and no more turn aside and brood" [4]—signalizes his progress to a precarious *stasis,* or at least to a less kinetic frame of mind, in which he tries to express the sound and unending movement of water, his sense of the life into which he must plunge. That his present *stasis* is precariously unstable is implicit in the way he tries to accept his fear and the necessary rôle of death in life; the language reflects an intention, an effort, more than achieved assurance:

> God becomes man becomes fish becomes barnacle goose becomes feather-bed mountain. Dead breaths I living breathe, tread dead dust, devour a urinous offal from all dead. Hauled stark over the gunwale he breathes upward the stench of his green grave, his leprous nosehole snoring to the sun.
> A seachange this, brown eyes saltblue. . . . Just you give it a fair trial. . . .
> . . . Evening will find itself.
> . . . Yes, evening will find itself in me, without me. All days make their end. . . .   [50.]

This is a passage less important for the symbolic relationships it suggests (father—sea—life, urine—death, etc.) than for the dramatic significance of its tone. Stephen's trust in the future is no mere involuntary drifting with the stream. As the rest of the chapter has established, he has some appreciation of the direction he must take and of the importance of

---

[4] From "Who will drive with Fergus now," which Joyce himself set and used to sing, and which was one of his mother's favourites: see Stanislaus Joyce, *My Brother's Keeper* [(New York: The Viking Press, Inc., 1958)], p. 143, and Patricia Hutchins, *James Joyce's World* (London: [Methuen,] 1957), pp. 186–7.

growing towards it as well as simply willing it. His attitude still remains tentative, largely a passive, but watchful, waiting. In order to crystallize its positive value, Joyce must direct us outside Stephen's consciousness, and this he does with the "objectively" rendered episode of the ship at the very end of the chapter. Revealed to Stephen's significantly "rere regardant" gaze, her sails "brailed up on the crosstrees, homing, upstream, silently moving, a silent ship." With the final hint that he too is silently moving homeward, Stephen is dismissed, and the stage is set for Bloom. . . .

. . . Unlike Stephen, Bloom is not much aware of his own individual character, nor is he concerned with establishing any special relationship between himself and "life." He *is* alive. Of course, as we have seen, we cannot take him as fully alive, an unqualified hero, but his common humanity does represent that "life" against which Stephen is placed.

Bloom engages with everyday life at many points—that is the primary and obvious significance of the Odyssean parallel: he is an "allround-man." More important, however, is the way in which he engages—the sense in which his completeness is a sign of moral vitality and his consciousness the expression of a man truly, if not ideally, alive. For all his comparative unselfconsciousness he is not unreflective; for all his absorption in everyday matters, he is far from completely absorbed by them. His active consciousness is the clearest basis of his moral stature and his dramatic significance; he is a modern Odysseus, expressing himself less in outward action than in inward awareness. Much of his pathos, much of the dramatic irony, derives from this limitation of his capacity for physical action, but neither this, nor the limitations of his intelligence and sensibility, destroy his fundamental dignity. This dignity, however, lies ultimately in his unselfconscious being, in what he *is* unknown to himself, which it is one of Joyce's prime intentions to reveal to us in "Circe" and "Ithaca." The most important difference between Bloom and Stephen is that while Stephen aspires to a special dignity of his own as an artist, he has not achieved it, where Bloom does possess his dignity, and all the more securely because he is never for one moment aware that he does—or that he possesses heroic dimensions.

His first appearance places him in careful *contrast* to Stephen. The first fact we learn about him is his liking for the inner organs of beasts and fowls: "most of all he liked grilled mutton kidneys which gave to his palate a fine tang of faintly scented urine." We recall Stephen's reflection on the previous page, at the end of "Proteus": "dead breaths I living breathe, tread dead dust, devour a urinous offal from all dead." Where Stephen can slip free of the dead hand of the past and accept the necessity of death only fitfully and with difficulty, Bloom accepts death

easily and transforms it into life.[5] One need not solemnly trace the symbolism of offal and urine through the whole book—though it is important to remember that Stephen and Bloom urinate together before they
part—in order to perceive this major difference between the attitude of
the two men to the dead past.[6] But so far this is not a realized difference,
only the symbol of one dramatically established in the acts and consciousness of Bloom as the action proceeds.

In "Calypso," where Bloom's racial and familial relationships are first
outlined, his awareness of them is inevitably his awareness of time. He
considers a prospectus for recultivating Palestine; his mind turns to a
sudden vision of the Holy Land as barren, exhausted, dead: "Grey horror seared his flesh. . . . Cold oils slid along his veins, chilling his blood:
age crusting him with a salt cloak. Well, I am here now." From the horror of the past he turns to the living flesh of the present: "to smell the
gentle smoke of tea, fume of the pan, sizzling butter. Be near her ample
bedwarmed flesh. Yes, yes." This does not represent the whole of his attitude to the past, of course, but already it is clear that he does not
agonize in the manner of Stephen. Even when he is immediately reminded that the ample bedwarmed flesh is waiting for Blazes Boylan,
and the thought of the future chills him like the thought of the dead
Promised Land, he does not remain fixed in his pain. His mind constantly shifts between past, present and future. The little discussion about
"metempsychosis" establishes one of the verbal symbols of this movement: they say we have forgotten the lives we are supposed to have lived
in the past, Bloom tells Molly; "some say they remember their past lives."
Bloom himself forgets and remembers as a human being active in the
present. If he recalls his ghosts, he salutes them and passes on. Where
Stephen fights and struggles and has suicidal impulses, Bloom wears the
past, and hence the present, more easily. At the end of "Hades," after he
has faced the shadow of death, his thoughts "turn aside and no more
brood": "Back to the world again. Enough of this place. . . . Plenty to
see and hear and feel yet. Feel live warm beings near you. Let them sleep
in their maggoty beds. They are not going to get me this innings. Warm
beds: warm fullblooded life." He recognizes the savagery of life, the
necessity even of killing ("Eat or be eaten. Kill! Kill!"), but, unlike
Stephen, he can accept this without the knowledge corrupting the springs
of action. He moves on always, rejecting the false *stasis* of imprisoning
frustration: "Life those chaps out there must have, stuck in the same

---

[5] But contrast Kenner's comment on this passage, p. 213.

[6] In his article on "Dante and Mrs. Bloom," *loc. cit.,* p. 89, Mr. Tindall briefly discusses the symbolism of urine, which he takes as water: "to Joyce water meant life and
making water was not only creating life but, by extention, creating art." This seems
questionable, both physiologically and poetically. Making water in this sense is to
eliminate waste-matter; urine is not the same as water; and Stephen creates neither life
nor art.

spot. Irish Lights board. Penance for their sins." To Bloom, life presents itself as an inescapable activity, the moral exigencies of which control the influence of the past as much as the influence of the past controls them.

Like Stephen, he recognizes the general patterns that circumscribe the life of the individual, though his awareness has a very different tone: "It's the blood sinking in the earth gives new life. Same idea those jews they said killed the christian boy. Every man his price." He preserves the same tone in his reflections about himself too:

> June that was too I wooed. The year returns. History repeats itself. . . .
> Life, love, voyage round your own little world. And now? . . .
>   All quiet on Howth now. The distant hills seem. Where we. The rhododendrons. I am a fool perhaps. He gets the plums and I the plumstones. Where I come in. All that old hill has seen. Names change: that's all. Lovers: yum yum.
>   . . . She kissed me. My youth. Never again. Only once it comes. Or hers. Take the train there tomorrow. No. Returning not the same. . . . The new I want. Nothing new under the sun. . . . Think you're escaping and run into yourself. Longest way round is the shortest way home. . . . All changed. Forgotten. The young are old. . . .   [376–377.]

Bloom's pathos here arises from his helpless recognition of ineluctability; it is the helplessness of humanity itself. As the contrasting echoes of Stephen's parable of the plums and of his speculations about the actualization of the self in experience suggest, Bloom's recognition is an experiential one, not a merely theoretical acceptance like Stephen's. For him, the life-cycle, the biological limits of the individual's experience, are a felt part of his actual life. He accepts the universe not because he has found any intellectual formula into which he can fit it, but for the more compelling reason that he simply has to. Inasmuch as he does so, moreover, he represents one of the values Joyce expresses in the work. Bloom's simple awareness of these natural patterns is not offered as stupidity or moral surrender, but as a kind of unthinking wisdom. Thus, when Bloom hears of Mrs. Purefoy's difficult lying-in, "his heavy pitying gaze absorbed her news. His tongue clacked in compassion. Dth! Dth!"—the suggestion of the life-cycle is Joyce's as much as, if not more than, Bloom's. Or again, when Bloom actually visits the hospital and hears of the death of a friend, he stands silent "in wanhope," whereupon the narrative comments in general terms on the inevitability of death. Even though Joyce makes no unqualified endorsement of Bloom, he does in this endorse his characteristic attitude. So that when Bloom's attitude to time and Stephen's are finally juxtaposed in "Ithaca," we should recognize the sense in which the former's is a criticism of the latter's. Standing beneath the stars and ready to part, they hear, as Bloom had heard among his thoughts of Dignam's death in the morning, the bells of St. George's church striking the passage of time:

What echoes of that sound were by both and each heard?

By Stephen, an echo of his unpurged remorse:

> *Liliata rutilantium. Turma circumdet.*
> *Iubilantium te virginum. Chorus excipiat.*

By Bloom, an echo of death, and yet also an incipient turn from it:

> *Heigho, heigho,*
> *Heigho, heigho.*   [704.]

His attitude can be easily mistaken for a completely passive resignation. In fact, it is something rather different, an *active* resignation, so to speak. Certainly, Bloom does not do obvious battle with his world, though we should remember that he has lost one job "for giving lip" and stands up to the Citizen where no one else does.[7] He does occasionally surrender to a sentimental and uselessly nostalgic acceptance of things as they are —his daughter, Milly, usually provokes this reaction: "A soft qualm, regret, flowed down his backbone, increasing. Will happen, yes. Prevent. Useless: can't move . . ." He submits without overt protest or resistance to the petty indignities that mark his social exclusion. On the other hand, his important acceptances are made with an awareness of the complexities; they are not easy resignations by any means. His proposals to Stephen for future meetings—meetings that William Empson has argued are to be regarded as having really taken place and to be the real point of the book[8]—are the product of his deep and pathetic desire for friendship. The proposals are, in fact, accepted by Stephen. Bloom, however, knows more than to take the arrangement at face-value:

> What rendered problematic for Bloom the realisation of these mutually selfexcluding propositions?
> The irreparability of the past: once at a performance of Albert Hengler's circus . . . an intuitive particoloured clown . . . had publicly declared that he (Bloom) was his (the clown's) papa. The imprevidibility of the future: once in the summer of 1898 he (Bloom) had marked a florin . . . for possible, circuitous or direct, return.
>
> Was the clown Bloom's son?
> No.
>
> Had Bloom's coin returned?
> Never.   [696.]

---

[7] J. Mitchell Morse also warns against over-estimating Bloom's passivity; see "The Disobedient Artist: Joyce and Loyola," *Publications of the Modern Language Association of America*, LXXII, 1957, pp. 1018–35, now chapter 6 of *The Sympathetic Alien* [(New York: New York University Press, 1959)]. As Mr. Morse points out, it is Bloom's moral *activity* that is the most striking thing about him, and he is in some ways set off, as predominantly a moralist, against the ambivalent and relativistic imagination of Stephen.

[8] William Empson, "The Theme of *Ulysses*," *Kenyon Review*, XVIII, 1956, pp. 26–52.

In short, if Bloom accepts the past as it has been and life as it is, it is not because he does not also desire them otherwise.

Probably the most important illustration of his whole general attitude is provided by his feelings about Molly's adultery. These change, or rather crystallize, during the course of the book, and in fact this crystallization is one of the central threads of the action. Bloom's first reactions are distress and emotional flight; when he sees Boylan in the street, for example, he meets the insupportable by escaping into the Museum, turning to the refuge of "cold statues" and "the Greek architecture." When he does allow his mind to dwell on the situation, it is with a certain self-pity and nostalgia: "Me. And me now." Later on, the art of song in the "Sirens" chapter induces another mood, more reflective, more detached, in which he is able to generalize his situation:

> Thou lost one. All songs on that theme. Yet more Bloom stretched his string. Cruel it seems. Let people get fond of each other: lure them on. Then tear asunder. . . . Human life. . . .
> Yet too much happy bores. He stretched more, more. Are you not happy in your? Twang. It snapped.   [277.]

His personal isolation is heavily emphasized in this chapter, of course, but it is an isolation which is partly an active movement of his mind towards a fuller understanding of his past and present situation (that the chapter is focused upon an *art*, and that Bloom's capacity to comprehend his situation is as limited as the elasticity of his string, are equally significant). But understanding of a sort he does achieve:

> I too, last my race. Milly young student. Well, my fault perhaps. No son. Rudy. Too late now. Or if not? If not? If still?
> He bore no hate.
> Hate. Love. Those are names. Rudy. Soon I am old.   [285.]

By evening ("Nausicaa"), he has begun to see Molly's behaviour in an even wider context as only one more illustration of the laws of attraction, of a universal natural process. And his reconciliation to her proposed tour with Boylan is significantly juxtaposed with his charitable thoughts about the Citizen who had abused and assaulted him. His mood is not quite a surrender to mere amoral natural processes; it includes a positive charity, a compassionate realization of the common human lot. The mocking sound of the cuckoo that concludes the chapter seems cheap, almost irrelevant, by comparison; its irony leaves his substance untouched. Still further, in "Circe" and "Eumaeus," he comes to recognize that his own sexual failure has a good deal to do with Molly's infidelity. Gradually he moves from *kinesis* to "a silent contemplation," which is summed up in "Ithaca":

> With what antagonistic sentiments were his subsequent reflections affected?
> Envy, jealousy, abnegation, equanimity.   [732.]

Envy of Boylan, jealousy of Molly, abnegation for complicated motives,
and equanimity because, finally, Molly's act is "more than inevitable,
irreparable."

> Why more abnegation than jealousy, less envy than equanimity?
> From outrage (matrimony) to outrage (adultery) there arose nought but
> outrage (copulation) yet the matrimonial violator of the matrimonially
> violated had not been outraged by the adulterous violator of the adulter-
> ously violated. . . .   [733.]

> By what reflections did he, a conscious reactor against the void of in-
> certitude, justify to himself his sentiments?
> [The naturalness of the attraction and the act]: the futility of triumph
> or protest of vindication: the inanity of extolled virtue: the lethargy of
> nescient matter: the apathy of the stars.   [744.]

The equanimity results in a final satisfaction in the warmth and beauty
of Molly's female "mute immutable mature animality"—the eternally
given, but never to be possessed, richness of the flesh.

> The visible signs of antesatisfaction?
> An approximate erection: a solicitous adversion: a gradual elevation:
> a tentative revelation: a silent contemplation.

> Then?
> He kissed the plump mellow yellow smellow melons of her rump, on
> each plump melonous hemisphere, in their mellow yellow furrow, with
> obscure prolonged provocative melonsmellonous osculation.

> The visible signs of postsatisfaction?
> A silent contemplation: a tentative velation: a gradual abasement: a
> solicitous aversion: a proximate erection.   [734-735.]

That Bloom's silent contemplative *stasis* is followed by a kind of *kinesis*
(characteristically weak and ambiguous, we might notice) marks the difference between the continuing process of life and the fixity of art. If
Bloom's slaying of the suitors by a victory over himself seems paltry or
despicable by contrast with Ulysses' more conclusive methods, we must
not therefore suppose that Joyce is being simply ironical at Bloom's
expense.[9] He rarely supports his characters in postures of moral violence;
his notion of true moral activity is less overtly militant. Bloom kills his
enemies, as Stephen hopes to do, within, and they are not Molly's suitors
so much as his own inner frustrating imbalance of envy, jealousy and
excessive abnegation. He wins a temporary equanimity, but clearly no
final victory. Life, Joyce implies, is not art; there is nothing concluded,
no absolute command possible.

[9] This *is* the view taken by [Douglas] Knight, "The Reading of *Ulysses*," [*ELH*, XIX
(March 1952)], pp. 72–3, 65–6. But [W. B.] Stanford [*The Ulysses Theme* (Oxford: Basil
Blackwell, 1954)], pp. 218–19, seems to me to be closer to the truth in his description and
evaluation of this part of the story.

Bloom's comparative freedom from guilt, remorse, nostalgia, jealousy, egotistic assertion and other nightmares of history is to be contrasted with Stephen's bondage. Similarly, his curiosity and openness to experience, unlike Stephen's search for "life," express a desire to place the past at the disposal of the future. Where Stephen is a novice, incapable as yet of using the past and so in search of a spiritual father, Bloom is oppressed by the complementary frustration that, as the last of his race, he has no one to whom he can hand on his spiritual gift.

The problem haunts him all through the book, emerging perhaps most explicitly as he sits with the young men in the hospital ("Oxen of the Sun") where he has been drawn by his compassion for Mrs. Purefoy and kept by his half-conscious attraction to Stephen. After a passage in which Mulligan mocks Stephen's divine analogies ("the black panther was himself the ghost of his own father"),[10] Bloom, contemplating the label on a bottle of Bass, passes to the "incorruptible eon of the gods." "What is the age of the soul of man?" Bloom relives his own youth—"he is young Leopold, as in a retrospective arrangement, a mirror within a mirror (hey, presto!), he beholdeth himself." But the mirror clouds; "now he is himself paternal and these about him might be his sons. Who can say? The wise father knows his own child." His intense regret that he has not fathered a living man-child, his unwilled frustration, reflects mirror-wise the deliberate contraception that forms the abstract theme of the chapter:

> No, Leopold! Name and memory solace thee not. That youthful illusion
> of thy strength was taken from thee and in vain. No son of thy loins is
> by thee. There is none now to be for Leopold, what Leopold was for
> Rudolph.   [413–414.]

For Bloom, as his "soul is wafted over regions of cycles of cycles of generations that have lived," the past is barren, "Agendath is a waste land," horrible and damned. But womankind, "link between nations and generations . . . sacred life-giver," still remains, with her potentialities for the future—"And, lo, wonder of metempsychosis, it is she, the everlasting bride, harbinger of the daystar, the bride, ever virgin. It is she, Martha, thou lost one, Millicent, the young, the dear, the radiant."

Bloom cannot understand, any more than Stephen, what he can offer the younger man. It is certainly not his good advice, nor anything he could formulate consciously; the essence of his gift is that he is unconscious of it—it is what he represents and is. Partly, of course, he is Stephen's possible "material" as an artist, the City against which Stephen reacts and which is therefore the necessary subject of his self-reflective art. More, however, he represents a relationship to the history of his own people that is analogous to Stephen's and yet unlike it. It is part of Bloom's relevance that, like Stephen, he also embodies a racial tradition

---

[10] For the identification of the black panther with Christ, see [A. M.] Klein ["The Black Panther: A Study in Technique," *Accent*, X, 1950].

(which is also a spiritual tradition), even though it is consciously present to him only in fragments.[11] His "defective mnemotechnic" links him with attitudes and patterns of life that he unwittingly re-experiences in his own circumstances. They are not Jewish in the narrowest sense; they have a wider reference, which emerges in "Circe," and to Bloom himself Christ is a symbol both of his values and the mixed tradition whence they derive: "Well, his uncle was a jew, says he. Your God was a jew. Christ was a jew like me." The racial parallel with Stephen is explicitly drawn in "Ithaca": both inherit a long and rich tradition, both are conscious only of fragments of it. Yet the contrast between the two men is equally explicit and equally important. Where Stephen consciously (and uneasily) rejects, Bloom accepts. Once, earlier, Bloom had impatiently criticized his father's beliefs and practices; now, they appear to him "not more rational than they had then appeared, not less rational than other beliefs and practices now appeared." As we shall see, this detachment is by no means the whole of Bloom's attitude, for much else in it is, as it should be, quite unconscious; his significance, nevertheless, is as an example, parallel to but contrasting with Stephen's case, of an involuntary involvement, an involuntary exile, but a real if unemphatic freedom.

Such contrasts between Bloom and Stephen would have little point without the relationship that lies at the centre of the whole book: they are here, as always, complementary counterparts, "fundamental and dominant," actuality and potentiality. The father-son theme is one metaphor for this; the theory about Shakespeare another; the figure of Christ, in whom are expressed the dichotomies of crucified citizen (Man) and crucified artist (God), of action and passion, of involvement and freedom, is yet a third. By its different aspects, the symbol of Christ links the diverse facts of the situation Joyce explores, but the meaning of Joyce's *symbol* lies in the facts it orders. Unless the values it relates and expresses are themselves realized, imaginatively established as denotations, the symbol remains empty and inert. Stephen cannot be portrayed as the suffering and crucified Artist redeeming the world; in the very terms of the book, he lacks the freedom, the love, and the capacity, and has only the desire to become an artist and the uneasy realization of what is involved. For the most part, he rejects. He is Christ as the "black panther," and the very incompleteness of his state provokes the metaphor of Lucifer. Stephen as Christ often passes over into Stephen as Satan: it is a sign of his immaturity that he is ready to adopt either rôle at any time. He is not quite *der Geist, der stets verneint,* of course; it is rather that his affirmations seem only velleities, or at best unachieved intentions. Bloom, therefore, must carry the heavier burden of significance—be not merely passive but active, not merely involved but free, not merely representa-

---

[11] J. Prescott has collected and annotated many of these fragments in his articles in the *Modern Language Quarterly*, XIII, 1952, pp. 149–62; and *Modern Language Notes*, LXVII, 1952, pp. 334–6.

tive of, but crucified by, his world, the scapegoat and redeemer, and tied all the while by close analogy and parallel with Stephen, so that the reader may perceive what Stephen must learn to perceive: the values Bloom represents and the deep similarity between the two of them. Bloom's ambiguous position, his example, his love, his freedom, if only he could understand them, are what Stephen must come to. For the parallels between the two men are fundamental: Bloom's exclusion from society reflects Stephen's spiritual exile from it (a situation neatly portrayed early in the book when they are both at the newspaper office). Each is an alien in the life of Dublin. They are both isolated by "parallax," each in his personal world, and only a full spiritual outgoing— or its symbol, art—can alleviate their condition. They both reject violence and the senseless agitations of the mob as incompatible with the freedom and order they seek. They are both keyless, citizen and artist, yet both "born adventurers" and committed to the essential isolation of their individuality. They both have personal courage, one in his pride, the other in his humility. Both strive to awake from the nightmare of history, though Stephen cannot yet realize what values he seeks, and Bloom cannot express what he means. But his attempts are the justification for the Christ metaphor—his positive courage in "Cyclops" for example, but more especially his unalienated integrity in "Circe." The most important structural parallel between the two protagonists, in fact, is that between Stephen's self-examination of the past, which is conducted consciously, and Bloom's, which is necessarily much less conscious; between "Proteus" and "Circe." The connections between these two chapters, with all that is implied by those connections, is what really establishes the metaphor of paternity.

The Advent of Bloom

by *Anthony Cronin*

Those who are intent on turning *Ulysses* into mere anagram and allegory are perhaps so because they are incapable of appreciating the "profane joy" with which ordinary mundanities are invested in it. Perhaps too they are unsympathetic towards the kind of life which in large part it portrays; incapable of savouring, for example, the citizen's language as Joyce himself savours it, to some extent even uninterested in the primary satisfactions we derive from language and the representation of life. Whatever Joyce's secondary purposes may have been, whatever elaborations of technique and allusion he indulges in, that is not where the true greatness of the book lies. Mr. Bloom may be Shakespeare; what is important to us is that he is Bloom. The fact that he is not only Odysseus but Shakespeare and Sinbad the sailor as well, does not account for his fascination: as if Joyce's talents lay simply in the ability to invent more and more "meaningful" parallels. Nor is the worth of the book to be suggested by explaining what it is really "about," as if Joyce was a nostrum vendor, a mystic or a philosopher. What the book is "about" may be important in the sense that every writer may have to be judged by the *quality* of his vision as well as by his ability to express it, though this is a debatable point which would require a lot of definition. It is irrelevant, if we mean by what it is "about" a mere attitude hidden in the hermeneutics which, if discovered, would only have the force of an attitude and not the force of art. To speak of the quality of a man's vision is not to speak of the worth of his mere, paraphrasable opinions about history or religion or our place in the cosmos: an ideology which could be discovered and exclaimed over like that of any other fashionable sage. Every recorded statement we have exhibits Joyce's total contempt for abstract ideas, his cheerful and not at all hag-ridden scepticism about religion, his indifference to the profundities of the new psychology. A good deal of confusion exists about the nature of his vision; he has been accused of everything from sentimentality, to indifference, to rage; but before asking what his book is about, it is equally, if not more im-

"The Advent of Bloom." Excerpted from Anthony Cronin, *A Question of Modernity* (London: Martin Secker & Warburg Ltd, 1966), pp. 69–81; 86–96. Copyright © 1966 by Anthony Cronin. Reprinted by permission of A D Peters and Company.

portant, to enquire into the almost totally neglected question of what in fact it is.

What it is can perhaps be seen more clearly by a preliminary examination of what it is not. It is to begin with unlike almost any other novel ever written. Almost all other novels are patterned dramatically. They are concerned not only with a situation, but with a situation that unfolds itself, a plot, which progresses through a chain of causation, often involving coincidence, frequently violence or at least death. Life in such books is to a greater or lesser degree subordinated to event. We get little or no static living, but only those events which contribute more or less to the main stream. Irrelevancies may be included but they are usually said to have had some influence on the behaviour of the characters in the crises of event. Life has to be contained within the pattern of event; it is therefore neater and smaller than real living. The events, being patterned, are also neater than the events in life, which have usually no pattern. Plot events are dialectic, being explainable in terms of each other, whereas events in life are frequently isolated and inexplicable, or, if explicable, they are so only in terms of an infinite conglomeration of factors which would stretch outside the book. The events out of which the pattern of event is made are both more clear-cut and more probable than the events in life, though the pattern as a whole is usually highly improbable.

The justification for this patterning in most serious works is presumably more than the amusement of the reader with a good story, the satisfaction of his aroused curiosity, or the gratification of his delight in violence or intrigue. The justification, if there is one, must rest both on the negative claim that much is allowable in letters that does not obtain in life, like speaking in iambic pentameters; and on the positive claim that the dramatic arrangement of life in a book is a means of producing pity, terror, catharsis or any other emotion that it is proper to feel in the presence of a work of art. The latter claim rests on the assumption that an artificial arrangement of life in a pattern of event and a curtailment of life in the interests of a pattern of event can be a source of aesthetic satisfaction.

Still the falsification of life remains. We may say that this falsification is tacitly admitted between the writer and the reader, just as a composer of opera tacitly agrees with the audience that people do not communicate by singing at each other; it exists all the same. There is no such falsification of life in *Ulysses*. Of course *Ulysses* is not just a "slice of life," as it was once assumed to be, though even as a slice of life, if that were conceivable, it would still be very great. (Samuel Beckett has said that Joyce thought it was perhaps "over-constructed": some of the commentators seem to suggest that it is constructed to the exclusion of everything but the construction and is the "greater" for that.) But the necessary limitations of Joyce's form do not result in a falsification of life as do those of the ordinary novel of self-sustaining event. In *Ulysses*, for the first time in fiction, life could be almost completely itself. Where in the novel of event each picture, each person, each happening, each thought has to be subordinated to the overall pattern, in *Ulysses* they are allowed their own importance. Nothing is a mere turning point in the narrative, a mere link in a chain of causation, a puppet called upon to give the story a twist or a push. Though there is event—there is a good deal of real drama in the episode of the funeral carriage: the stony silence with which, as Irish Catholics believing in the last sacraments, his companions greet Bloom's assertion that sudden death is the best, and the unfortunate reference to suicide—it has its own right to exist independently. Conversation, anecdote, thought, desultory impression, image and happening are freed at last from their long subordination to plot. They do not have to play a part; or to suffer drastic curtailment because they are counted as irrelevant. Of course they have to have some significance: *Ulysses* would be a terrifying monstrosity if they had not. Each is, in fact, an epiphany, to use Joyce's own term, of greater or lesser importance; but their importance is not that of mere contributing factors to a story. This is the texture of life, not the artificiality of contrived event; and, as a result, *Ulysses* is a prose work much of which one can read as one does a poem, for the epiphanies and the words themselves, not for the sake of a story to which they contribute, though they do, of course, contribute to the total impression the book makes.

Succeeding in this, Joyce has succeeded in eliminating the underlying falsehood of the novel. Though there may be a tacit agreement between the reader and the writer that things do not happen as the novel suggests, that they are not so isolated, nor clear-cut, nor interlocked, nor dramatic; and that most of life is composed of experiences which do not serve the novelist's purposes, there nevertheless remains a residual feeling on the reader's part that things ought to be like this, that fiction is in some way better than fact, a feeling that is bad for fact, for living, and, one might add, bad for fiction too. The various confusions about "naturalism" and "realism" do not help matters. Zola, the great prophet of naturalism, is full of the most preposterous melodrama. Nor, for all that we hear about the influence or non-influence of *Ulysses*, has the novel, even the so-called serious novel, altered very much, if at all, in this respect: event is still preponderant at the expense of texture.

But along with this liberation of ordinary living from the shackles of plot, goes an enormous extension of the range of life included. If one of the simplest but most important functions of the writer is to extend the recorded area of human experience, Joyce has flung the frontiers further out than any writer of this century—and it is to the particular honour of this century that whole new tracts of human experience, never before explored, have been brought under the amending and meliorating rule of the artist's compassion. Whatever his secondary purposes may have been, whatever intertwining strands of meaning and experience *Ulysses* contains, whatever the point of the story, if there is a point, all his statements go to show that Joyce considered it a major, indeed *the* major part of his vocation as a writer to speak the truths that had never before been spoken. As his brother points out, he was a realist and an extremist who had had the advantage over most writers of having to conduct his after-dinner discussions about life in a country in which the dinner itself was often lacking. From the time when he told Stanislaus that "he had no doubt that most artists, even the greatest, belied the life they knew," so that "literature . . . was a parody of life" and came to believe, according to Stanislaus, that "the poetry of noble sentiments, the romantic music, and the dramatic passions, with a dominant love theme, which culture offered him as a true poetic insight into the universal problems of human life, did not fit in with life as he knew it"—his primary purpose as an artist was clear. He ended his first adolescent manifesto with a quotation from Ibsen: " 'What will you do in our society, Miss Hessel?' asked Rorlund—'I will let in fresh air, pastor,' answered Lona." And in *Ulysses* itself he writes of the "secrets, silent, stony" which "sit in the dark palaces of both our hearts: secrets weary of their tyranny: tyrants willing to be dethroned."

Part of this process was technical: ordinary living had to be freed from the distortions of plot, from the skimping and twisting essential in the novel of event, of men and women in dramatic conflict, so that it could achieve its own entelechy. But along with this liberation from the tyranny of narrative went a tremendous extension of the amount of life included. Joyce includes so much that had never been included in art before, of man not only in his basic sexuality but in his basic sordidity as well, that he must stand as one of the great liberators of the human spirit from the tyranny of its own secrets. And not only did he bring such things within the scope of expression; he brought them, which is more important, within the scope of art.

A man's message is his way of seeing. Instead of asking whether Bloom will or will not get his breakfast in bed in the morning, and what, if anything, is the significance of the meeting between Bloom and Stephen, it is perhaps better to ask what spirit pervades and informs *Ulysses*. The mood of a book should operate on the reader more surely and a great deal more subtly than anything that could be described as its message.

"The theme of *Ulysses* is simple," says Mr. Richard Ellmann in his book, *James Joyce*, "casual kindness overcomes unconscionable power." Mr. Harry Levin in *James Joyce*, however, will have nothing to do with such calendar mottoes. He thinks that the book offers no hope and no comfort, that there is only the author's creative intensity, beating down "like an aroused volcano upon an ancient city, overtaking its doomed inhabitants in forum or temple, at home or at brothel, and petrifying them in the insensate agonies of paralysis." (Incidentally, it is difficult to make out from Mr. Levin's celebrated study whether he enjoyed reading the book or not.) Mr. Hugh Kenner thinks the book is a gargantuan, ironic machine, and he favours the dilemma of Modern Industrial Man, the dead remains of classical and Christian civilisation being incapsulated in the speech of the characters, whose language is the language of eighteenth-century Dublin, in order to show how the mighty are fallen. That the language of the nameless narrator of the Cyclops episode is the language of eighteenth-century Dublin one is inclined to doubt. It is sufficiently obvious that neither he nor the citizen are Industrial Men, or industrious men either, for the matter of that. Many people have found the book terrible. George Orwell believed that it was "the product of a special vision of life, the vision of a Catholic who has lost his faith. What Joyce is saying is, 'Here is life without God. Just look at it!' " (Apart altogether from whether we really feel that Joyce is saying anything like this when we read the book, it is perhaps worth remarking here that though all the evidence goes to show that he was a cheerful sort of unbeliever, it is rather to be doubted whether, as Mr. Eliot has pointed out to the present author, anybody brought up as an Irish Catholic could ever, deep in his being, envisage the world as "godless.") Mr. William Empson thinks that Bloom's isolation and Stephen's megalomania are so monstrous that, if the book is to be bearable, it must have a happy ending. He thinks Joyce meant to indicate that Stephen went to bed with Molly, the first woman not a whore he had ever been to bed with, and that this not only produced an enormous improvement in his character, but was the means of restoring conjugal relations between the Blooms.

All this disagreement would seem to suggest that there is a deep inherent difficulty in deciding what are the values of the book, even, let us say, to put it perfectly simply, in deciding whether it is a cheerful book or a very gloomy one.

The values with which we are surrounded in life are, so to speak, concentric: near at hand are those of the parental, or, later, the human circle in which we move, outside them the values of society and beyond that again what are alleged to be the values of God or of the grave. Before discussing his larger vision it would be as well to see whether Joyce accepts, rejects, endorses or modifies the ordinary close-at-hand values of society and it is perhaps instructive to compare him with a famous, and in many ways remarkable, novelist who is said to have attacked them. . . .

Thackeray quite obviously expects the reader to share his beliefs, his prejudices and his values: his book [*Vanity Fair*] is written in the assurance that there is a common ground and that it is quite easily reached by people of good will. Joyce does not seem to have any prejudices whatever about values or beliefs. As far as can be seen, initially at least, what he expects from the reader is only a level of literacy and a freedom from atavistic reaction to sexual abnormality, dirt, drink, dishonesty, failure (how failure sets Thackeray off, one way or the other!) and all societal obstacles to admiration or compassion, or at least a cool regard. The people of *Ulysses* are a pretty battered lot. Debt, drink, idleness afflict practically all of them, Stephen included. Bloom is not idle, but he is not very industrious either, and his record of false starts and lost jobs in Cuffe's, Wisdom Hely's, Thom's and elsewhere certainly amounts to failure, a failure from which only the nine hundred pounds and the insurance policy inherited from his father protect him. Parts of his past, the making up to Mrs. Riordan, for example, or the suggestion to Molly that she should pose in the nude for the rich dilettantes in Merrion Square, are not very creditable in terms of the sort of values we imbibe from Thackeray or indeed any of the writing of the past. Nor would the rest of the people in the book appear, by these standards, very prepossessing. The three old men who foregather in the Ormonde would not have much to say for themselves in most courts of judgment of life. Ben Dollard of the bass baritone has squandered his substance and reduced himself to penury; Bob Cowley is in the hands of the bailiffs, Simon Dedalus's daughters are near starving while he drinks. Yet there seems to be nothing much on their consciences that a ball of malt and a bar of a song will not amend. Is Joyce's attitude towards them condemnatory, compassionate or indifferent? Are we supposed to admire them as they evidently to some extent admire themselves?

The first thing one is forced to conclude is that if *Ulysses* is an examination of hell, or futility, or an unredeemed decay, or anything else of that nature—which it is frequently alleged to be—it presents some very curious characteristics. Here is a passage from *Stephen Hero* which is an illuminating contrast to the tone of *Ulysses*. Stephen has gone to the Adelphi Hotel to look for Cranly. He finds him in the billiard-room and sits down beside him to watch the game:

> It was a three-handed game. An elderly clerk, evidently in a patronising mood, was playing two of his junior colleagues. The elderly clerk was a tall stout man who wore gilt spectacles on a face like a red shrivelled apple. He was in his shirt-sleeves and he played and spoke so briskly as to suggest that he was drilling rather than playing. The young clerks were both clean-shaven. One of them was a thickset young man who played doggedly without speaking, the other was an effervescent young man with white eye-brows and a nervous manner. Cranly and Stephen watched the game pro-gress, creep from point to point. The heavy young man put his ball on the floor three times in succession and the scoring was so slow that the marker came and stood by the table as a reminder that the twenty minutes had passed. The players chalked their cues oftener than before and, seeing that they were in earnest about finishing the game, the marker did not say

anything about the time. But his presence acted upon them. The elderly clerk jerked his cue at his ball, making a bad stroke, and stood back from the table blinking his eyes and saying "Missed that time." The effervescent young clerk hurried to his ball, made a bad stroke and, looking along his cue, said "Ah!". The dogged young man shot his ball straight into the top pocket, a fact which the marker registered at once on the broken marking-board. The elderly clerk peered for a few critical seconds over the rim of his glasses, made another bad stroke and, at once proceeding to chalk his cue, said briefly and sharply to the effervescent young man "Come on now, White. Hurry up now."

The hopeless pretence of those three lives before him, their unredeemable servility, made the back of Stephen's eyes feel burning hot. He laid his hand on Cranly's shoulder and said impetuously:

"We must go at once. I can't stand it any longer."

If this is hell, and it is, we are out of it in *Ulysses*. There is no one in *Ulysses* whose life is a hopeless pretence or who presents an aspect of unredeemable servility. Indeed there is scarcely anyone who does not bear himself with panache, with gaiety, with scurrility or with pride. Bloom, though insulted, certainly feels no inferiority. And it is instructive to compare the mood of the portraiture in *Ulysses* with Joyce's treatment of the same people in *Dubliners*. It comes as something of a shock to realise that the Ignatius Gallagher whose scoop we hear about in the *Freeman's Journal* office is the vulgarian who appeared from London in "A Little Cloud." The Lenehan of *Ulysses* is a great deal less insufferable (and more cheerful) than the Lenehan who hangs about while Corley extracts money from the slavey in "Two Gallants.") Martin Cunningham, Jack Power, McCoy, Tom Kernan are all treated harshly and satirically in the earlier book but with what almost amounts to gentleness in the later. But the strangest blossoming concerns someone who had appeared only in the *Portrait* and *Stephen Hero*. Simon Dedalus now at last attains those legendary dimensions that the *Portrait* had grudgingly hinted at. He is given size, humour, style and pathos; it is made quite clear that he retains his daughter's amused affection even though he refuses her the money he proceeds to spend in the Ormonde; and his song in that place is given its full worth of beauty. We see him well away now on his downward path, in the glory of his scandalous autumn, and we leave him in full voice.

Joyce openly enjoys his material in *Ulysses* and grants it a worth which, for any but satirical purposes, is denied to it in *Dubliners*. I have no wish to suggest that the book is Pickwickian or that Simon Dedalus is a first cousin of the Cheeryble brothers; nor that the book presents a happier view of experience simply because it is funnier than *Dubliners* or the *Portrait*. But the humour of *Ulysses* can scarcely be other than sympathetic, for the simple reason that most of it is made by the characters themselves. It is their tongues and imaginations, the vitality of their language, the grotesquery of their wit which, as much as anything else, draw us back to the book and make it, whatever else it may be, one of the funniest in the language.

And there can hardly be any question but that Joyce enjoys them just as they enjoy themselves. The Citizen is well aware that he is giving a performance, albeit straightfaced, and he is certainly enjoying himself. In *Dubliners* the comedy is of a kind that gives Joyce and the reader bitter and mordant amusement—the asinine conversation about the doctrine of infallibility in the story, "Grace," for example—but which the characters themselves can hardly be said to share. *Dubliners* may be comic; it is anything but humorous. If the man who wrote *Dubliners* has looked upon the Gorgon's head, the man who wrote *Ulysses* has certainly not been turned to stone.

And it is often forgotten how much of *Ulysses* explores the lives of people other than simply Bloom and Stephen: when Joyce's narrowness of scope as a novelist is complained of, it should be remembered how skilfully and often how movingly he touched in the whole background of a minor character's life: Martin Cunningham's wife, J. J. O'Molloy's attempts to borrow money, the Dignam household, Mrs. Breen's marriage, Father Conmee's complacency, Zoe's patter. Hundreds of such details, flitting across Bloom's mind or emerging from some conversation, evoke, seldom without compassion, the lives of a dozen others.

The people of *Ulysses* are not a cross-section of the bourgeois world: they are Joyce's father's world, that narrow world of drink and song, of debt and redemption, of vulgarity, wit and seedy gentility that his father inhabited. It is through singing that they are, for the most part, acquainted; and Joyce himself loved song. "The humour of *Ulysses* is his; its people are his friends. The book is his spittin' image," he said to Louis Gillet after his father's death. And, apart from their feeling for song, the people of *Ulysses* are by no means without their virtues: their ready understanding of misfortune, their willingness to help each other beat the rap, their refusal to judge each other by the standards of mere respectability are apparent. *Ulysses*, says Mr. Harry Levin in his book, *James Joyce: A Critical Introduction*, is an epic "entirely lacking in the epic virtues of love, friendship and magnanimity," but he seems to be forgetting or ignoring something deeply important in the characters' attitude to each other:

> For a few days tell him, Father Cowley said anxiously.
>
> Ben Dollard halted and stared, his loud orifice open, a dangling button of his coat wagging brightbacked from its thread as he wiped away the heavy shraums that clogged his eyes to hear aright.
>
> What few days? he boomed. Hasn't your landlord distrained for rent?
>
> He has, Father Cowley said.
>
> Then our friend's writ is not worth the paper it's printed on, Ben Dol-

lard said. The landlord has the prior claim. I gave him all the particulars.
29 Windsor Avenue. Love is the name?
    That's right, Father Cowley said . . . But are you sure of that?
    You can tell Barabbas from me, Ben Dollard said, that he can put that
writ where Jacko put the nuts.
    He led Father Cowley boldly forward linked to his bulk.
    Filberts I believe they were, Mr. Dedalus said, as he dropped his glasses
on his coatfront, following them.

And along with their readiness to help, however desultory, idle or
unreliable it may be, they have a gaiety and courage in face of their own
usually well-deserved misfortunes, which is part of an attitude to life
that may at bottom be weak and self-deceiving, but which also augurs a
certain generosity and recklessness of spirit not markedly characteristic
of the bourgeois world. Apart from Stephen's student friends and the
librarians these people are all, or nearly all, failures of one kind or another. Even the editor of the *Freeman* is, according to Ned Lambert, a
"sad case" of "incipient jigs." That Joyce should have thought an exposure of their limitations and weaknesses worth the full weight of so much
of the book is inconceivable. Many judgments on the people of *Ulysses*
seem to proceed from a sort of upset liberalism or shocked Protestantism
which finds them and their humour an outrage, but these judgments are
certainly not shared by Joyce himself. Yeats was nearer the mark when
he agreed that *Ulysses* was "cruel" but added that it was "our Irish
cruelty, and also our kind of strength." A great deal of the humour of
these people is admittedly cruel, but then it is *Galgenhumor,* the product
of misfortune, and those who find it too cruel would probably find most
Irish humour so, from Lever's to Samuel Beckett's, and might profitably
even take a closer look at some of the humour of Somerville and Ross.
    The confusion of morality with mere respectability which is almost en-
demic in the English mind is entirely absent in Joyce, and the vulgarity
of judgment by mere status is entirely absent from his book. The people
of *Ulysses,* though they belong, very roughly speaking, to a certain social
class, form an almost completely classless community. Though the realities of money and survival are known to them, the irrelevancies of the
social structure are not important to Joyce. Nor does *Ulysses* contain any
lingering traces of a morality—sexual, social, monetary or hygienic—
unconsciously adopted from respectable society and silently assumed to
be held in common with the respectable reader. Joyce has shifted the
process of judgment of human behaviour altogether away from that
governed merely by social reflex. And this is one of the ways in which
he is a specifically modern writer, reflecting the real consciousness of
our time; for whatever else may be said about it, and with all its vulgari-
ties, its violences, its half-baked caricatures of serious creative purposes
on its head, ours is a time of liberation from merely societal values. That
his book is in large part governed by this spirit of tolerance and libera-

tion is all the more remarkable in that it is populated not by artists or anarchists or beats or professional rebels of one kind or another, but by some of the outwardly ordinary people of Dublin in 1904. It is as if the lid had been pulled off ordinary society to reveal the falsity of the lie that people are divided into the respectable and the criminal: to reveal in all its outrageousness the unbiddable eccentricity, weakness, humour and unreliability of man. . . .

It is striking how clearly Joyce, in his own career, sums up the *fin de siècle* and its immediate aftermath, the advent of modern literature. There is an aesthetic revolt. A brave, proud, Satanic but "languid" young man scorns the world as it is and rejects its paths in favour of his own right to follow and create an ideal beauty. The *fin de siècle* artist turns his back on the meanness, squalor and ignobility of the world. Then suddenly in the aftermath we find modern art as never before concerned with that world and attempting to bring all that very squalor within its compass: within, that is to say, in some way or other, the compass of "beauty."

Stephen is right to revolt against and abandon the Dublin he knew, and the parental environment into which he had been born. While remaining personally within it he was unlikely to accomplish much. "When the soul of man is born in this country there are nets flung at it to hold it back from flight. You talk to me of nationality, language, religion. I shall try to fly by those nets." Physically and spiritually of course he did. *Ulysses* is in no sense a double apostasy. Its author is not finding sustenance or illumination in the spiritual values of its characters. But he is in their human value, and in their human reality. In the Proteus episode, while Stephen is communing with himself on the strand, contemplating a visit to his uncle, he reflects on his family. We hear, in this reflection, his real, "consubstantial father's voice" for the first time, commenting on his in-laws:

> O weeping God, the things I married into. The drunken little costdrawer and his brother, the cornet player. Highly respectable gondoliers. And skeweyed Walter sirring his father, no less. Sir. Yes, sir. No, sir. Jesus wept: and no wonder by Christ.

And Stephen imagines also his uncle's greeting:

> Sit down or by the law Harry I'll knock you down.
> Walter squints vainly for a chair.
> He has nothing to sit down on, sir.
> He has nowhere to put it, you mug. Bring in our Chippendale chair. Would you like a bite of something? . . . the rich of a rasher fried with a herring? Sure? So much the better. We have nothing in the house but backache pills.

And he reflects:

> Houses of decay, mine his and all. You told the Clongowes gentry you had
> an uncle a judge and an uncle a general in the army. Come out of them,
> Stephen. Beauty is not there.

Yet, if the purpose of Stephen's revolt, and, in whatever sense, the purpose of the artist, was the creation or extraction of some form of beauty,
and if *Ulysses* was the justification of that revolt and the fulfilment of
that purpose, then beauty must lie there, even in those "houses of decay"
which are its subject. If, to put it simply, the book was his father's "spit-
ting image," it is in the contemplation of that image that beauty must lie.

Ulysses executes a complex movement of reconciliation and acceptance:
towards the world of its author's father, towards the "sordid and deceptive" world of ordinary living; and, because the self, having abandoned
the heroic lie, is now seen to be part of that world, towards the self as
well. For Stephen and, ultimately, because art achieves the general
through the particular instance, for us, they are one and the same. He
had been tempted to reject the world of mundane, sordid and deceptive
detail, as well as his father's houses of decay, in favour of an ideal beauty.
That to reject the mundanities and sordidities of this world is also to
reject a great deal of the self, every human being knows, in whom "the
monster" who favours the ideal has not grown to dominatingly "heroic
proportions." It was through the concept and the creation of Leopold
Bloom that Joyce, with many characteristic ironies and subtleties, but
also with an immense simplicity, achieved the multiple apotheosis he
desired.

"There is," says Lenehan, "a touch of the artist about old Bloom. He's
a cultured allroundman, Bloom is. . . . He's not one of your common
or garden . . . you know . . . There's a touch of the artist about old
Bloom."

There is indeed, for "As we . . . weave and unweave our bodies, Stephen said, from day to day, their molecules shuttled to and fro, so does
the artist weave and unweave his image." And a few pages later we are
reminded of another Jewish character in the same young man's assertion
that Shakespeare "drew Shylock out of his own long pocket."

There are many parallels between Bloom and Stephen, just as there
are many resemblances between Bloom and the mature Joyce. Boylan
stands in relation to Bloom as Mulligan does to Stephen: accenting his
isolation, making a mockery of his attitudinisings, representing a worldly
glitter and a sexual flamboyance which neither Bloom nor Stephen possesses.

> Wit. You would give your five wits for youth's proud livery he pranks in.
> Lineaments of gratified desire.

To a large extent, though not nearly to the same extent as Stephen,
Bloom rejects the values of the society within which he moves. Both are
humiliated; both are excluded, partly by choice and partly by force. Both

are infidels, though both are concerned with and coloured by the ancient faiths within which they were nurtured. Both of them have deep and complex feelings about the histories of their races and their ancestral religions; but, nevertheless, to both of them history is a nightmare from which one must struggle to awake. Both have reason to feel remorse about the dead.

But their contrasts in resemblance are no less interesting than the resemblances themselves. Whereas Stephen is almost overwhelmed by his remorse, Bloom recovers his balance comparatively easily. In the brothel Bloom finds the thought of his ancestral background a source of strength; Stephen finds the thought of his merely another source of remorse. Parallel to Stephen's dramatic defiance of convention and society runs Bloom's comic, often shaken, often degraded, seldom dignified, never wholly triumphant, but still stubborn, courageous and, in the main, successful attempt to achieve the same end: to be oneself. But Bloom has merely to remain himself, whereas Stephen has to become. Confronted like Stephen by mockery, assault, the temptations of the flesh, Messianic ambition and remorse, Bloom, unlike Stephen, has attained to a certain magnanimity.

In general, where we find a resemblance, in circumstance or personality, between the two, and when we see its end, we can say that the difference is that Bloom is more mature than Stephen and seems to body forth— with some irony of course and some caricature, but nonetheless fairly faithfully—the differences between Stephen and the mature Joyce.[1]

But Bloom had to be made inclusive not only of the circumstantial Joyce, but of the human nature that Joyce and all men shared. If the pretences to heroism were to be stripped away and *Ulysses* was to be the first great masterpiece of unheroic literature; if Bloom was to survive as the first great anti-hero, standing in for all unheroic men, including the self, if the "silent secrets" sitting in the dark palaces of all men's hearts which were "weary of their tyranny" were to be dethroned, the avatar had to be subjected to and his power of survival tested against the most open and the most cruel tests.[2]

---

[1] Bloom is of course important also, as an instrument of Joyce's return to his father's world, though it is also true that he emphasises his differences from it. He, who "knows your old fellow" is also "middler the Holy Ghost," the third person of the blessed Trinity, mediator between the son and his consubstantial father's world. This theme is made so plain and is so constantly returned to that to suggest it as a central motif in the book is not to indulge in any arcane exegesis. It is not necessary for any of the three characters to become other than they are, in order that we may grasp Bloom's middle position between Dublin and Trieste, between the father and his associates in Ireland and the artist in the Austro-Hungarian empire—where, incidentally, old Virag, Bloom's father, was born. Joyce came to delight in the existence and the creative possibilities of his father's world, but he did not desire to be part of it. Hence his hero is Bloom, the common man who is also the outsider, and Dubliner who is also a stranger.

[2] There is a sense in which Bloom stands in for all humanity: like Kafka's K, Chaplin's

This frequently ridiculous, often humiliated man is seen in every possible intimacy and exposed to every possible nuance of contempt. He is put to flight by physical threats; he is cuckolded; he masturbates before our eyes; most of the atavisms born of fear and shame by which we are accustomed to react to others and judge ourselves are flouted. Nor does Joyce spare him his humour. From the episode of John Henry Menton's hat to the silly questions about Gibraltar in the coffee stall, he is exposed to it. Even such ambiguous qualities as his wariness at fence sometimes desert him in favour of a boyish and ridiculous vanity for the truth. And the cruellest cut of all is reserved till last. Molly may or may not be Gea Tellus or the Great Earth Mother; she is certainly Bloom's wife. She knows him through and through and she spares him nothing. If she remembers his romantic insistence on Howth Head, she also remembers his peculiar request in Harold's Cross Road. Joyce's purpose in ending the book with Molly's monologue has been much debated; yet it seems fairly obvious that if his purpose was the total exposure of Bloom, and the exposure of him in the most candid light, no tribunal could equal in intimate knowledge and ultimate frankness the thoughts of his woman.

Yet the remarkable thing is that in some way Bloom survives all this, even Molly's inquisition, though shakily as usual. "Let them go and get a husband first that's fit to be looked at," Molly says of the Miss Kearneys; and she recognises that he is in some sense or other superior to his mockers:

> . . . theyre a nice lot all of them well theyre not going to get my husband again into their clutches if I can help it making fun of him then behind his back I know well when he goes on with his idiotics because he has sense enough not to squander every penny piece he earns down their gullets and looks after his wife and family goodfornothings . . .

Her final "yes" may or may not have the allegorical implications her admirers have read into it; it may or may not be a "yes" to life; it is certainly a repetition of her original acceptance of Bloom.

Nor does the reader withhold his assent, as the long book draws to a close and we get to know Bloom through intimacies of body and soul

---

tramp or Beckett's old man. Endlessly interesting, unmistakably real though he is in the personal detail which is piled up, he is yet sufficiently outside his immediate environment to take on a certain universality. His position is ambiguous in several respects. Though no anarchist, he is at least a failure. He stands far enough outside the society to present a contrast and suggest, however comical it may be, a conflict: in this he again resembles K, anxious to cooperate but denied the opportunity, or Chaplin's tramp, gazing wistfully at the lighted ballroom, or Beckett's old men who are anonymously fed and maintained in their solitude. That Bloom should be Odysseus, Sinbad the sailor, the wandering Jew and whatnot, may help to confer this universality upon him. It is done in more important ways by a series of carefully arranged ironies and ambiguities in his personal position: orphaned son and bereaved father, worldly wise and yet a failure, Irish and non-Irish, husband yet cuckold, faithful and faithless.

to which no other character in literature had ever previously been subjected. Joyce set out to show man in a light he had never been seen in
before; to expose him to a gaze more omnipresent and more exacting
than any to which he had ever previously been exposed. He weighted the
circumstances against his man; he put him in situations which normally
arouse only our contempt; he exposed him to the jibes of the cruellest
wits in Europe; he brought the elaborations of his own irony gleefully
to bear upon him. Yet it is the measure of his success in his ultimate purpose that the man not only survives but survives triumphantly, as the first
great hero of unheroic literature; that he arouses not only our compassion and sympathy, our affection and humorous understanding, but, before his long chapter of humiliations is over, our profoundest respect.

That Bloom's own qualities, often overlooked by criticism, and always
derided by the other characters, had something to do with this miracle
we must admit; though they are certainly not the whole story. He is at
least averagely kind. He performs, for example, most of what are known
in Catholic theology as "the corporal works of mercy" during the day:
he visits the sick, comforts the afflicted, buries the head, shelters the homeless, etc. Though no combatant, he can bring himself to assert vital truths
in the teeth of the opposition.

> But it's no use, says he. Force, hatred, history, all that. That's not life for
> men and women, insult and hatred. And everybody knows that it's the
> very opposite of that that is really life.
> What? says Alf.
> Love, says Bloom. I mean the opposite of hatred.

And he pays for this, and for similar pronouncements, in more ways
than one. It is typical of Joyce's method that it is the enunciation of
this simple and terrible truth that brings down upon him Hynes's cruel
and brilliant sneer about his own abilities as a lover—"I wonder did he
ever put it out of sight"—just as it is his display of learning in Lenehan's
story of coming home beside Molly in the sidecar which exposes him to
the jibe, so amusing to the teller that he momentarily collapses with
laughter, about "that's only a pinprick."

His own humour, his irony, his subtlety and his intelligence are, in
general, easy to underestimate. His mind only works in clichés in the
coffee stall scene when he is tired, and it does not seem to have been
noticed that he is here making a mistaken attempt to impress Stephen as
a sort of literary man and thinker. What he utters are the clichés of
editorial journalism, particularly provincial journalism of a sort that is
written in Ireland to this day, though it was probably more widespread
everywhere in 1904. It is just the sort of language we might expect Bloom
to use in order to impress Stephen intellectually at the beginning of their
acquaintance. (The general unpopularity of this extremely funny and
engaging section of the book with critics who are not particularly well

acquainted with Ireland, may stem from their lack of recognition of the
precise kind of language he is talking.) Before that, as Dr. S. L. Goldberg
has pointed out (he is very good on Bloom's process of thought, suggesting that his stream of consciousness, far from being "jellyfish," is actually
composed of illuminating and rewarding epiphanies), Bloom's quiet ability to think for himself, his equanimity without insensitivity, above all,
perhaps, his combination of moral seriousness with a generally humorous,
caustic, but tolerant cast of mind are remarkable enough. Joyce's purpose
would not have been well served either if Bloom had been merely the
sort of stupid, acquiescent, bumbling mediocrity which earlier criticism
often made him out to be. It was necessary that he should be deprived
of certain dignities and exposed in certain lights, that he should be the
opposite of Napoleonic and often the apotheosis of the foolish, but it
would not have done, either, to make him out merely a dull cretin. In
his kindness and his gropings after better things he is surely as human
as in his *niaiseries*. Joyce had to be fair twice over.

Nor is he dull in any other sense. The fact that he is not a scurrilous
wit like most of the others, that he is grave and quiet in demeanour and
talks seriously when he believes the issues are serious, should not disguise
the fact that his mind has a constant and perhaps predominantly humorous cast:

> All kinds of places are good for ads. That quack doctor for the clap used to
> be stuck up in all the greenhouses. Never see it now. Strictly confidential.
> Dr Hy Franks. Didn't cost him a red like Maginni the dancing master self
> advertisement. Got fellows to stick them up or stick them up himself for
> that matter on the q.t. running in to loosen a button. Fly by night. Just
> the place too. POST NO BILLS. POST NO PILLS. Some chap with a
> dose burning him.

But it must be repeated that it is in no way primarily because of his
intellectual or moral qualities that Bloom so arouses our interest and
so commands our affection. (It should not, really, except to critics, be
necessary to prove that he does the latter: no character in contemporary
fiction has such a widely variegated personal following.) I mean my
Ulysses to be a good man, said Joyce to Frank Budgen right enough; and
we can see that he is, however strange the definition of goodness might
seem by orthodox standards, but it is not this in the end. When we ask
what it is, we are forced ultimately, I think, to recognise that here is the
familiar: the worn, familiar, comical, shabby, eroded but not collapsed
face of humanity. In his vulnerability, his weakness, his secrecies, his
continuous but uncertain ability to remain upright, his clinging to a
few props, his constantly threatened dignity, Bloom commands that affection in the midst of comedy which we give to our own image, stained and
worn as it is. Joyce has given him an almost infinite complexity as well;
because the book is technically, for all its faults, a *tour de force*, we learn

about Bloom as we learn about nobody else in fiction while we go along. And his creator has also breathed life into him and surrounded him, on this one day, with a world masterfully rich in the comic and in living detail. But his ultimate triumph was to extract this ordinary poetry of humanity from him; and it is a strange one, for his creator was Stephen Dedalus, that well-known aesthete.

Joyce's movement, as he was subsequently to demonstrate at length, was circular. By "the commodious vicus of recirculation" one came back to where one started, to the father and the race. He had, in particular (as, it is alleged, has all humanity in general), a fallen father, "foosterfather." The fall began in the dark wet winter of Parnell's downfall and death, when John Joyce began that long downward progress in which the instincts of a dandy and a gentleman, a Corkman and a boaster, a whiskey-drinking "praiser of his own past" were to consort oddly with, and to succeed only in accelerating, that decline into "squalor and insincerity" of which Stephen Hero speaks. The two falls, Parnell's and his Parnellite father's, were forever after symbolically one in Joyce's mind. He was to harmonise them humorously and to entwine them with all other falls and fathers in *Finnegans Wake*. In *Ulysses* he has achieved out of the resentments and limitations of adolescence, even out of the justified attitudes of revolt and the judgments he was entitled to make about his spiritual and carnal inheritance, an attitude of compassion, tolerance and delight, which returns to that inheritance what it gave him: pride, humour, a love of song, a sense of style and a knowledge of the obverse of these coins, the degradations, the inescapable Irishnesses of life. The contrast between Stanislaus's attitude to his father, as expressed in *My Brother's Keeper*, and Joyce's is almost a parable of the difference between the viewpoint of the good man and the artist. The one is a judgment, harsh, clear and unforgiving. The other is an acceptance.

Yet, important though this movement was for Joyce—this achievement, like Shakespeare (according to Stephen), of the spiritual paternity of his own father—it is not the whole story. Like "the greyedauburn Shakespeare," walking in Fetter Lane Joyce was "weaving and unweaving his own image" and seeing himself as he then was "by reflection from that which then I shall be"; and he was also attempting to incorporate and to redeem aspects of our common humanity which had never been incorporated victoriously into literature before. It is here that Leopold Bloom enters, contrasted in his humility yet his continuing, if comic, integrity, with Stephen Dedalus; the self-image transmuted into an Irish Jew with ancestry somewhere in central Europe, with "a touch of the artist" and yet without the artist's redemption from the conditions of ordinary living. For Bloom does represent ordinary living, though isolated and set apart. He is pragmatic, yet a visionary; mean and careful, yet often in trouble out of generosity or fineness of spirit; betrayed and betraying, yet loyal after his fashion in the primary instances of love; ridiculous, yet dignified; spat upon, yet victorious; sensitive yet complacent, with the complacency which turns out in the end to be one of humanity's great defences, a clinging to the moment and the necessities of the moment, a form of continuing courage. All this adds up to the inescapable Jewishness of life. Bloom is not heroic, in the old sense. Nor is he abysmal, in the old sense, as any character in literature with certain of his characteristics would have had to be before him. In him, for the first time, our unpromising, unpoetic, unheroic image is found to have surprising possibilities for pride and for poetry.

The greatness of *Ulysses* is partly technical.[3] A new prose form has been achieved, free from the distortions of dramatic narrative, and not dependent for its intensity on dramatic confrontations and resolutions. Yet it has intensity: a matter of language, of density of life, of immediacy of texture; in a word, of poetry. That the texture is yet "ordinary" proves that intensity, poetry, resides here too, its extraction being a matter of language and of the pitch of interest with which the ordinary is contemplated and then evoked.

In this sense it can hardly be otherwise than "on the side of life," ordinary, continuing life, as against dogmatisms of one kind or another. Such poetry cannot avoid possessing, in Coleridge's word, geniality; and if this were all that were to be said it would still be enough. Poetry is enough. The book does not have to be "about" anything, except, of course, Leopold Bloom.

Yet over such a large area, an uncoloured contemplation and evocation of life is tantamount to impossible. There remains the question of the author's vision. One cannot prove syllogistically that the temper of the book is what Joyce called "the classic temper," that it is an act of acceptance and an act of *pietas*. One can only appeal to the reader's response to its abounding humour, its creative zest, its ability to anneal the spirit (all of which are inseparably bound up with its poetry and its "geniality"); and one can only try, as I have tried, to show that Joyce meant it to be received in this way and that, in part, he wrote a saga about a young man who achieved this classic temper. It is not necessary to seek profundities of meaning in *Ulysses*. Criticism has performed no service for Joyce by the suggestion that we must unravel the book before we can understand it; and that patience, skill and drudgery in unravelment are the primary qualities required of its ideal reader. They are not the sort of qualities commonly found in those most remarkable for receptivity and generosity of response to art or anything else. The suggestion that they are essential is part of the academic claim to indispensability—let alone

[3] *Ulysses* and *The Waste Land,* published so near together in time, began in English that attempt to find new forms to accommodate more images in a new relationship, which remains characteristic of much of the most interesting work of this century, though not always of the most praised.

usefulness—which has followed in our time as a result of the vesting of academic interests in literature. Yet it is also the duty of the critic to seek to interpret a book in the spirit in which it is written. Whether the facts that *Ulysses* is partly a strange act of *pietas* on Joyce's part; that Bloom, as well as being plain Leopold Bloom of Eccles Street, is a mediator between the artist and mankind; or that the book is a work of abounding comedy, full of "profane joy," make it greater than if it were a work of hatred and disgust, is a question difficult to answer. We can only fruitfully say that all great works of art are full of intensity, and that there is not therefore so much difference between opposing visions as criticism may be tempted to suggest.

It is certain, however, that if we can describe *Ulysses* in this way, we claim it to be more important than it would be if the whole enormous structure had been raised in support of some theory about metempsychosis, some illumination of comparative myth, or some conviction about the decline of Western man. It is in the redemption of our common and ordinary humanity from its own "deceits and sordities," and the totality as well as the poetic intensity of its statement of the conditions of ordinary living, that its originality and its importance for us lies. More than any other book, *Ulysses* marks the end of heroic literature, and with the advent of Bloom, man takes on a new poetic interest for his complex mundanity rather than as an actor of greater or lesser strength and tragic resonance. The resonance is there, and the tragedy as well as the triumph, but they are otherwise revealed. In no previous work, to take but one of his characteristics, had a "good" man been shown who was not altogether "normal" sexually.

We are rightly suspicious of the notion of progress, but there is a sense in which there is progress in the arts. We cover more ground, we say what has not been said; partial and limited like the visions of other artists of other eras though ours may be, we extend both the ordinary recorded area of human experience and the reclaimed area of poetic compassion; and we in our time have been honest. *Ulysses* has faults, of eccentricity, of mere display, of mechanical thoroughness. Yet in the way it encompasses ordinary living and the way it gives to much that had been denied it the intensity and texture of poetry, *Ulysses* is a landmark, perhaps the most important single event in the great breakthrough that has been achieved in this century.

Why Molly Bloom Menstruates

by Richard Ellmann

The denouement of Ulysses has been much disputed. What seems to end the book is that Bloom, who nodded off at the end of the "Ithaca" episode, and his more wakeful wife Molly, both snore away in the arms of Morpheus, or as Joyce puts it, in the arms of Murphy. But is this really the end? Did Joyce have no future in mind for his characters? The question is particularly likely to be asked because *A Portrait* is often said to find its sequel in *Ulysses* where Stephen appears after an interval of about two years. But *A Portrait* seems self-contained, it celebrates the birth first of Stephen's body and then of his soul, it brings him from inchoate to real selfhood, from possibility to decision. If he reappears in *Ulysses,* and I won't deny that he does, he is there for a different purpose, not to present his further adventures.

What then does happen to Bloom and Stephen? One critic declares that Stephen goes out into the night and writes—*Ulysses*. But *Ulysses* is not the work of Stephen, any more than *Hamlet* is the work of Hamlet; it issues from that mind of which Stephen, Bloom, Molly, and even Mulligan and Boylan are only aspects. Two other critics regard the ending as proleptic, but the events they foresee are not the same. William Empson remembers that Stephen, after refusing to stay the night, agrees to exchange with Mrs. Bloom Italian for singing lessons, and proposes that Stephen returns on 17 June or anyway in the next few days, with his grammar book. The mutual instruction then takes a predictable turn. Bloom tolerates the affair, Empson feels, because he wants desperately to have a son, even if through the agency of another man.

On a practical level, this theory offers a number of difficulties. Apart from Molly's impending concert tour, which will make other alliances than with Boylan complicated for her, Empson leans heavily upon what appears to be a mere gesture of politeness on Stephen's part. Having been rescued from a jam, and having turned down an invitation to stay the night, he avoids twice refusing his host pointblank by appearing to accept a vague and unscheduled exchange of lessons. But Bloom recognizes—

"Why Molly Bloom Menstruates." From *Ulysses on the Liffey,* by Richard Ellmann (London: Faber and Faber Ltd., 1972), pp. 159–76. Copyright © 1972 by Richard Ellmann. Reprinted by permission of Oxford University Press, Inc. and Faber and Faber Ltd. One of Mr. Ellmann's footnotes has been shortened.

and Joyce at once underlines the recognition—that Stephen's return is problematic. That Molly dandles the idea as an erotic fancy does not make it more likely. The notion of a Stephen–Molly affair outside the book is so skimpily supported that it becomes a nineteenth-century parlour game like "Describe Desdemona's girlhood" or "Fortinbras's reign in Denmark."

The other theory for 17 June is exactly opposite. According to it, Bloom, instead of relaxing further his marriage tie, tightens it and becomes a proper husband. Edmund Wilson proposed this idea some years ago in an uncharacteristic burst of optimism; he contended that Bloom's request for breakfast in bed proved that Bloom was once more becoming master in his own house. A difficulty with this oatmeal theory is that it rests heavily upon the notion that not to make breakfast himself is Bloom's assertion of male authority. This in turn would be more convincing if Bloom had seemed put upon when he made breakfast on the morning of June 16, but actually he likes cooking and doesn't feel degraded by it. Moreover he has apparently done it, except when ill, during the whole of their married life, including the period when they enjoyed complete conjugal relations. Need he feel degraded? After all, if cooks are always women, chefs are always men.[1] His request for breakfast may be just what it appears to be, an expression of fatigue after a late night which is most unusual for him. Molly indicates that she expects to return to the usual pattern after one morning's exertions. At any rate, it seems an unwarranted assumption that breakfast in bed will restore anyone's sexual relations to normalcy. It is harder to reject Wilson's theory than Empson's, but both suffer from a desire, vestigial even among modern readers of novels, to detain the characters a little longer in their fictional lives. Yet a warning must be taken from Eugammon of Cyrene, who tacked his unfortunate sequel onto the *Odyssey*.

Joyce declared in his aesthetic notebook that the excellence of a comedy depended upon its joy, which in turn depended upon its fulfilment of desire. To the extent that a work was not sufficient to itself, it was deficient in joy. He could scarcely then have intended to encourage speculation about the future of his characters. He meant what he said in a letter, that in the "Ithaca" episode Bloom and Stephen become like the stars at which they gaze, and that in "Penelope" Bloom and Molly with him are off to eternity. The conjugal future at 7 Eccles street no longer interests him, any more than future doings of Odysseus and Penelope interest Homer or of Dante and Beatrice interest the author of *The Divine Comedy*. Joyce leaves possibilities at the end like dangling threads, just as Homer leaves an unfulfilled prophecy of Tiresias, but he has his mind set on other things. At the end of his Linati schema Joyce shows Bloom going off to *"Alta Notte"* ("Deep Night") and Stephen to *"Alba"*

---

[1] Mary Ellmann, in *Thinking About Women* (New York and London, 1968).

("Dawn"), but since these opposites coincide, the point is that there is no more to say. If Joyce had wanted to, he could certainly have given the book either Empson's or Wilson's conclusion: to please Empson he might have let Stephen stay the night, to please Wilson he could have had husband and wife resume complete sexual relations for the first time in eleven years. He does neither of these, though in Homer Telemachus presumably sleeps in the palace and Odysseus and Penelope share a bed. Instead of sexual intercourse in the present, Joyce has Molly think of a sexual scene in the past. He did so not because Flaubert had prescribed to the writer of fiction, *ne pas conclure,* but because he had another conclusion in mind.

He said himself that "The last word (human, all too human) is left to Penelope. This is the indispensable countersign to Bloom's passport to eternity." Beyond eternity his characters could scarcely be expected to go. The episode was, he said, the book's *clou,* the star turn of the show. In a jocular mood he said also that "Ithaca" was the true ending of the book because "Penelope" had neither beginning, middle, nor end. But it is not so formless as that, since it begins with a capital letter and ends with a full stop. Moreover, the first word in the book is *Stately* and the last *Yes,* the first and last letters of each being reversed so that the serpent has his tail in his mouth at last.[2] It would be more accurate to say that the form of "Penelope" is ungirdled than that it is nonexistent. Molly's countersign may be deciphered, and an explanation given for her thoughts of Mrs. Riordan, an elderly widow now dead, for her menstruation, and for her memories of adolescence on Gibraltar. These prove necessary rather than improvisatory.

Coming after the dry, impersonal, and pseudoscientific order of most of the "Ithaca" episode, the final monologue offers a personal, lyrical efflorescence. It is the only episode to which Joyce assigns no specific hour—the time is no o'clock, or as he said in one schema, it is the time indicated mathematically by the slightly disproportioned figure ∞ or lemniscate lying on its side—the number of eternity and infinity. It might be more exact to say that the ruins of time and space and the mansions of eternity here coexist, at least until the very end. Molly presents herself without portentousness as spokesman for nature. Like the Wife of Bath, she contends that God has not endowed us with sensual proclivities if these are not to be indulged. "Nature it is," she insists, falling into the fallacy

---

[2] Joyce probably regarded S as a male letter (Gerty MacDowell relates Bloom to a snake staring at its prey), and Y as a female one. (He said in a letter that "yes" was a female word.) For this literary symbolism he had precedents in Mallarmé and Rimbaud, not to mention Dante. It may be noted here that he draws another circle by making the *Telemachiad* begin with S and end with P, and the *Nostos* begin with P and end with S.

Compare *Stephen Hero,* p. 32: ". . . he put his lines together not word by word but letter by letter. He read Blake and Rimbaud on the values of letters and even permuted and combined the five vowels to construct cries for primitive emotions.

of identifying virtue with what is natural that Hume had criticized. (Joyce too knew it was a fallacy; Richard Rowan in *Exiles,* when Robert poses a "law of nature," retorts, "Did I vote it?") Yet Molly's nature is not indiscriminate; as she sees and represents it, nature is choosy—Darwin thought it choosy too. Still she is acceptant enough to plant the almost desert globe of the "Ithaca" episode with vegetables and people and animals and curious objects. Most of all, she covers it with flowers. In the Linati plan, the part of the body allotted to "Penelope" is fat ("Eumaeus" having offered nerves, and "Ithaca" bones). Philosophy is fleshed. Stephen had recalled earlier the medieval legend that Aristotle was enticed by a "light o' love" to let her bit, bridle, and ride him, and Molly's nature, so much more earthy, trivial, sexualized, and lyrical than Aristotle's or Hume's, appears as a final penetration by the wisdom of the body of the wisdom of the mind. (Molly's only acquaintance with Aristotle is the apocryphal and semipornographic *Aristotle's Masterpiece*; she malaprops his name into "some old Aristocrat or whatever his name is.") *"Ich bin das Fleisch das stets bejaht,"* Joyce says of her, confirming her as the opposite pole to Mulligan's denying spirit. But her yeasaying is mixed with much naysaying—until the very end of her monologue, "Yes" and "No" (with a great many "knows" for good measure) are rivals for pre-eminence. Her final affirmation is a victory over strong resistance.

Molly Bloom's birthday is 8 September, and in tribute to this anniversary, and to the symbol of eternity-infinity, Joyce writes her monologue in eight sentences. "It begins and ends," Joyce wrote Budgen,

> with the female word *yes.* It turns like the huge earth ball slowly surely and evenly round and round spinning, its four cardinal points being the female breasts, arse, womb and cunt expressed by the words *because, bottom* (in all senses bottom button, bottom of the class, bottom of the sea, bottom of his heart), *woman, yes.* Though probably more obscene than any preceding episode it seems to me to be perfectly sane full amoral fertilisable untrustworthy engaging shrewd limited prudent indifferent *Weib.*

He delights in mythologizing Molly as Gea-Tellus, then, by bringing her down with a thump onto the orangekeyed chamberpot at 7 Eccles street, in demythologizing her into an old shoe.

Molly's animadversions begin with thoughts of Mrs. Riordan, a widow whom Bloom befriended:

> Yes because he never did a thing like that before as ask to get his breakfast in bed with a couple of eggs since the *City Arms* hotel when he used to be pretending to be laid up with a sick voice doing his highness to make himself interesting to that old faggot Mrs Riordan that he thought he had a great leg of and she never left us a farthing all for masses for herself and her soul greatest miser ever was actually afraid to lay out 4d for her methylated spirit telling me all her ailments she had too much old chat in her about politics and earthquakes and the end of the world let

us have a bit of fun first God help the world if all the women were her
sort down on bathingsuits and lownecks of course nobody wanted her to
wear I suppose she was pious because no man would look at her twice I
hope Ill never be like her a wonder she didnt want us to cover our
faces . . .

Joyce's purpose is served by having Molly establish her own point of view
against its counterpart, Mrs. Riordan's prudery, the latter associated with
miserliness and piety here, as earlier in the book with occultism and aes-
theticism. Molly might seem to run more danger from the opposite fac-
tion, of Mistress Moll Flanders. She says herself, however, that she is not
a whore or a slut, and she is right. Only the most rigorous interpretation
of adultery—Christ's in the Sermon on the Mount, "Whosoever looketh
on a woman to lust after her hath committed adultery with her already in
his heart"—could consider Molly's friendships, except that with Boylan,
and perhaps that with D'Arcy, as adulterous. The book makes clear that
this first relationship is something new. June 16 may in fact be the first
day that Boylan and Molly have had "carnal," as Bloom puts it. It may
also be, though this is never established, the day in June that Bloom and
Molly climaxed their courtship by proposal and consent among the rhododendrons on Howth sixteen years before. Joyce plays on the coincidence without bearing down too hard. Fidelity and infidelity coexist.

Essentially Molly is right about herself—she is not the wholly sexual
being that to Boylan she must appear to be. She hopes that he is pleased
with her, but she is not really pleased with him. She complains about his
too familiar manners in slapping her on the behind—"I'm not a horse
or an ass am I"—but she remembers that Boylan's father was a horse-
trader and hopes this fact may explain his conduct. Boylan writes bad
loveletters ending, "Yours ever Hugh Boylan." Molly detects that he is
basically a "strange brute" with an unconscionableness that Stephen had
earlier described as the *sentimental* desire to "enjoy without incurring the
immense debtorship for a thing done." So while Molly is not planning to
break with Boylan, she is not expecting the relationship to last, and
thinks of other men as more perceptive and congenial. For the same reason she rejects sado-masochism, in books about flagellants, "Sure theres
nothing for a woman in that." She steers between Mrs. Riordan's maso-
chistic prudery and Boylan's loutishness.

Bloom has as much trouble as Ulysses had in winning recognition as
Penelope's husband. Joyce complained once of his wife that she did not
appear to see much difference between him and other men, though in
fact Nora Joyce remarked to a friend that her husband was like nobody
else. The seeming (though not real) inability to differentiate finely is
characteristic of Molly, who falls into calling the various men she has
known by the pronoun "he," without much further identification. (Stephen Dedalus did the same in "Proteus": "She she she. What she?" But
he had no particular woman to think about.) Against Stephen's effort

to make women mythical, "handmaidens of the moon," "wombs of sin," and the like, Molly regards men as either natural or unnatural. Basically she is earth to Bloom's sun, modifying his light by her own movements. She is thoroughly aware of his many failings, but notes also a few virtues. He is kind to old women like Mrs. Riordan, he has a few brains, he was handsome when young, he wipes his feet on the mat. On the other hand, his atheism, his socialism, his talk of persecution, put her off. She gradually acknowledges his pre-eminence by the frequency with which she returns to thinking about him. As compared with Boylan, her husband is the more complete man, with the supreme virtue that he wishes her well. She cannot say as much for Boylan. Molly, as the earth, prefers in Bloom the more complete to the less complete example of a biological species.

In the book's characterology, Molly is needed to contribute a quality not often present in either Bloom or Stephen, her naturalness and spontaneity. The two men are thoughtful, detached, Bloom because he sees all round, Stephen because he looks deep in. Molly's monologue is therefore less an addition than a correction. The "Ithaca" episode had offered a heliocentric view of Bloom, Molly offers a geocentric one, the two together forming the angle of parallax (a word which had baffled Bloom earlier in the day). Bloomsday becomes everymansday, and everywomansday, in that all necessary elements of desirable life have been gathered together. None of the principal figures is complete in himself, but together they sum up what is affirmable. At the end we are brought back to the earth, to spring, to vegetation, and to sexual love.

Molly has a capacity for intense yet fastidious feeling which makes Joyce's altitudinous ending possible. The peroration of her monologue is morose delectation, theologically speaking, but moroseness plays no part in it. She is thinking of that day among the rhododendrons on Howth when she and Bloom came to an understanding, but she marvellously collocates such elements as land and sea to have them all "swimming in roses."

> I love flowers Id love to have the whole place swimming in roses God of heaven theres nothing like nature the wild mountains then the sea and the waves rushing then the beautiful country with fields of oats and wheat and all kinds of things and all the fine cattle going about that would do your heart good to see rivers and lakes and flowers all sorts of shapes and smells and colours springing up even out of the ditches primroses and violets nature it is

She quickly resolves the questions of belief and incertitude which have dogged Stephen and western philosophy, and with which Bloom has bothered her, by finding them not worth asking:

> as for them saying theres no God I wouldnt give a snap of my two fingers for all their learning why dont they go and create something I often asked him atheists or whatever they call themselves go and wash the cobbles

off themselves first then they go howling for the priest and they dying and why why because theyre afraid of hell on account of their bad conscience ah yes I know them well who was the first person in the universe before there was anybody that made it all who ah that they dont know neither do I so there you are they might as well try to stop the sun from rising tomorrow the sun shines for you he said the day we were lying among the rhododendrons on Howth head in the grey tweed suit and his straw hat the day I got him to propose to me yes first I gave him the bit of seedcake out of my mouth and it was leapyear like now yes 16 years ago

This recollection of the seedcake, which Bloom also experienced in the "Lestrygonians" episode, is vaguely reminiscent of something else, and if we remember that *Finnegans Wake* speaks of the apple in the Garden of Eden as the seedfruit, there is a momentary connection with the apple which Eve passed to Adam as Molly to Bloom. This is what St. Augustine called the happy fault, *felix culpa,* but Bloom calls it *copula felix,* happy not because it brought about redemption by Christ, but in itself. As in Dante's Earthly Paradise, Adam and Eve have been absolved of original sin. Moist with spittle, the seedcake offers its parallel also to the host, and the lovers' rite is contrasted with the black mass of "Circe."

my God after that long kiss I near lost my breath yes he said I was a flower of the mountain yes so we are flowers all a womans body yes that was one true thing he said in his life and the sun shines for you today yes that was why I liked him because I saw he understood or felt what a woman is and I knew I could always get round him and I gave him all the pleasure I could leading him on till he asked me to say yes and I wouldnt answer first only looked out over the sea and the sky I was thinking of so many things he didnt know of Mulvey and Mr Stanhope and Hester and father and old captain Groves and the sailors playing all birds fly and I say stoop and washing up dishes they called it on the pier and the sentry in front of the governors house with the thing round his white helmet poor devil half roasted and the Spanish girls laughing in their shawls and their tall combs and the auctions in the morning the Greeks and the jews and the Arabs and the devil knows who else from all the ends of Europe and Duke street

Duke street is in Dublin. East and West join here, as in "Circe" greekjew and jewgreek meet, with the Arabs added here to the pot:

and the fowl market all clucking outside Larby Sharons and the poor donkeys slipping half asleep and the vague fellows in the cloaks asleep in the shade on the steps and the big wheels of the carts of the bulls and the old castle thousands of years old yes and those handsome Moors all in white and turbans like kings asking you to sit down in their little bit of a shop and Ronda with the old windows of the posadas glancing eyes a lattice hid for her lover to kiss the iron and the wineshops half open at night and the castanets and the night we missed the boat at Algeciras the watchman going about serene with his lamp and O that awful deep-down torrent O and the sea the sea crimson sometimes like fire

Water and fire combine, and so does the crimson sea of the straits of Gibraltar with Molly's menstruation, about which she has complained earlier, as if the natural forces of earth and woman were synonymous. This synthesis was prepared long before in the book; in the "Proteus" episode Stephen brooded on the oddity of God's transubstantiation into flesh occurring in so many communions in so many times and places:

> And at the same instant perhaps a priest round the corner is elevating it. Dringdring! And two streets off another locking it into a pyx. Dringadring! And in a ladychapel another taking housel all to his own cheek. Dringdring! Down, up, forward, back.

Then in "Nausicaa," Bloom meditated on the same identity-variety in the process of menstruation:

> How many women in Dublin have it today? Martha, she [Gerty]. Something in the air. That's the moon. But then why don't all women menstruate at the same time with same moon, I mean? Depends on the time they were born, I suppose. Or all start scratch then get out of step.

These two passages seem at first to be idle. But Joyce is establishing a secret parallel and opposition: the body of God and the body of woman share blood in common. In allowing Molly to menstruate at the end Joyce consecrates the blood in the chamberpot rather than the blood in the chalice, mentioned by Mulligan at the beginning of the book. For this blood is substance, not more or less than substance. The great human potentiality is substantiation, not transubstantiation, or subsubstantiation. It is this quality which the artist has too, in that he produces living human characters, not ethereal or less than human ones. It is human blood,[3] not divine. Menstruation is Promethean.

> and the glorious sunsets and the figtrees in the Alameda gardens yes and all the queer little streets and pink and blue and yellow houses and the rosegardens and the jessamine and geraniums and cactuses and Gibraltar as a girl where I was a Flower of the mountain yes when I put the rose in my hair like the Andalusian girls used or shall I wear a red yes and how he kissed me under the Moorish wall

Molly confuses, or rather conflates, an incident when in her early youth she lay on the rock of Gibraltar beside Lieutenant Mulvey, with the moment of her courtship by Bloom on another eminence, the hill of Howth.

And now her reference to all the men she has known as "he" has a sudden relevance: Mulvey glides into Bloom in the next line: "and I thought well as well him as another." In Homer, Tiresias had prophesied that Ulysses would, after some years with Penelope, set sail once again but return at last to Ithaca. Dante, however, as Keats said, brought "news" of Ulysses, for in the *Inferno* Ulysses tells Dante of a last, presumptuous

---

[3] Molly's menstruation also establishes that she is not with child by Boylan.

voyage beyond the pillars of Hercules and out into the unknown and for him fatal sea. In Molly's mind, Mulvey, who was her Ulysses on Calpe's mount at Gibraltar, blends into Bloom, her Ulysses on Howth. She stamps an Irish visa on Ulysses' Greek passport. There is also an Italian visa, for Dante and Beatrice in Canto XXVII of the *Paradiso* look down on the straits of Gibraltar just as Bloom-Mulvey and Molly do. It is now clear why Molly Bloom had to be born so far from Ireland, at the pillars of Hercules.

In the last non-sentences of her monologue, Molly, having as she said got Bloom to propose to her, joins activity to passivity, aggression to surrender:

> and I thought well as well him as another and then I asked him with my eyes to ask again yes and then he asked me would I yes to say yes my mountain flower and first I put my arms around him yes and drew him down to me so he could feel my breasts all perfume yes and his heart was going like mad and yes I said yes I will Yes.

But why then does Molly end with an act of sixteen years before? She seems to burst the confines of her present situation, and fly from her jingly bed to a time which is beyond present time and a place beyond present place. In fact, she bursts through them to "that other world" mentioned by Martha Clifford, which is not death but an imaginative recreation, like *le temps retrouvé* of Proust. Like Adam and Eve's, it is a paradise lost, for as Proust says, the only true paradise is the one we have lost. According to Dante, Adam and Eve's paradise lasted only six hours, Bloom and Molly's is about the same. At the beginning of Molly's monologue she had thought of Mrs. Riordan predicting the end of the world, and here, in memory and imagination, the world does end and is created afresh. Joyce said that this episode had no art, but his book is consummated by the principle that art is nature's self. Molly, like Gerty MacDowell, like Bloom, like Stephen, has a touch of the artist about her, but that is because art is a natural process, which begins and ends with impure substance, and bids the dead to rise. There is sadness too, since Molly's present is so bleak in comparison with that lost paradise where, as Yeats said, all was "blossoming and dancing." The sadness is muted, however. Time and space are, at least for an instant, mere ghosts beside eternity and infinity.

Not Stephen then—though he defined the eucharistic element of art—but Molly, re-bears paradise, and Bloom, who earlier evoked the same scene, is her husband in art as in law. But Joyce has other nuptials in mind as well. "Penelope" ends the second half of the book as "Scylla and Charybdis" ended the first. The idea that Stephen brought to birth in "Scylla" is that Shakespeare's life provided him with the matter of his plays and poems, or in grander terms, that art is nature. Molly, by demonstrating that nature is art, may be seen as reaching across nine chapters of the book to offer Shakespeare her hand. As Shakespeare says in *A Winter's Tale*, "o'er that art/Which you say adds to nature is an art/That nature makes." [4] Deliberate and spontaneous creation are joined.

As if to render this contract more licit, Joyce in the "Circe" episode had Bloom and Stephen look together into a mirror, and see there not their own faces but the beardless face of Shakespeare. The cuckolded Shakespeare and Bloom, the betrayed Shakespeare and Stephen, are more closely akin than anyone would have suspected. All three out of victimization, as Molly out of present deprivation, create their artistic moments. There is a famous late-nineteenth-century edition of Shakespeare edited by F. J. Furnivall, which is known as the *Leopold Shakespere*, and Joyce makes this strange amalgam credible, with Stephen, now fused with Bloom, also a part of it. He announces the nuptials of Mrs. Marion Bloom and Mr. Leopold Shakespeare.

But another ingredient is necessary for art as for nature. Bloom's statement that the very opposite of hatred is truly life is borne out by Molly's last words, for it is love which empowers the imagination to overcome time, just as it is love which, in Wallace Stevens's words, "tips the tree of life." The first nine episodes of the book ended with a vision of the act of love as the basic act of art. The last nine episodes end with a vision of love as the basic act of nature. Joyce affirms this union of the two halves of his book by uniting the ship, which appears so heraldically and mysteriously at the end of the "Telemachiad," with the straits which appear at the end of the "Return." The ship sails through the straits, even navigation constituting an amorous movement. The ship is the *Rosevean,* and its name is taken up in Molly's epithalamion where she thinks about wearing a white rose or a red. Thus is fulfilled Stephen's prophecy in the "Oxen of the Sun," "Desire's wind blasts the thorntree but after it becomes from a bramblebush to be a rose upon the rood of time." Yeats, Dante, and Joyce all agree, though Joyce corrects Dante (and Plato) by placing sexual love above all other kinds of love. Red-rosed Molly and Bloom, himself a flower, fertilize the terrestrial paradise. Their youth and age, their innocence and experience, blend. In their dark bed at dead of night the summer sunlight shines.

The narrative level of the book has by this time become less important, and Joyce will not pursue his characters literally because he has negotiated their symbolic reconciliation. On the ethical level Bloom and Stephen have succeeded in taking the city of Dublin by exposing enthusiasm and superstition there, and by disclosing a truer way of goodwill and freedom. Molly's hardwon approbation confirms their enterprise. On the historical level, the characters have awakened from the Circean nightmare of history by drawing the past into the present (a timeless present)

---

[4] The whole passage in *The Winter's Tale*, IV, iv, 86–97, is relevant. . . . In the same vein, Dante has Virgil explain in the *Inferno*, XI, that "Vostr'arte a Dio quasi è nipote," that is, that God's child is nature whose child is art.

and making it an expression of love instead of hatred, of fondness rather than remorse. Art has been shown to be a part of nature, and in all its processes an imitation of natural ones. These processes have their summit in love, of which the highest form is sexual love.

Joyce outflanks the individual lives of his characters by these ultimate implications. But he outflanks them also by making each episode a part of the body. It seems at first that this slow accretion of a human form was gratuitous, but it must now be seen to be essential. Stephen says that literature is the eternal affirmation of the spirit of man, but pure spirit is something never endorsed in this book. For the body of man must be affirmed with his spirit. So the pervasive physicality of *Ulysses* goes with its spirituality. The identity of the archetypal man whose body the whole book limns is never given; it can scarcely be Bloom, since the book is larger than he; it must include Molly and Stephen, a trinity and a unity. On the analogy of Blake's giant Albion, the androgynous man who stands within and behind and beyond might be called Hibernion. One day he will be Finnegan.

In the final stages of his book, Joyce, with all his boldness, shows a certain embarrassment and reticence. He speaks of love without naming it; he celebrates art as an essential part of nature, but offers his proofs without ceremony or explanation; his moral criticism of his time is sharp yet couched entirely in images; without warning he raises his narrative from a literal to an anagogic plane. He is determined that his book, unlike some of the works of his master Tolstoy, should not be didactic. What claims he has to make for various possibilities in experience he puts forward with the utmost delicacy. That we are all members of the one body, and of the one spirit, remains implicit rather than explicit. This message he will give us only obliquely and in Greek, in Dublin Greek.

The Language of the Outlaw

by Harry Levin

Thinking of Swift, said Thackeray, is like thinking of an empire falling. To think about Joyce is to allow our thoughts to dwell upon a buried city. As they have traversed the stages of his career, we have seen the soaring aspirations of young Icarus lead to the underground labyrinth of the aging Dædalus. We see how his subject broadens as his style darkens: the hero of the *Portrait of the Artist* is the author, the hero of *Ulysses* the common man, of *Finnegans Wake* mankind. The past which Joyce tries to recapture, in the throes of his "traumaturgid" [496] nightmare, is not personal reminiscence but collective experience. The burial mound of his sleeping giant contains an enormous and heterogeneous time capsule. H. C. Earwicker's subconscious mind is the historical consciousness of the human race. Thus modern culture, rounding out Vico's cycle, cowers before the thunder and returns to the cave—to Plato's cave via Saint Patrick's purgatory. [80] With contemporary ruins accumulating above ground, we seek refuge in the underworld of Homeric shades, in the eternal places of Dante's hell, in Shakespeare's dark backward and abysm of time, in the subterranean passages of Sir Thomas Browne, in the hollow caverns under Wagner's foreboding earth, in Lewis Carroll's rabbit-hole of fantasy, Henry James' deep well of memory, T. S. Eliot's contrived corridors of history, or Thomas Mann's *coulisses* and abysses of the past.

Happily, an Irish wake is apt to rise above its melancholy occasion. Here is Joyce talking to himself: [189–190]

> Sniffer of carrion, premature gravedigger, seeker of the nest of evil in the bosom of a good word, you, who sleep at our vigil and fast for our feast, you with your dislocated reason, have cutely foretold, a jophet in your own absence, by blind poring upon your many scalds and burns and blisters, impetiginous sore and pustules, by the auspices of that raven cloud, your shade, and by the auguries of rooks in parlament, death, with

"The Language of the Outlaw." From Harry Levin, *James Joyce: A Critical Introduction.* Copyright 1941 by New Directions, Norfolk, Conn., © 1960 by New Directions Publishing Corporation. Reprinted by permission of the author, New Directions Publishing Corporation, Faber and Faber Ltd., and Lawrence P. Pollinger, Ltd.

Superscripts refer directly to pages in the Viking Press edition of *Finnegans Wake,* or, in the case of *Ulysses,* to the 1961 Random House edition.

every disaster, the dynamatisation of colleagues, the reducing of records to ashes, the levelling of all customs by blazes, the return of a lot of sweetempered gunpowdered didst unto dudst but it never stphruck your mudhead's obtundity (O hell, here comes our funeral! O pest, I'll miss the post!) that the more carrots you chop, the more turnips you slit, the more murphies you peel, the more onions you cry over, the more bullbeef you butch, the more mutton you crackerhack, the more potherbs you pound, the fiercer the fire and the longer your spoon and the harder you gruel with more grease to your elbow the merrier fumes your new Irish stew.

The parenthesis is the outcry of the great writer who has come too late. In the times of the Tuatha De Danaan, the legendary tribe that left Greece to colonize Ireland and to be driven into the hills by the later conquests of the Celts, he might have been the Dagda, their poet, priest, and king, whose harp enchanted all his listeners and whose appetite was equal to untold messes of pottage. In a time when universities are bombed and books are burned, the confiscation of the banned English edition of *Ulysses* by the New York post office authorities is an omen of "the levelling of all customs by blazes." The last of the bards, half blinded and long exiled, Shem stirs a magic cauldron at the funeral feast of civilization. His international potpourri is brewed from an Irish recipe, with a dash of everything else he has ever read or heard. *Ulysses* is seasoned with the same ingredients, but *Finnegans Wake* is the richer concoction. The old themes of the artist and the city are combined in the person of the mythical hod-carrier, the builder of cities. Dublin is now merely the local habitation for history itself. Artifice, by a supreme effort, is bent upon creating a language of its own.

The thwarted filial impulse, still prompting Joyce to look up to some intellectual godfather, goes beyond Homer to the scholar who refined Homer out of existence, beyond the authority of Aquinas to the skepticism of Bruno, and beyond Shakespeare's immediacy to Swift's detachment. If a poet is a maker, a prose writer is *altus prosator*—in the Latin of a venerable Irish hymn attributed to Saint Columba—the sublime begetter.[185] As the son becomes a father, he ceases to be a disciple and becomes a rival. Like "Great Shapesphere," [295] he emulates God and rivals nature. The note of banishment, which Stephen Dedalus overheard in Shakespeare, is sounded defiantly. The reception of *Ulysses* has lengthened the distance between Joyce and Ireland, or any other English-speaking country. Ruefully, in *Finnegans Wake*, he glances back at "his usylessly unreadable Blue Book of Eccles." [179] There are moments of startling candor, when he doubts his mission and questions himself: "Was liffe worth leaving?" [230] Or conversely, *à la Henri Quatre*, "was Parish worth thette mess." [199] When he addressed his friend, John Sullivan, whose remarkably pure tenor range was better appreciated abroad than at home, it was "a Banned Writer to a Banned Singer." So much public apathy and so little critical discernment, together with such excruciating treatment at the hand of the publishers and censors, tangibly reinforced his sense of persecution. "A hundred cares, a tithe of troubles," moans the river, "and is there one who understands me?" [627]

Since Joyce lived to write, though he never wrote for a living, he went on writing to please himself, with an almost paranoid disregard of any other reader. The authors of the so-called *Exagmination,* it must be acknowledged, were more of a claque than an audience, like Victor Hugo's friends on the first night of *Hernani.* Yet Joyce's disregard was touchingly sensitive to the slightest sign of outside interest. His friends report that his last year was clouded by the indifferent response to *Finnegans Wake*—as if it could have been otherwise. The indifference was quite natural, and so was his disappointment. What was unnatural is that he should have cultivated both for seventeen years "with a meticulosity bordering on the insane." [173] His work in progress he came to regard as "that letter selfpenned to one's other, that neverperfect everplanned." [489] To be a writer under such circumstances, for Shakespeare, would have meant "speechless death"; for Joyce's garrulous fellow Parisian, Gertrude Stein, it meant a chance to be "alone with English." For Joyce, exile meant a renewal of silence and, under the tutelage of the Defense of the Realm Act, a new and diabolical cunning: "Mum's for's maxim, ban's for's book and Dodgesome Dora for hedgehung sheolmastress." [228]

The silence behind *Finnegans Wake,* like the silence that Carlyle preached in forty volumes, is the oracular sort that requires comment. Having abandoned his hopes of direct communication, Joyce turned his efforts to symbolic expression. "In a Symbol there is concealment and yet revelation," opined Carlyle's oracle, Dr. Teufelsdroeckh, "hence, therefore, by Silence and by Speech acting together, comes a double significance." But this augmented meaning will be hardly audible to those whose patience is not intrigued by the metaphorical diction of Vico's heroic age. To say that Joyce's writing smells of the lamp is to make a pallid understatement. It reeks of the thurible. No writer, not Flaubert himself, has set a more conspicuous example of the cult of style. Joyce's holy grail, *la dive bouteille,* is Shem's inkbottle. For its sake he has given up his church along with his city, and by its virtue he would recover them. In the discipline and tradition of literature, perhaps, he finds compensations for the rootlessness of his life. "Suffoclose! Shikespower! Seudodanto! Anonymoses!" he exclaims, transported by his own ingenuity.[47] He has identified himself with the greatest writers; he has recapitulated the development of English prose; now he must synthesize his language.

English was only an acquired speech to the artist as a young man. Latin was an educational and ecclesiastical idiom. Gaelic was one of those nets that Stephen flew by. The hard years of Trieste and Zurich were weathered by teaching English and other foreign languages in the cosmopolitan babel of the Berlitz schools. Joyce's synthetic language had to distort, if not disown, the tongue of Shakespeare and Swift; it had to preserve the hieratic intonations of the liturgy, excite the enthusiasms of a literary movement, and reverberate with the polyglot humors of the professional linguist. To fulfil these conditions, it had to assume what I. A. Richards calls a severance of poetry and belief: it had to be "sanscreed." [215] A ripe specimen of patriotic eloquence, quoted in the newspaper episode of *Ulysses*,[142-143] compares the plight of the Jews under the Pharaohs to that of Ireland in the British Empire. *Why will you jews not accept our culture, our religion and our language?"* the high priest asks Moses. The answer, when Joyce himself declaims it, even through the imperfections of an acoustical recording, is his *apologia* for the nomadic life of the banished writer. His expatriation is an exodus, a deliverance from slavery. The bearer of the curse is destined to be the bringer of the word:

> —*But, ladies and gentlemen, had the youthful Moses listened to and accepted that view of life, had he bowed his head and bowed his will and bowed his spirit before that arrogant admonition he would never have brought the chosen people out of their house of bondage nor followed the pillar of the cloud by day. He would never have spoken with the Eternal amid lightnings on Sinai's mountaintop nor ever have come down with the light of inspiration shining in his countenance and bearing in his arms the tables of the law, graven in the language of the outlaw.*

Saint Patrick, who spent forty days on a mountain in his turn, fasting and praying for the conversion of Ireland, stands by the side of Moses in the hierarchy of *Finnegans Wake*.[307] Here the implied relation of the Irish to the Israelites is that of Stephen to Bloom, of artist to prophet. Inspiration, in the most transcendental sense of the word, holds both terms of the comparison together. A work of art, according to those tenets of esthetic mysticism which Joyce so devoutly professed, is among the varieties of religious experience. His earliest sketches were epiphanies and his choice of a career was a kind of ordination. His maturest work still conforms to the Catholic pattern: as Valery Larbaud observed, it is closer to the Jesuit casuists than to the French naturalists. And, if Joyce's naturalism seems to stem from the confessional, we may also observe that his symbolism is deeply rooted in the sacrament of the mass. The black mass of *Ulysses* follows the *confiteor* of the *Portrait of the Artist*. The hero of *Finnegans Wake,* in the character of a cricketeer named "Hosty," is again united with the body of Christ. "How culious an epiphany!" [508] The church is broad enough to touch the extremes of confession and mystery, both the appalling frankness and the labored obscurity with which Joyce alternately expresses himself. As the artist's stature enlarges, he is no longer a visionary but a demiurge, no longer waiting for revelations but arranging them. With godlike equivocation he can reveal or conceal, mystify or make manifest, fashion myths and forge words.

Words are the stuff that Earwicker's dream is made on. The darker shadings of consciousness, the gropings of the somnolent mind, the states between sleeping and waking—unless it be by Proust—have never been so acutely rendered. But Joyce's technique always tends to get ahead of his psychology. *Finnegans Wake* respects, though it garbles and parodies, the literary conventions. It brims over with ad libs and misplaced confidences and self-conscious stage-whispers. Now and then it pauses to defend itself,[112] to bait the censorship,[179] or to pull the legs of would-be commentators.[453] It mentions the working title,[497] throws in such items as "The Holy Office" [190] and "Gas from a Burner," [93] and freely discusses the suppression of *Dubliners*.[185] It includes a brief outline of *Ulysses*[229] and even a letter to the author from a dissatisfied reader.[113] In reply, frequent telegraphic appeals from the author to his "abcedminded" readers[18] (". . . stop, please stop, do please stop, and O do please stop respectively . . ." [124]) punctuate[232] the torrent[379] of his soliloquy[560] periodically.[609] These *obiter dicta* cannot be traced, with any show of plausibility, to the sodden brain of a snoring publican. No psychoanalyst could account for the encyclopedic sweep of Earwicker's fantasies or the acoustical properties of his dreamwork.

The strangest feature of this dream vision is that it lacks visual imagery. Joyce's imagination, as his light is spent, concentrates on the "mind's ear." [477] Though he offers us a *"verbivocovisual presentment,"* [341] it is no easier to visualize a Mookse or a Gripes than to gather a clear-cut impression of slithy tove or a mome rath. "Ope Eustace tube!" is his sound advice.[535] When he promises us a view of Dublin, he enjoins us to listen: "Hush! Caution! Echoland!" [13] The isle is full of noises. Gradually, after we have become accustomed to the darkness, we recognize familiar voices. From the pedantic jargon[121] and childish lisping,[396] the young men's blarney[407] and old women's chatter,[101] we distinguish Earwicker by his intermittent stutter[45] and catastrophic hiccup.[454] He is usually submerged in a welter of dialects and documents—pidgin English,[485] American slang,[455] vulgar Latin,[185] liturgical responses,[470] legal forms,[545] advertisements,[181] riddles.[170] To this confusion of tongues the radio lends a spasmodic continuity, comparable to the influence of the film on *Ulysses*. The loudspeaker, with its summons to sales and revolutions, its medley of raucous chamber music and prefabricated repartee, its collaboration between Dædalean engineering and blind static, is the medium of *Finnegans Wake*. With a "tolvtubular high fidelity daildialler," [309] we tune in on the "sponsor programme" from Howth Castle, "Haveth Childers Everywhere." [531]

Everyone who has played Joyce's captivating phonograph record from "Anna Livia Plurabelle" will agree that the best introduction to his book is to hear him read it aloud. Yet even the author's expressive brogue cannot convey all the inflections, unless it is supplemented by the text. If he ever appeals to the eye, it is to the eye of a reader. A full reading must be simultaneously oral and literary, "synopticked on the word," [367] dividing our attention between vocal and verbal images. Joyce is interested in both the sound of a word and the figure it cuts on the page. In a disquisition on the alphabet, when he tells us "how hard a thing it is to mpe mporn a gentlerman," he would remind us that, since *beta* has the value of V in modern Greek, B must be indicated by a *mu* and a *pi*.[120] When he speaks of school days, his book takes on the temporary appearance of a schoolbook. One set of marginalia, in pompous capitals, exhibits Vico's terminology. The other set, in shrewd italics, betrays Joyce's own accents. The footnotes are infantile *scholia*. "Traduced into jingish janglage for the nusances of dolphins born" recalls the *in usum Delphini* of an edition of the classics notorious for its expurgations.[275] A geometrical diagram demonstrates the equivalence of one delta-shaped triangle lettered *ALP* to another, or of mother to daughter.[293] An uncivil nose and a pair of crossbones, childishly scrawled at the end of the chapter, are the least abstruse of Joyce's symbols.

The impatient reader, perpetually admonished to look out for typographical ambushes and to keep listening for surreptitious rhythms, may come to feel that *Finnegans Wake* is a grim business. Actually it is a wonderful game—by no means a private affair, but one in which many may join, each with his own contribution, and the more the merrier. This realization may prove equally disturbing to the reader whose conception of art is rather grim. He should realize that all art is a game, the object of which is to make the problems of life and death—with as much insight, skill, and originality as possible—a source of enjoyment. For enjoying *Finnegans Wake*, we need scarcely insist, the prerequisite is not omniscience. It is no more than a curiosity about Joyce's unique methods and some awareness of his particular preoccupations. His work is enriched by such large resources of invention and allusion that its total effect is infinite variety. But, when we are able to scan the variety, we notice that it is controlled by a few well-defined themes and a number of characteristic devices. Myriads of minute details boil down to a handful of generalizations.

The very reverse, of course, is true of the process of composition: it takes the bare elements and exposes them to unceasing elaboration. Writing is primarily a basis for rewriting, and revision is a form of self-caricature. Every word of the first draft is subject to a series of gross exaggerations. Each successive version, even after publication, is a palimpsest for further accretions. We can well believe that the final version of one chapter, previously published as "Anna Livia Plurabelle," cost Joyce more than 1600 intensive working hours. His "warping proccess" [497] enables him to expand and condense at a single stroke; the alteration of a letter will widen the orbit of a phrase. By including all the alternatives, rather than choosing and discarding, he eliminates the writer's chief torture, hesitation between phrases. Incidentally, he throws economy to the winds. Since the essence of his method is not to select but to accumulate, his readers seldom have that feeling of inevitability which is the touchstone of a more reserved style. They feel a continual surprise. Sooner or later, they feel the reservation voiced by Dr. Johnson, when he said of James Macpherson's earlier attempt to revive the spirit of Finn MacCool: "Sir, a man might write such stuff for ever, if he would *abandon* his mind to it."

The differences in mood between *Ulysses* and *Finnegans Wake* are underlined by the contrast between the Homeric poems and that prodigious literary hoax, "Makefearsome's Ocean." [294] Joyce's recourse to the Ossianic poems, like his use of the counterfeit word, "hesitancy," evinces a growing addiction to the idea of forgery. Jim the Penman is forging, with a vengeance, the uncreated conscience of his race. His creative ideals have found their unforeseen fulfilment in "an epical forged cheque on the public for his own private profit." [181] The artist, god of his own world, is no better than a criminal in this one, Joyce obliquely admits; the finest literary imitations of life are fakes. It should be unnecessary to add that the only person who has the right to accuse Joyce of being "a low sham" [170] is himself, and that his accusation is a self-searching testimonial of sincerity. However unintelligible he may seem, he is never incoherent. His idiom is based on a firm command of the usages of popular speech. His habit of sudden generalization is backed by his facility with proverbs. Look at Shem's "bodily getup": "all ears, . . . not a foot to stand on, a handful of thumbs, . . . a deaf heart, a loose liver, . . . a manroot of all evil . . ." [169]

Consciously, by extending his range of reference, Joyce limits our appreciation of his work. Because *po-russki* means "in Russian" in Russian, "Paud the russky" is at once an apology for, and an explanation of, a macaronic Anglo-Russian interlude about the Crimean War.[335] "Pratschkats at their platschpails," for old women by the Liffey, is wasted on us, if we do not know that *prachka* and *plach* are Russian for "laundress" and "crying." [101] But the words we know should teach us not to conclude, from the words we miss, that Joyce can be vague or loose. Whenever we happen to catch the overtones, we are impressed by his philological accuracy and logical rigor. With *Finnegans Wake* the circular exposition of *Ulysses* is carried to its logical conclusion, which is no conclusion at all. The peculiarity of Joyce's later writing is that any passage presupposes a reading knowledge of the rest of the book. On the other hand, to master a page is to understand the book. The trick is to pick out a passage where a breakthrough can be conveniently effected. For this sort of exercise, such set-pieces as the "Tales Told of Shem and Shaun" are both revealing and entertaining. "When a part so ptee does duty for the holos we soon grow to use of an allforabit." [18]

A book must have a beginning, a middle and an end; but a dream may be a jumble of excluded middles. The first page of *Finnegans Wake* is an orderly thematic statement, and the following pages bring their own tautologies and encores. But the reader must be prepared for continuous digression, instead of consecutive narration. Instead of a table of contents, he may take his bearings from a rough summary of the miscellaneous chapters. The first episode of the first section is an epical invocation;[3] the second episode sets Earwicker's peccadillo to the ribald strains of "The Ballad of Persse O'Reilly";[30] the third prolongs the hearsay after closing hours;[48] and the fourth proceeds, with due solemnity, to the trial.[75] All four are unified by the theme of Earwicker's fall; the fifth episode takes up the question of Anna's letter.[104] The sixth consists of twelve leading questions and evasive answers, passing in review the hero (HCE), the heroine (ALP), their tavern (the Bristol), their city (Dublin), their man of all work (Joe), their maid of all work (Kate), their twelve patrons (variously denominated Murphys, Doyles, or Sullivans), their daughter (Isabel), the theory of history (Vico), the theory of love (Swift), the theory of time and space (illustrated by Shem's fable of the Mookse and the Gripes), and the signature of the author (*"Semus sumus!"*) respectively. Shem is the villain of the next episode, unmasked by his twin in an allegorical debate between Justius and Mercius.[169] The rhythm of the river, emerging toward the end of the seventh, is fully orchestrated in the eighth episode, the haunting "Anna Livia Plurabelle" colloquy.[196]

There are four lengthening episodes to the second section, and again to the third. If a dream may be assigned to a definite location, the first section was located in and around the Phoenix Park; the second is at Chapelizod, and the third will be on the hill of Howth. The second section starts to be the program of a play, "The Mime of Mick, Nick, and the Maggies," with cast, credits, and a lively synopsis.[219] When the diversion ends in a thunderstorm, the party retreats into the book of childhood.[260] The third episode takes us on a voyage of discovery, with the patrons of Earwicker's pub as Viking sea-farers.[309] The fourth eavesdrops upon the romance of Tristan and Isolde, through the censorious ears of the quartet of old men ("Mamalujo").[383] After the watchman has told the hour, the third section gives Shaun a chance to tell his fable of the Ondt and the Gracehoper.[403] He is back again, in a second episode, with his sermon.[429] Shaun, by now "Yawn," is his father's boy, and his "dream monologue" leads naturally to Earwicker, as Shem's has led to his mother. The third episode marks the climax with a keen over the barrow of the hero.[474] The fourth, a half-waking evocation of the slumbering household, should be carefully scrutinized for its clues to the literal situation.[555] The fourth section is a brief coda, which heralds the dawn and completes the Viconian revolution.[593]

This enumeration, if it clarifies anything, confronts us with something more like vaudeville than narrative. The deafmute dialogue of a prehistoric comedy team, Mutt and Jute,[16] is revived on the day of judgment by Muta and Juva,[609] and provides a *divertissement* by Butt and Taff in the midst of the battle of Sebastapol.[338] The tabloid scandal of "Peaches" and "Daddy" Browning is warmed over to suit Earwicker's fancy.[65] One red herring after another, pursued by the dreamer, turns out to be an *idée-fixe*. While the main themes are never absent from the background, the foreground is always crowded with topical matters. In the middle distance, ordinarily the center of interest, the action is shadowy and capricious. Avid for a story, the reader will find little in Joyce's "meandertale" [18] to reward his pains. He will track down Saint Michael and Satan to their picture-frame on the wall of Earwicker's bedroom, and rationalize the Garden of Eden into a mantelpiece in the Adelphian style of the brothers Adam.[559] The penultimate episode, he will find, is as detailed a survey of domestic arrangements as the corresponding inventory of *Ulysses*. He will find a more substantial residue of human sympathy in the most tenuous sketch of *Dubliners* than in the whole of *Finnegans Wake*.

And tastes will differ, when he complains of being given an intolerable deal of sack to wash down his half-pennyworth of bread. The richness of Joyce's symbolism helps us to tolerate the realities of the situation. Considered for its vestiges of naturalistic fiction, a night with the Earwickers is weary, flat, and stale. Its most dramatic event, signalized by the vulgar name of a quaint fountain in Brussels,[267] occurs when a child wets his bed.[427] Its *dénouement* is the interruption of Earwicker's connubial performance by a rooster,[595] whose chiliastic "cocorico" is anticipated by numerous alliterations in K.[193] Joyce's perverse passion for the inert and the undistinguished could not have directed him to a less eventful subject. Nor could he, having sacked history and despoiled language, have endowed this unpromising material with more liveliness and distinction. From his own Olympian imaginative level, he causes the all but unmentionable trivialities of daily and nightly routine to produce earth-shaking consequences. Earwicker's flatulence produces Vico's thunder.[258] Pedestrian readers will not forgive a novelist or a dramatist for such conceits, though they accept them from a humorist or even a poet. When we come to sum up Joyce's work, however, we must admit that it was never strong in scenic description, sympathetic characterization, or the other virtues of the novel. His peculiar strength lay in speculation, introspection, and an almost hyperesthetic capacity for rendering sensations. These are poetic attributes, and his successes are the achievements of a poet—in arranging verbal harmonies and touching off emotional responses.

Joyce demands the same degree of absorption that Yeats and Donne receive. We are bound to be disappointed, if we approach him with the notion of extracting a quintessential content from the encumbrances of form. The two, in *Ulysses*, were intended to coalesce. Where they fail to do so, it is because he has imposed a formal requirement that is too rigid to be satisfied without hindering the advance of the plot. The Siren episode is too cluttered up with verbiage to be an effective scene, and too broken up with comment to be an authentic fugue. The drastic solution of this dilemma, in *Finnegans Wake*, is to subordinate content to form: to forego the normal suspenses and sympathies that bind the reader to the book, reduce the plot to a few platitudes that can be readily stylized, and confer complete autonomy upon words. They are now matter, not manner. Nothing could be farther from the fallacy of imitative form than Joyce's latter tendency toward abstract content. We are borne from one page to the next, not by the expository current of the prose, but by the harmonic relations of the language—phonetic, syntactic, or referential, as the case may be. The mythological themes, recurring, varying, modulating into a new context, have a consistency of their own. When we have an index to them, we shall comprehend the book.

The relation between chapters is abrupt and arbitrary, as with the movements of a symphony. As with music, as with any composition in time, the structure seems to dissolve into the texture, when we examine it closely. At close range, *Finnegans Wake* seems to realize the aspiration of the other arts toward the condition of music. The obvious musical analogies are misleading, for they imply a limitation, rather than an enlargement, of our means of expression. They encourage a doctrine of pure poetry, or prose that exists solely for the sake of euphony. Joyce is a consummate master of the music of words, but he is also a master of "the music of ideas," the complex orchestration of associated images which symbolist poets have taught us to appreciate. His innovation is to harmonize the two modes. Now, when you bring discordant sounds and associations together, you have created a pun. If the associations remain irrelevant, it is a bad pun; if they show an unlooked-for relevance, it is better; if the relevant associations are rich enough, it is poetry. The Elizabethans regarded this as a legitimate rhetorical resource. The Victorians degraded it into a parlor trick. Joyce has rehabilitated the pun for literary purposes. Again, as he was fond of pointing out, he has a theological precedent: the church itself was founded on a pun ("thuartpeatrick" [3]).

Having laid down such vast reserves of potential association, Joyce can easily and adroitly pun his way through 628 pages. From Saint Peter and his rock, on one excursion, he can move on to a Greek wine, by a devious route that stops at Petrarch, Laura, laurel, Daphne, and Mavrodaphne.[20a] Often these roundabout progressions, like the motions of the mind, disclose unexpected shortcuts. Who would have expected the initial letter of "victory," translated into Morse code and timed to the opening bar of Beethoven's *Fifth Symphony,* to become a symbol by which millions live and die? The dream convention is Joyce's license for a free association of ideas and a systematic distortion of language. Psychoanalysis insinuates its special significances into his calculated slips of the tongue. Under cover of a drowsy indistinctness and a series of subconscious lapses, he has developed a diction that is actually alert and pointed, that bristles with virtuosity and will stoop to any kind of slapstick. His neologism is the joint product of the three types of verbal wit that Freud has discriminated—condensation, displacement, allusion.

Joyce perceived that all attempts to make the subconscious intelligible break down into nonsense. This, of course, did not deter him. He perfected a species of "double-talk," like the convincing gibberish of certain comedians, superficially adjusted to the various norms of discourse, and fundamentally nonsensical. The twofold ambiguity is that, by playfully harping on his obsessions, Joyce makes a modicum of sense. He can contradict himself with a clear conscience and a straight face. Consider his most sustained *double-entendre:* Shaun preaching a sermon on chastity to twenty-nine adolescent girls is really Earwicker professing a more than fatherly love for his daughter. The psychological censor has dictated a sanctimonious tone, and the chapter is scrupulously modelled on the soundest lenten homiletics; but prurience will out. "Oop, I never open momouth but I pack mefood in it," Shaun leers genially.[437] Recommending safe books for the *jeune fille*—to quote one of his few safe examples—he debauches the household words of Dickens into "Doveyed Covetfilles" and "the old cupiosity shape." [434] After the sermon in the *Portrait of the Artist,* and the youthful tragedy of Stephen's first recoil from carnal sin, Jaunty Jaun's homily comes as a monstrous satyr-play.

How did Joyce manage to concoct these "messes of mottage?" [183] By accentuating the purely formal values of words, and by linking them together with as many devices as he could manipulate. Some of these devices are auditory—rhyme,[371] alliteration,[250] assonance,[216] onomatopoeia.[258] Others are morphological—back-formations,[266] infixes,[191] etymologies,[120] spoonerisms.[189] Others are alphabetical—acrostics,[88] anagrams,[140] palindromes,[496] inversions.[311] Still others, more sportive, run through a sequence of words by changing a letter at a time,[142] or weave groups of related names into narratives—one still runs across specimens of this *genre* in school magazines. The material ranges the Joycean gamut from Irish counties ("cold airs")[595] to Ibsen's plays ("peers and gints")[540] and musicians ("peer Golazy" and "mere Bare").[360] Insects and philosophers collaborate in the cosmic irony of the Ondt and the Gracehoper, by this procedure, and hundreds of rivers accommodate themselves to the main stream of the Liffey. Other devices are peculiar to Joyce—like the four polysyllables terminating in the pretentious suffix *-ation,* which he employs now and then to call the discussion to order.[372]

The official guide to his vocabulary is Lewis Carroll's student of semantics, Humpty Dumpty, who could explain all the poems that were ever invented and a good many that hadn't been just yet. Through "portmanteau-words" Joyce is able to instil a Freudian undertone in his small talk. The extra compartment permits the transient word to assimilate local color: a Siberian atmosphere turns the Bristol into an "isbar" and the *spécialité de la maison* into "irsk irskusky." [70] "Potapheu's wife" lends a touch of domestic warmth to an otherwise chilling story.[193] The adjective, "lidylac," applied to curtains, has an appropriate aroma of lavender and old lace.[461] And what better word than "umbroglia" could have been coined to fit the foreign policy of the late Neville Chamberlain? [284] "Umprumptu" [93] colors Humpty Dumpty's fall with a tinge of onomatopoetic spontaneity; "wenchyoumaycuddler" is more specific than it sets out to be.[608] A typical phrase, which telescopes Joyce's prepossessions, is "viceking's graab": Ireland is both the grave of Norse heroes and the spoil of the British viceroy.[18] When, "by the waters of babalong," we sit down and laugh, we are exiled to that border region which is disputed by wit and poetry.[103] "The flushpots of Euston and the hanging garments of Marylebone" have a retrospective poignance that is not unworthy of T. S. Eliot.[192] And, in a fresher vein, the paragraph about the sleeping infant Isobel, "like some losthappy leaf," is a delicate lyric that suggests Hopkins' "Spring and Fall." [556]

On the whole, there were not many obstacles to keep Swift from living up to his definition of style: "proper words in proper places." The wear and tear on language since his time, the corruptions of usage, the vulgarizations of journalism, the affectations of scholarship, have so relaxed the standard that we are no longer surprised to find proper words in improper places. Joyce, with Swift's feeling for linguistic elegance and sense of outraged propriety, has a very different language to handle; the style of *Finnegans Wake,* which shocks us into an awareness of the difference, may be defined as "improper words in proper places." Joyce utilizes the malapropism as the literary expression of social maladjustment, the language of the outlaw. The boyish inscription in a closet of Clongowes Wood College, *Julius Caesar wrote The Calico Belly,* was more than a reduction to absurdity; it was a protest against things as they are. But the genius of Mrs. Malaprop offers a means of escape, as well as a mode of criticism, and sometimes casts a temporary glamor over familiar things. Joyce revised the nursery rhyme, "Ride a cock horse," to advertise "Anna Livia Plurabelle." The one quality she had in common with the fine lady was music, so that is the one word of the last line that does not undergo a sea-change: *Sheashell ebb music wayriver she flows.*

Portmanteau-words and malapropisms can be isolated and analyzed; heavier luggage and longer passages are more securely embedded in the text. When every word of a simple declarative sentence is subjected to the same sort of alteration, the result is not too complex. "Nobirdy aviar soar anywing to eagle it" is simply an ornithological fashion of stating that nobody ever saw anything to equal it.[505] Most of Joyce's sentences are acted upon by more complicating forces. The result is a polyphonic phrasing which takes its key from its most consistent combination of sounds and meanings, but may be modified by substitution or addition at any point. One of the simplest questions of the book is, "How hominous his house, haunt it?" [560] Here the subdominant would be "How ominous his house, ain't it?" The tonic, through the allusive and alliterative influence of the key-word, "house," has introduced "home" and "haunt." The dominant augments the chord by bringing out the latinate adjective for humanity and shifting the question to an injunction. There is a further consonance between "ominous" and "haunt," and between the whole sentence and the main theme. In comparison with the contrapuntal possibilities of this way of writing, the Siren scene from *Ulysses* is plain-song.

Another instance, more strictly measured, is a line from Shaun's account of the Gracehoper's despair: "Was he come to hevre with his engiles or gone to hull with the poop?" [416] Here the honors seem fairly divided between crossing the North Sea and finding out someone's destination in the next world. Not quite fairly. "Hevre" is equally Havre and heaven, as "engiles" refers impartially to the ship's engines and God's angels; but hell hides behind the redoubled opacity of Hull, and "poop" is literal because of the blasphemous suggestion about the Pope. Since the answer to the equation is already hinted by the symmetrical relationship of both parts of the two clauses, no meaning is lost by the displacement, and a certain emphasis is gained. Every sentence is a wilful divagation from the expectations raised by the last. While the rhythmic undercurrent is pulling us in one direction, the drift of associations carries us the other way. By listening carefully, we can make out a number of recurrent lilts and metrical patterns, pulsating through the fluctuations of verbalism. Bear in mind this concise formulation of Vico's doctrine: [215]

> Teems of times and happy returns. The seim anew.

The children's hour is responsible for a variation: [277]

> We drames our dreams tell Bappy returns. And Sein annews.

The *Götterdämmerung* has a terrifying effect on the words, and leaves the tune unchanged: [510]

> —Booms of bombs and heavy rethudders?
> —This aim to you!

By the time the Phoenix arises, it is an old story, and we are ready—as in the song about Old Man Finnegan—to begin again: [614]

> Themes have thimes and habit reburns. To flame in you.

The system of *leitmotif* borrows more heavily from literary echoes than *Ulysses*, although the cadences of nature are a crucial exception. Rain has its own distinctive rhythm, which adapts itself to an impression of Earwicker's drunken discomfort, as he tosses about at the end of an episode: [74]

> Liverpoor? Sot a bit of it! His braynes coolt parritch, his pelt nassy, his heart's adrone, his bluidstreams acrawl, his puff but a piff, his extremities extremely so.

Later on, when deeper slumber has made him deaf to the rain, he is personified as a bridge crossing Dublin Bay:[266]

> Rivapool? Hod a brieck on it! But its piers eerie, its span spooky, its toll but a till, its parapets all peripateting.

The "hitherandthithering waters of" the Liffey are presented with endless versatility;[265] Earwicker is represented by the incremental repetition of "The House That Jack Built." [511] "John Peel," as a drinking song, owes its authority to a hunting print on display at the Bristol.[31] There are doubtless a number of signs advertising Guinness' stout. The ubiquitous slogan is broadcast on the final day: hustled from your graves, when the conquering hero appears in triumph, you are informed that "genghis is ghoon for you." [593] The noble motto of the Order of the Garter is quoted,[113] only to be flouted,[495] and the Lord's prayer is taken in vain by Kate, the cross-grained housemaid, with searing Joycean blasphemy.[530] Joyce, in his echolalia, is revisited by fragments and reminiscences so profusely scattered and so deeply charged, that his maltreatment of them is a culminating gesture of dissent from a lifelong disciple of the fallen archangel. His work is a gargantuan burlesque, not of any other given work, but of the entire cultural heritage.

Often his allusions to other writers justify themselves by enlivening a trite refrain: "Walhalloo, Walhalloo, Walhalloo, mourn in plein!" is a manifest improvement upon Victor Hugo's *"Waterloo, Waterloo, Waterloo, morne plaine!"* [541] On the Belgian battlefield, which it lets you keep in sight, it heaps Valhalla, a war cry, full mourning, and full morning. Joyce is not afraid to hinge the critical point of an episode on an elusive reference. He sketches out the setting for Earwicker's downfall, without mentioning the arsenal, by parodying an epigram that Swift wrote when it was built:

> Behold a proof of Irish sense,
>   Here Irish wit is seen!
> Where nothing's left that's worth defence,
>   They build a magazine!

Joyce falls short of the biting Anglophobia of his model, though he touches, somewhat self-consciously, on Swift's visit to England in the matter of tithes: "Behove this sound of Irish sense. Really? Here English might be seen. Royally? One sovereign punned to petery pence. Regally? The silence speaks the scene. Fake!" [12] The nearer Joyce comes to a scene or an emotion, the more prone he is to indulge in literary byplay. When Earwicker's *cri du cœur* is muffled in a travesty of *Macbeth*, we may assume a studied evasion on the author's part, a determination to detach himself from his characters at all costs: "For a burning would is come to dance inane. Glamours hath moidered's lieb and herefore Coldours must leap no more. Lack breath must leap no more." [250]

These distractions are quite deliberate. If Earwicker's plight really held our attention and solicitude, we should consider them heartless, far-fetched, and even cheap. Joyce shows no more concern for his hero than a geneticist for a fruit-fly; he happens to be interested in the peculiarities of the *genus* earwig. Indifferent, he pares his fingernails, having reached the stage of artistic development that passes over the individual in favor of the general. The divine, far-off event toward which Joyce's doomsday book moves is a "general election." [253] By associating ideas and multiplying parallels he is attempting to universalize his limited subject-matter. Universality, insofar as he can be said to have attained it, is a mosaic of particulars. When he reverts to basic situations, primary emotions, and final values, he is willing to take them for granted. His serious interest is focussed on the manifold permutations of shape, color—in the last analysis—language. Of the romance between his hero and heroine he has a good deal to say, but no more to express than the schoolboy who carves "HCE loves ALP" on a tree-trunk. Instead of selecting the *mot juste,* Joyce accumulates a Rabelaisian catalogue of epithets: ". . . neoliffic smith and magdalenian jinnyjones . . . martial sin with peccadilly . . . solomn one and shebby . . . Regies Producer with screendoll Vedette." [576]

Here the characters, grotesquely magnified and romantically draped, are lay figures. The real romance is between Joyce and the language. Even when his subject is moribund, his writing is alive. The result of his experiments fits in surprisingly well with the conclusions toward which critical theories and poetic practice, propaganda studies and pedagogical tests, semantics and logical positivism, have lately been pushing us. We used to lament that words were such a shadowy approximation of objective reality. We have learned to look upon them as objects of immediate apprehension, more real in themselves than their penumbras of meaning. They were always symbols, to be sure, but we had fallen into the careless habit of confounding the symbol with its referents. Joyce, conceding the priority of the word to the thing, renews our perception of language as an artistic medium. When he sought words, in the hospital chapter of *Ulysses,* to reproduce the origins of life, he was foiled by the intervention of literary history, embryology, and other excrescences. Turning from representation to presentation, he allows nothing to intervene between the prose of *Finnegans Wake* and the flow of the Liffey.

Joyce's book, with more reason than Jules Romains' interminable pot-boiler, is describable as a *roman-fleuve.* Its most authentic voice is the prosopopoeia of the river, rippling upwards to the surface of consciousness in all her feminine moods and changes. When Anna Livia is introduced, she is a vivacious young girl in a shower of spring rain: "Arrah, sure, we all love little Anny Ruiny, or, we mean to say, lovelittle Anna Rayiny, when unda her brella, mid piddle med puddle she ninnygoes nannygoes nancing by." [7] Later she makes a mature appearance, conveying words of maternal comfort to the feckless Shem, "babbling, bubbling, chattering to herself, deloothering the fields on their elbows leaning with the sloothering slide of her, giddgaddy, grannyma, gossipaceous Anna Livia." [195] By the end, her remembrance of girlhood ("just a young thin pale soft shy slim slip of a thing" [202]) has been transferred to her daughter *con variazioni* ("just a whisk brisk sly spry spink spank sprint of a thing" [627]). A shower, a stream, a freshet, the river rises until it drowns out the other sounds. Meanwhile, on the banks of the Liffey, two old washerwomen gossip about Earwicker and his family, proceeding "to make his private linen public" until nightfall has transformed them into a tree and a stone:[215]

> Can't hear with the waters of. The chittering waters of. Flittering bats, fieldmice bawk talk. Ho! Are you not gone ahome? What Thom Malone? Can't hear with bawk of bats, all thim liffeying waters of. Ho, talk save us! My foos won't moos. I feel as old as yonder elm. A tale told of Shaun or Shem? All Livia's daughtersons. Dark hawks hear us. Night! Night! My ho head halls. I feel as heavy as yonder stone. Tell me of John or Shaun? Who were Shem and Shaun the living sons or daughters of? Night now! Tell me, tell me, tell me, elm! Night night! Telmetale of stem or stone. Beside the rivering waters of, hitherandthithering waters of. Night!

This paragraph, the last of the first section, is among the few that yielded to a committee of seven French translators, collaborating with Joyce. Their task, like Urquhart's with Rabelais, was to translate a style— *double entendre* for pun, "*le parc de l'Inphernix*" for "the Fiendish Park"—where a literal translation would have been meaningless. They proved, at all events, that the application of Joyce's technique is not restricted to English. Assonance is easier in French, and orthography is harder:

> *N'entends pas cause les ondes de. Le bébé babil des ondes de. Souris chauve, trottinette cause pause. Hein! Tu n'es pas rentré? Quel père André? N'entends pas cause les fuisouris, les liffeyantes ondes de. Eh! Bruit nous aide! Mon pied à pied se lie lierré. Je me sens vieille comme mon orme même. Un conte conté de Shaun ou Shem? De Livie tous les fillefils. Sombre faucons écoutent l'ombre. Nuit. Nuit. Ma taute tête tombe. Je me sens lourde comme ma pierre-stone. Conte moi de John ou Shaun. Qui furent Shem et Shaun en vie les fils ou filles de. Là-dessus nuit. Dis-mor, dis-mor, dis-mor, orme. Nuit, nuit! Contemoiconte soit tronc ou pierre. Tan rivierantes ondes de, couretcouranies ondes de. Nuit.*

Difficulties of the opposite kind were met by C. K. Ogden, when he turned the same passage into Basic English, as an accompaniment to Joyce's recording. His problem was not to imitate the suggestiveness of the original, but to reduce it to direct statement. Hence he is forced to ignore harmonies and conceits, and to rule out ambiguities, sometimes rather arbitrarily. There is not much left:

No sound but the waters of. The dancing waters of. Winged things in flight, field-rats louder than talk. Ho! Are you not gone, ho! What Tom Malone? No sound but the noise of these things, the Liffey and all its waters of. Ho, talk safe keep us! There's no moving this my foot. I seem as old as that tree over there. A story of Shaun or Shem but where? All Livia's daughters and sons. Dark birds are hearing. Night! Night! My old head's bent. My weight is like that stone you see. What may the John Shaun story be? Or who were Shem and Shaun the living sons and daughters of? Night now! Say it, say it, tree! Night night! The story say of stem or stone. By the side of the river waters of, this way and that way waters of. Night!

This self-denying paraphrase juxtaposes the simplest and the most complex English, Mr. Ogden's language of strict denotation and Joyce's language of extreme connotation. Both are reactions against our modern Babel, and Mr. Ogden has hailed Joyce as "the bellwether of debabelization." While his enemies have attacked him for conducting a campaign to disintegrate literature, his friends have rallied to "the revolution of the word." In sober fact, Joyce is neither an obscurantist nor a logodedalist, neither a destroyer nor a creator of language. He could scarcely achieve his microscopic precision and polysemantic subtlety unless he were a neutral. His restless play of allusion depends, to the vast extent of his knowledge, on the acceptance of a linguistic *status quo*. Within his top-heavy frame of reference, everything must be in its place. Whatever is capable of being sounded or enunciated will find its echo in *Finnegans Wake*: Joyce alludes glibly and impartially to such concerns as left-wing literature,[116] Whitman and democracy,[263] Lenin and Marxism,[271] the Gestapo,[332] the Nazis,[375] the Soviets,[414] and the "braintrust."[529] The sounds are heard, the names called, the phrases invoked, as it were by a well-informed parrot. The rest is "SILENCE."[501]

Quinet

by Clive Hart

The more repetition a book contains, the less easy it must obviously be for the writer to create motifs whose recurrence will arrest the attention of the reader. In writing a book so consistently repetitive as *Finnegans Wake,* Joyce set himself the considerable technical problem of creating, for major architectonic or thematic purposes, a few outstanding motifs which would not be entirely swamped by the general flow of mutating material. His simplest solution to this difficulty was to turn aside from his normal custom of building up motifs from insignificant little phrases and to construct, or borrow, a number of very long motifs which, by virtue of their unusual proportions might readily be picked out even on a casual reading—if anyone ever reads *Finnegans Wake* casually. The misquotation from Quinet* is in some ways the most remarkable of these long motifs.

Stuart Gilbert quite correctly defined the technique of *Finnegans Wake* as *"pointilliste* throughout." [1] The development of a style which involved the manipulation of ever smaller and more autonomous units eventually led Joyce to the point where, as I have suggested above, he could insert short, detached phrases in any one of a number of places in the text. Yet in spite of the unusually fragmentary nature of Joyce's own mature literary methods, he seems never to have abandoned his youthful admiration for "supple periodic prose" in the work of other writers. Even as late as 1935 he stuck to his unpopular assertion that Newman was the greatest of English prose-stylists.[2] This love of simplicity in others may well have been a psychological reaction against the complexity of his own writing very similar to that which induced him momentarily to lower his defences and publish *Pomes Penyeach.* In a somewhat lyrical mood he incorporated the

"Quinet." From *Structure and Motif in Finnegans Wake,* by Clive Hart (London: Faber and Faber Ltd., 1962), pp. 182–200. Reprinted by permission of Northwestern University Press and Faber and Faber Ltd. A few of Mr. Hart's footnotes have been deleted.

* [Edgar Quinet (1803–1875) French historian and romantic nationalist. A violent anticleric, he was dismissed from his teaching post at the Collège de France for advocating the annihilation of Roman Catholic influence in France.—Ed.]

[1] S. Gilbert, *James Joyce's Ulysses,* London, 1952, p. 96.
[2] *Letters,* p. 366.

Quinet sentence into the text of *Finnegans Wake* in the original French (281). While this is the only quotation of any length to be included in the book, it is interesting to note that Joyce has misquoted no less than six times, almost certainly due to faulty memory:[3]

> *Aujourd'hui, comme aux jours de Pline et de Columelle, la jacinthe se plaît dans les Gaules, la pervenche en Illyrie, la marguerite sur les ruines de Numance; et pendant qu'autour d'elles les villes ont changé de maîtres et de nom, que plusieurs sont rentrées dans le néant, que les civilisations se sont choquées et brisées, leurs paisibles générations ont traversé les âges et se sont succédé l'une à l'autre jusqu'à nous, fraîches et riantes comme aux jours des batailles.*

The sentence is taken from the *Introduction à la philosophie de l'histoire de l'humanité* [1827], a general and attractively written essay which Joyce probably found congenial, but which he does not seem to have used in *Finnegans Wake* in any other way.[4] The version in *Finnegans Wake* reads as follows:

> *Aujourd'hui comme aux temps de Pline et de Columelle la jacinthe se plaît dans les Gaules, la pervenche en Illyrie, la marguerite sur les ruines de Numance et pendant qu'autour d'elles les villes ont changé de maîtres et de noms, que plusieurs sont entrées dans le néant, que les civilisations se sont choquées et brisées, leurs paisibles générations ont traversé les âges et sont arrivées jusqu'à nous, fraîches et riantes comme aux jours des batailles.*

Joyce's change of *jours* to *temps* renders the echoes at the beginning and end of the sentence less exact; the changes of punctuation and the substitution of *noms* for *nom* are not serious (though *nom* is the more usual French), but by reading *entrées* for *rentrées,* Joyce has surely thrown away much of the sentence's power to suggest the cyclic nature of history. The final change—*sont arrivées* for *se sont succédé l'une à l'autre*—may perhaps be intentional, since it considerably improves the rhythmic balance, but this is in any case just the kind of stylistic improvement we should expect Joyce to make unconsciously when quoting from memory.

There is rather more to the sentence than its simple content might suggest, for it may be interpreted as a type-example of imitative form on a small scale—an idea which may never have occurred to Quinet, but of which Joyce makes full use. A brief analysis will show how well suited it is to Joyce's purposes. Perhaps the most immediately obvious thing about the sentence is that, like *Finnegans Wake,* it is a closed circle. After the word *Aujourd'hui* with which it begins, we step immediately back into the past: *comme aux temps de Pline et de Columelle.* For Vico, whom

---

[3] *See* the plate between pp. 128 and 129 in Mrs. Maria Jolas' *A James Joyce Yearbook,* Paris, 1949, which reproduces an even more corrupted version in Joyce's hand; this shows clear signs of having been written out from memory.

[4] *Œuvres Complètes,* Paris, 1857, vol. II, pp. 367–8. . . .

Quinet studied and translated, the days of Pliny and Columella, when western Rome was on the way toward its destruction, represented the *ricorso* period of transition between two great historical cycles and formed the prelude to a new Theological Age. The historians presiding over the sentence are a symbolic brother-pair who, apart from the role they play in the five variations of the motif, appear twice more in *Finnegans Wake* (255, 319). They are particularly relevant to II.2, where the brother-battle is beginning to be openly expressed during the geometry and history lessons. The symbolic flowers, clearly identified throughout the book with the tempting young girls, follow hard on the heels of these illustrious "twins." Having rapidly established the primary male and female principles, Quinet now lets the sentence move forward again in time from late Roman days, so that it passes over what are in fact three Viconian Ages (post-Roman times, feudal Europe, Vico's own times) until it "rearrives" (*sont arrivées*) at the next Age of dissolution and changeover which Joyce obviously equates with the twentieth century (*jusqu'à nous*). A return to the past is implied in the concluding phrase, *comme aux jours des batailles*, echoing the words *comme aux temps* [or *jours*] *de Pline et de Columelle* with which the sentence began; the cyclic pattern, the BELLUM-PAX-BELLUM (281) is thus clearly established. This verbal echo further justifies Joyce's identification of the twin historians—who might otherwise seem to be no more than passive onlookers—with the eternal combatants. The continuity of the female element, the flowers, is expressed through a neat counterpoint of form and content: even in the central phrases of the sentence, where the transitory nature of the rough male City is under discussion, the rhythm is fluent and gentle.

Joyce was essentially an indoor man, a city dweller. All his books before *Finnegans Wake* are urban. Nature in the Wordsworthian sense seems to have meant little to him, and although in *Finnegans Wake* river and mountain, flower and tree are for the first time used as major recurrent symbols, they are little more than stylised icons which rarely develop into sensuous, living images. In *A Portrait*, the rural setting of Clongowes Wood College is barely mentioned and fulfills no important function as it might have done in, say, a Lawrence, while the more recently published pages from *Stephen Hero*,[5] dealing with rural Mullingar, show how out of touch Joyce felt when he attempted to write naturalistically about events in settings outside his native city. The biographies have little to say about holidays spent away from city life, and the *Letters* contain very little mention of the natural world (except, of course, for the frequent allusions to the Liffey, which formed an essential part of Joyce's urban Dublin). Mr. Frank Budgen insists that Joyce detested flowers, and indeed even the graceful periwinkle, hyacinth and daisy of Quinet's sentence are prized

---

[5] M. Magalaner (ed.), *A James Joyce Miscellany, second series,* Carbondale, Ill., 1959, pp. 3–8.

more for the abstractions they embody than for their sensuous qualities. Soon after Joyce begins to rework the sentence, he transforms the flowers into a giggling group of lewd schoolgirls, and then into a variety of other rapidly mutating symbols. This is not to say that the book would be better otherwise. In too many places it is already dangerously near to a sentimentality which any softening of Joyce's hard, stylised approach to natural objects could only tend to exaggerate.

The Quinet motif is intimately bound up with the "change-of-sex" theme, the "MUTUOMORPHOMUTATION" (281), as I shall presently demonstrate. First, however, a few comments about Joyce's numerology are needed. All the numbers up to seven, and a few beyond that, are associated with major characters, or groups of characters. The following are the most important identifications:

0 Anna, "Mother Zero"; a female symbol
1 Earwicker, the ithyphallic father
2 Isolde and her "looking-glass" girl; the pair of tempting girls in the Park; the washerwomen (All of these pairs are of course equivalent.)
3 the English soldiers who apprehend Earwicker in the Phoenix Park
4 the Old Androgynes
5 the Four, with their Ass
6 the twelve customers often seem to be made up of six men, each playing two parts (e.g., "a choir of the O'Daley O'Doyles doublesixing the chorus," 48)
7 the "Rainbow-girls," allied to the "2"
10 the Father and Mother in union (see 308, and SK 162–3)
12 the Customers
28 the "February-girls"—an expanded form of the "7" (The algebraical sum of $7 = 28$.)
29 Isolde, the leap-year-girl
40 always associated with Anna; possibly her age at the naturalistic level
111 Anna's three children multiplied by a trick of notation; also the kabbalistic total of "A–L–P" ($A = 1, L = 30, P = 80$)[6]

These are the primary identifications, but Joyce likes the idea of cosmic reciprocity and hence whenever possible he balances a numerical group of one sex with an identical group of the opposite sex, so creating an analogy with the concept of "anti-particles" in modern physics.[7] Thus the female duo is reflected in the Shem-Shaun partnership, while the three soldiers —who seem to be Shem, Shaun, and a form of their father, HCE—are balanced by a female trinity made up of Isolde, her mirror-image, and "their" mother, Anna Livia. In the Quinet sentence, the female duo and

[6] See S. L. MacGregor Mathers, *The Kabbalah Unveiled*, London, 1887, p. 3.
[7] It will be noticed that "4" and "10" are the only numbers which Joyce makes intrinsically androgynous; 4 is the "perfect number," . . . and the algebraical sum of $4 = 10$.

the male trio are made to appear in their inverted forms, but each of these groups plays a part which is a combination of the activities of the "primary" "2" and the "primary" "3"—the tempting of the sinner and his subsequent apprehension. Thus the belligerent Pliny and Columella, whose rather feminine-sounding names seem to have suggested to Joyce that they were inverts,[8] solicit homosexually, while the three nymphomaniac flowers peep through the shrubbery as do the spying soldiers. Joyce makes this point in a marginal gloss: the two historians are *"Dons Johns"*—two gallants—while the three flowers are *"Totty Askins,"* that is, they are both juvenile ("totty") seducers who ask for the attention of the males whom they always rebuff, and also three enemy (English) soldiers. This succinct identification of the girls and the soldiers is further emphasised in the right-hand note, "BELLETRISTICS," which seems to be Joyce's coinage for Amazons with a literary bias.

Isobel writes two footnotes to Quinet, in the second of which she suggests that the flatus of his very spiritual style be transmuted into the rather more solid matter to be found on Anna Livia's cloacal scrap of tissue:[9]

> Translout that gaswind into turfish, Teague, that's a good bog and you, Thady, poliss it off, there's a nateswipe, on your blottom pulper.

Joyce takes Isobel's advice and parodies the sentence in five places in *Finnegans Wake,* thus "translouting" it into his Irish "turfish" and thoroughly assimilating it into the book. (I have used the word "parody" here for want of a better. Joyce is not really parodying Quinet at any point, but refashioning his sentence word by word to suit new contexts—an altogether different art for which no adequate term seems to exist. The five "parodies" are more like free translations into various dialects of "Djoytsch.") Stylistically, Quinet's sentence is direct, lyrical, and simple —in short, all that *Finnegans Wake* is not. By the time Joyce was composing his last book, he was long past the stage when he could comfortably write such simple stuff at this, however much he may have admired it. The result is that all his reworkings inevitably annihilate Quinet's rather too self-conscious grace and delicacy. As I shall show below, Joyce has in every case considerably elaborated and extended the original material, but it is interesting to see how the necessity to compose within a more or less predetermined form has very largely curbed his habit of expansion and interpolation. The first three parodies (those on pages 14–15, 117, and 236) were incorporated relatively early in their respective chapters, and although in successive manuscript versions the surrounding passages have in each case been greatly developed and expanded, the parodies have remained almost untouched. In their earliest forms they read as follows:

[8] E.g., "medams culonelle" (351).
[9] Cf. the Russian General's cleaning himself with a sod of Irish turf (353).

Since the high old times of Hebear and Hairyman the cornflowers have
been staying at Ballymun, the duskrose has choosed out Goatstown's cross-
roads, twolips have pressed togatherthem by sweet Rush, townland of
twinlights the whitethorn and redthorn have fairygayed the mayvalleys
of Knockmaroon and though for rings round them during a hundred
thousand yeargangs, the Formoreans have brittled the Tooath of the Danes
and the Oxman has been pestered by the Firebugs & the Joynts have
thrown up wallmutting & Little on the Green is childsfather of the city,
these paxsealing buttonholes have quadrilled across the centuries and here
now whiff to us, fresh & made-of-all-smiles as on the day of Killallwhoo.
[British Museum Add. MS 47482 A, ff. 101–2. This was the first of the
parodies to be written, and dates from 1926. See *Letters*, p. 246.]

Since nozzy Nanette tripped palmyways with Highho Harry there's a
spurtfire turf a'kind o'kindling whenoft as the souffsouff blows her peaties
up and a claypot wet for thee, my Sitys, and talkatalka till Tibbs have
eve: and whathough billiousness has been billiousness during milliums of
millenions and our mixed racings have been giving two hoots or three
jeers for the grape, vine, and brew and Pieter's in Nieuw Amsteldam and
Paoli's where the poules go and rum smelt his end for him and he dined
off sooth american this oldworld epistola of their weatherings and their
marryings and their buryings and their natural selections has combled
tumbled down to us fersch and made-at-all-hours like an auld cup on tay.
[Add. MS 47473, f. 102. This version dates from the second half of 1927,
when Joyce was revising the *Criterion III* text of I.5 for *transition* 5,
August 1927. See J. J. Slocum and H. Cahoon, *A Bibliography of James
Joyce 1882–1941*, London, 1953, pp. 99, 101, sections C.64, and C.70.]

Since the days of Roamaloose and Rehmoose the pavanos have been
stridend through the struts of Chapelldiseut, the vaulsies have meed and
youdled through the purly ooze of Ballybough, many a mismy cloudy has
tripped tauntily along that hercourt strayed reelway and the rigadoons
have held ragtimed revels on the plateauplain of Grangegorman; and
though since then sterlings and guineas have been replaced by brooks and
lions and some progress has been made on stilths and the races have come
and gone and Thyme, that chef of seasoners, has made his usual astewte
use of endadjustables and what not willbe isnor was, those danceadeils
and cancanzanies have come stummering down for our begayment through
the bedeafdom of po's greats, the obcecity of pa's teapuc's, as lithe and
limb free limber as when momie played at ma. [Add. MS 47477, f. 21.
This was the third of the parodies to be written, and dates from 1930.
See *Letters*, p. 295. It is interesting to note that in all later versions the
word "stilths" has been corrupted to "stilts."]

The fourth parody (354) is a special case, since the passage in question
went through two stages of composition before it occurred to Joyce to turn
it into a fresh treatment of Quinet:

Forfife and formicular allonall and in particular till budly shoots the
rising germinal badly. [Add. MS 47480, f. 68.]

> When old the wormd was a gadden opter and apter were Twummily
> twims and if fieforlife fells farforficular allonalls not too particular so till
> budly shoots the rising germinal let bodley chew the fat of his auger and
> budley bite the dustice of the piece. [Add. MS 47480, f. 67; it is possible
> that "auger" should read "anger."]

Joyce worked this up into a parody of Quinet for the *transition* text; once
again the earliest version of the parody is almost identical to the final
printed text:

> When old the wormd was a gadden and Anthea first unfoiled her limbs
> Wanderloot was the way the wold wagged and opter and apter were
> samuraised twimbs. They had their mutthering ivies and their murdhering
> idies and their mouldhering iries in that muskat grove but there'll be
> bright Plinnyflowers in Calomella's cool bowers when the magpyre's babble
> towers scorching and screeching from the ravenindove. If thees liked the
> sex of his head and mees ates the seeps of his traublers he's dancing
> figgies to the spittle side and shoving outs the soord. And he'll be buying
> buys and gulling gells with his carme, silk and honey while myandthys
> playing lancifer lucifug and what's duff as a bettle for usses makes cosyn
> corallines' moues weeter to wee. So till butagain budly budly [*sic*] shoots
> thon rising germinal let bodley chew the fatt of his anger and badley bide
> the toil of his tubb. [Add. MS 47480, f. 105; J. J. Slocum and H. Cahoon,
> *A Bibliography of James Joyce 1882–1941*, London, 1953, p. 101, section
> C.70.]

The final parody (615) was apparently one of the last passages of *Finnegans Wake* to be composed, since it was not added to Book IV until after
the proofs had been set up. The printed text is almost exactly the same as
the MS insertion.[10] (The decision to include the quotation in French in
II.2 also seems to have been made quite late.)

The original quotation and all the finished parodies are closely associated in the text with commentaries on them which rehearse the basic situation, or much of it, in fresh terms, and in some cases can almost be said
to represent further minor variations on the motif. The paragraph following the quotation in II.2 discusses Quinet's ideas with vivacity and dis-
respectful wit:

> Margaritomancy! Hyacinthinous pervinciveness! Flowers. A cloud. But
> Bruto and Cassio are ware only of trifid tongues the whispered wilfulness,
> ('tis demonall!) and shadows shadows multiplicating (il folsoletto nel falso-
> letto col fazzolotto dal fuzzolezzo), totients quotients, they tackle their
> quarrel. Sickamoor's so woful sally. Ancient's aerger. And eachway both-
> wise glory signs. What if she love Sieger less though she leave Ruhm
> moan? That's how our oxyggent has gotten ahold of half their world.
> Moving about in the free of the air and mixing with the ruck. Enten eller,
> either or.

---

[10] British Museum Add. MS 47488, ff. 195–6.

One can sense in the outburst of exclamation points the relief with which Joyce, for all his praise of Quinet, turned again to the freedom of his own manner. That the sentence in its original and parodied forms is an important touchstone for the whole of *Finnegans Wake* is suggested by the marginal gloss to this commentary: "SORTES VIRGINIANAE"—for those with eyes to see, all our fates are to be found written in the Book of the Virgins, whose mystic invincibility (deriving perhaps from invincible ignorance) seems to be implicit in Joyce's translation of their names. These names once again allude to the masculine, soldierly aspect of the flowers, for Hyacinthus was a homosexual Spartan boy, "Margaritomancy!" may be read "Margaret, a man, see!" and Joyce seems to derive *pervinca* from *pervinco*.

In a charming prelude to the first parody (14), the basic materials of the sentence are presented in a pastoral setting. The polar principles underlying the scene of battles, death and regrowth, are to be found "neath the stone pine" where the "pastor lies with his crook." [11] The androgynous twins are a pair of grazing sheep—"pricket" and "pricket's sister"—while the "herb trinity" seem once again to be female, as on page 281: "amaid" (14). The eternal scene having been set—"Thus, too, for donkey's years"— the parody of Quinet may follow: "Since the bouts of Hebear and Hairyman . . ."

Joyce's inevitable elaborations have allowed the flowers to increase their number to six: "cornflowers . . . duskrose . . . twolips . . . whitethorn . . . redthorn . . . may-,'" while the garden in which they grow is now located in Ireland. The parody is pregnant with cross-references to other themes and motifs, as we should expect. The word *"riantes"* of the original is rendered by "made-of-all-smiles," which recurs in the next parody as "made-of-all-hours" (117), thus suggesting both the girls' timeless qualities and their constant sensual willingness; the important figure 1000 appears here as "chiliad"; the round of twenty-nine words for "Peace" (470–71)—which forms a complete cycle in itself, and recurs in III.3 as twenty-nine words for "Dead" (499.04)—is heralded in both forms by the phrase "paxsealing buttonholes," implying that the flowers both bring peace and seal up with wax the Letter of life that they help to write. (There is, as I shall show, a constant and close association of the Letter with Quinet's sentence.) The most important of the cross-references, however, is the inclusion of the old dance to the rhythm of which the flowers are made to arrive *jusqu'à nous*: "quadrilled across the centuries." The dance is continually used in *Finnegans Wake* as a symbol of communication and of cyclic progress. When they chant "Peace," the leap-year girls dance widdershins around Shaun-Osiris, as if around a phallic may-pole

---

[11] The crook is Eve, made from Adam's bent rib; cf. *"Hic cubat edilis. Apud libertinam parvulam"* (7).

and, even more significantly perhaps, they execute a sacred "trepas" [12] when they change this chant to "Dead," on the occasion of his *sparagmos* (499). I have already mentioned Joyce's repeated assertion that the cyclic scheme of *Finnegans Wake* "is like a rumba round my garden." Quinet's flowers grow in the garden of the world as civilisations clash and break, so that in the "rumba" of historical progress we may now perhaps hear a suggestion of the rumble of "toppling masonry."

Into the commentary which follows the first parody, Joyce pours all the superfluity of material that could not be squeezed into the parody itself; useful ideas apparently flowed all too fast. This is one case where the very richness of Joyce's thinking became something of an embarrassment to him. He had already blown the sentence up to more than one and a half times its original length (119 words against Quinet's 75) and had left only the vaguest rhythmic similarity. The decoration of the classical model with a mass of baroque ornamentation had to stop before poor Quinet disappeared altogether. But, as usual, Joyce manages to turn difficulty to his own advantage, for repetition "in outher wards" is, after all, what he is looking for most of the time in *Finnegans Wake*; if he has too much material for any given thematic statement, he simply repeats himself until the material is exhausted. This new flow of rich and evocative symbols gives further valuable insights into the primary situation. The rhythmic superiority of Joyce's free style is at once apparent:

> The babbelers with their thangas vain have been (confusium hold them!) they were and went; thigging thugs were and houhnhymn songtoms were and comely norgels were and pollyfool fiansees. Menn have thawed, clerks have surssurhummed the blond has sought of the brune: Elsekiss thou may, mean Kerry piggy?: and the duncledames have countered with the hellish fellows: Who ails tongue coddeau, aspace of dumbillsilly? And they fell upong one another: and themselves they have fallen. And still nowanights and by nights of yore do all bold floras of the field to their shyfaun lovers say only: Cull me ere I wilt to thee!: and, but a little later: Pluck me whilst I blush! Well may they wilt, marry, and profusedly blush, be troth! For that saying is as old as the howitts. Lave a whale while in a whillbarrow (isn't it the truath I'm tallin ye?) to have fins and flippers that shimmy and shake. Tim Timmycan timped hir, tampting Tam. Fleppety! Flippety! Fleapow!
>   Hop!

In the second parody, on page 117, the brother-pair, who had been in-carnated on page 14 as cavemen equivalents of Heber and Heremon, take on the form of a music-hall song-and-dance team: "Since nozzy Nanette tripped palmyways with Highho Harry . . ." The three flowers, on the other hand, no longer figure as individuals, but as a collective symbol, the Letter: "this oldworld epistola." In identifying the flower-girls with their Letter, Joyce is even more literally putting into practice Isolde's sugges-

---

[12] *Trépas* (Fr.) = death.

tion in her second footnote on page 281. It is significant that while this is the version in which the Quinet-Letter identification is made most explicit, it is also the parody which departs most from the rhythms and general organisation of the original (except for the special case on page 354); Joyce is opting for more "turfish" and less French. It is particularly rich in allusions to other motifs and their associated symbols, the most salient of these being the cup-of-tea-and-pot still-life which is usually in evidence somewhere in the middle-ground whenever the Letter is under discussion. The water for the wetting of the tea and the consequent creation of a new world is heated over the fire of "Pat's Purge" (117)—an amusing conceit by means of which Joyce closely associates the tea symbol with the ubiquitous Phoenix-Magic-Fire theme. Bridget and Patrick enter with their constant litany of "tauftauf"–"mishe mishe," modified here to "souffsouff" and "talkatalka," and since Bridget and Patrick are a constantly recurring brother-and-sister pair, their solemn ritual is evidently to be identified with the theatrical frivolities of "Nanette" and "Harry."

The survival of the Letter-posy over the "billiousness" of infirm "mixed racings" is developed in a very direct statement of the Viconian cyclic principle:

> this oldworld epistola of their weatherings and their marryings and their buryings and their natural selections has combled tumbled down to us fersch and made-at-all-hours like an ould cup on tay.

The scene of the rise and fall of masculine glory has meanwhile been shifted from Ireland (15) back to Europe—"Pieter's in Nieuw Amsteldam and Paoli's where the poules go"—or perhaps even farther afield—"he dined off sooth american"—but wherever the comedy may be played out, the slow progress of history is seen to be like nothing so much as the gigantic drinking party of *Finnegans Wake*: "two hoots or three jeers for the grape vine and brew." The whole of this parody is in fact a further stage in Joyce's reduction of the nightmare of history to a "shout in the street."

The *jours des batailles*, which in the first parody were metamorphosed into an Irish bloodbath on the "eve of Killallwho," are now no more than a storm in "an ould cup on tay." [13] Joyce is identifying the fighting in the field with the sexual battle which assures the continued existence of the race of flowers, and in so doing he is postulating the ultimate interdependence of Quinet's opposed principles of war and peace, mortality and continuity. This is yet another example of the far-reaching ways in which *leitmotivs* work for Joyce, for without the structural correspondence "*jours des batailles*–ould cup on tay," which the motif establishes, Joyce's point would be lost.

In the brilliantly concise version of the sentence on page 236, the two

---

[13] See F. M. Boldereff, *Reading Finnegans Wake*, New York, 1959, pp. 182ff. for some interesting comments on the function of tea-symbolism in *Finnegans Wake*.

Roman historians have been transformed into the traditional founders of their city—"Roamaloose and Rehmoose"—a rather less pacific couple. After having quadrilled across the centuries which separate I.1 and II.1, the flowers have been refined away until nothing remains of them but the essence of their dances—the pavans, waltzes, reels, and rigadoons—while the scene of their seductive frolics has once more been shifted back to Ireland. The alternations of Irish and overseas backgrounds to the parodies (14–15, Ireland; 117, Europe and South America; 236, Ireland; 354, Eden; 615, "our mutter nation") parallel the many other oscillations of locality in *Finnegans Wake*—Tristan's loves in Brittany and Ireland, Shem's trips to Australia, Shaun's to the United States. Later on in the sentence, after it has moved forward in time, the older dances mentioned above are seen to have developed into the crazy modern gaiety of the Parisian cancan ("cancanzanies"), which stimulates the frustrated Earwicker to the point of *bégayement* ("begayment").

The destruction of the expendable male aspects of the world is equated with the preparation of food—"Thyme, that chef of seasoners, has made his usual astewte use of endajustables" (236)—which is one of the favourite pastimes of fat-bellied Shaun to whom the "dimb dumbelles" (236) pander at every turn. (The dumb-bell—the mathematical sign for infinity, ∞—is, of course, an especially suitable symbol for Joyce's immortal but empty-headed and vulgar flower-girls.) The seasoning of history's stew is just one more aspect of the "Eating the God" theme which Joyce took over from Frazer, and, after all, says Joyce, no matter how often the Host may go a progress through the guts of a communicant, the true God remains whole, inviolate. However destructive and degenerate Shaun's gourmandising may seem, nothing is really destroyed in the process; the laws of conservation always hold, so that "whatnot willbe isnor." History, like the kaleidoscope of *Finnegans Wake*, simply rearranges a number of "endadjustables," and the sharing out of the God among the congregation, though it symbolises the continuity of life, is no more than a juggling with the distribution of the same particles of Being. Through past eons and past epochs (236) the flower-dancers have continued to survive the *jours des batailles* which are no longer equated, as on page 117, with the lively and "fizzin" (308) cup of tea, but with the struggles of the ageing Anna to remain fertile. Book II is the Book of the Children; Anna has been replaced, and we watch the pitiful spectacle of the already mummified woman playing at the motherhood of which she is no longer capable (236). The cup of tea that was once her most important fertility symbol reappears in this parody, but only in association with the deaf, purblind, and obsessed old man of a past age, who has been supplanted just as his wife has: "the bedeafdom of po's taeorns, the obcecity of pa's teapucs." Furthermore, as Joyce uses back-slang for the cup ("teapucs"), we may fairly assume that it is upside down and hence, like Omar's glass, empty. The word "teapucs" may also contain the "specs" necessary to combat pa's approaching blindness; there seems to be at least one physical defect that Earwicker shares with his myopic second-best son, Shem.

In the preceding paragraph, Anna Livia's *billet doux* ("billy . . . coo") is identified with the Missal used at the communion, but when an office from it is sung—"and sing a missal too"—this is discovered, rather surprisingly, to be no more than the latest version of Quinet. Joyce could hardly have made greater claims for his motif.

The fourth parody is by far the most difficult of the set, and at the same time one of the most significant. The supreme importance of Quinet's sentence in *Finnegans Wake* is emphasised by the use to which Joyce puts this version—namely, to conclude the central "Butt and Taff" conversation as the two speak in unison for the first and only time. The passage is so dense with meaning that it will be as well to quote the final polished text in full:

> When old the wormd was a gadden and Anthea first unfoiled her limbs wanderloot was the way the wood wagged where opter and apter were samuraised twimbs. They had their mutthering ivies and their murdhering idies and their mouldhering iries in that muskat grove but there'll be bright plinnyflowers in Calomella's cool bowers when the magpyre's babble towers scorching and screeching from the ravenindove. If thees lobed the sex of his head and mees ates the seep of his traublers he's dancing figgies to the spittle side and shoving outs the soord. And he'll be buying buys and go gulling gells with his flossim and jessim of carm, silk and honey while myandthys playing lancifer lucifug and what's duff as a bettle for usses makes coy cosyn corollanes' moues weeter to wee. So till but-again budly shoots thon rising germinal let bodley chow the fatt of his anger and badley bide the toil of his tubb.

This is the only occasion on which Quinet's single sentence has been broken down by Joyce into more than one—a fact which must be accounted for by the peculiar circumstances of the parody's genesis. The flowers have been transported away from time and space and made to blossom in the Garden of Eden, the site at which so many of Joyce's motifs are allowed to play themselves out. It will be seen that Pliny and Columella are once again present in person and that Anna Livia herself makes a third with her girls, in the guise of Aphrodite Antheia. In this passage, however, Joyce has gone far beyond Quinet, on to whose little sentence he has piled allusion after allusion to virtually every major theme in *Finnegans Wake,* including the Fall, ritual murder, blindness, Wagnerian Magic-Fire, the dance, Irish nationalism, homosexuality, simony, and micturition.

On page 615, where the last of the parodies immediately precedes the fullest and most important version of the Letter, the association of the two motifs is given its final and simplest expression. Since Book IV is the Age of Vico's *ricorso,* in which dawn begins to disperse many mists, Joyce reverts to a rather closer adherence to the rhythms and content of the original sentence. Pliny and Columella reappear almost undisguised, and the three flowers flourish again in the forms which Quinet gave them. Even here, however, there are numerous complexities. Columella doubles with Columkille, thus making another link in the long chain of correspondences that Joyce is always at pains to establish between Ireland and Rome.[14] The three flowers, from Gaul, Illyria, and Numancia, now show by their names that they in fact owe allegiance to more than one nation: the hyacinth from Gaul ("all-too-ghoulish") is also Italian ("Giacinta"); the Illyrian periwinkle has French ancestry ("Pervenche"); the Spanish daisy among the ruins of Numancia is half English ("Margaret"). In the last analysis they all belong to Ireland: "our mutter nation."

The most interesting change in this final parody is the inclusion for the first time of a clear symbol of male immortality. "Finnius the old One" also endures through the "hophazzards" of history. Though the manifestations of the masculine principle seem more transient than those of the feminine, the underlying essence of Finn the Giant is no less real or indestructible than that of Anna Livia with her twenty-nine tributaries. Finn will wake again at "Cockalooralooraloomenos." (This is one of the last appearances in *Finnegans Wake* of the cockcrow motif which throughout the book forms a trinity with the thundervoice (Father) and the Word "whiskey" (holy spirit), and shares with them the privilege of awakening the fallen hero to new life.)

The tea-table with cup, saucer, and teapot is now reset as the morning breakfast-table at which eggs are to be eaten: "there'll be iggs for brekkers come to mournhim" (12). At least one version of the Letter is written on the shells of these eggs—"there's scribings scrawled on eggs" (615)—and as they are broken open to be eaten, we at last understand how it is that the "punctuation" of the Letter is supplied by the fork of the Professor at the Breakfast Table (124), although the attempt to eat boiled eggs with a fork seems to brand the Professor as one of the absent-minded variety. As always, Joyce aims for a duality of function in his symbolism, so that the "piping hot" morning teapot is made to serve also as Molly-Josephine's orange-keyed night-utensil, the "Sophy-Key-Po" of 9. Having so firmly established the association of the Letter with the eggs on which it is written, with the generative power of tea, and with the cycle of ingoing and outgoing water, Joyce then hatches the complete text (615–19).

---

[14] Cf., for example, "The seanad and the pobbel queue's remainder" (434).

James Joyce in His Letters

by Lionel Trilling

In 1935, near the end of a long affectionate letter to his son George in America, James Joyce wrote: "Here I conclude. My eyes are tired. For over half a century they have gazed into nullity, where they have found a lovely nothing."

It is not a characteristic utterance. Joyce was little given to making large statements about the nature of existence. As Dr. Johnson said of Dryden, he knew how to complain, but his articulate grievances were not usually of a metaphysical kind. They referred to particular circumstances of practical life, chiefly the lets and hindrances to his work; at least in his later years, such resentment as he expressed was less in response to what he suffered as a person than to the impediments that were put in his way as an artist.

And actually we cannot be certain that Joyce did indeed mean to complain when he wrote to George of his long gaze into *"nulla"*—his letters to his children were always in Italian—or that he was yielding to a metaphysical self-pity when he said he had found in it *"un bellissimo niente."* The adjective may well have been intended not ironically but literally, and Joyce can be understood to say that human existence is nullity right enough, yet if it is looked into with a vision such as his, the nothing that can be perceived really *is* lovely, though the maintenance of the vision is fatiguing work.

To read the passage in this way is in accord with our readiness nowadays to see Joyce as preeminently a "positive" writer, to be aware of the resistance he offered to nullity through his great acts of creation. From the famous climactic epiphany of *A Portrait of the Artist as a Young Man,* in which life "calls" in all imaginable erotic beauty and is answered in ecstasy, he went on to celebrate human existence even in the pain, defeat, and humiliation that make up so large a part of its substance. He consciously intended Molly Bloom's ultimate "Yes" as a doctrinal statement, a judgment in life's favor made after all the adverse evidence was in. He contrived a rich poetry out of the humble and sordid, the sad repeated round of the commonplace, laying a significant

"James Joyce in His Letters," by Lionel Trilling. Reprinted from *Commentary* (February 1968), by permission, and by permission of the author. Copyright © 1968 by the American Jewish Committee.

·, nameless, unremembered acts of kindness and of
ιe point that Joyce as a young man could speak of
lative praise, with particular reference to *The Ex-*
.he power of his own work derives from the Words-
discovering a transcendence by which life, in con-
y, is affirmed.

tell the whole story of the relation in which Joyce
was not only resistant to it but also partisan with it.
He loved it ... ght to make it prevail. The transcendent affirmation
of hypostasized life went along with a profound indifference, even a hostility, to a great many of the particularities in which the energies of
life embody themselves. He could speak in thrilling archaic phrase of
"the fair courts of life," yet the elaborations of developed society were
for the most part of no account to him, and to much of the redundancy
of culture as it proliferates in objects and practices that are meant to be
pleasing he was chiefly apathetic. His alienation from so many of the
modes and conditions of human existence is sometimes chilling.

Among life's processes, that of entropy makes an especial appeal to
Joyce. The "paralysis" which is represented in *Dubliners* as the pathol-
ogy of a nation at a particular moment of its history was also known to
him as a general condition of life itself, and if he found it frightening,
he also found it tempting. *Dubliners* does indeed have the import of social criticism that its author often said it was meant to have. This "chapter in the moral history" of his nation levels an accusation to which the
conscience of his race, when at last it will have been forged in the smithy
of his soul, must be sensitive. But if the devolution of energy to the
point of "paralysis" is, in a moral and social view, a condition to be
deplored and reversed, it is also for Joyce a sacred and powerful state
of existence. The attraction it had for him is nearly overt in the first
story of *Dubliners,* "The Sisters," and in the last, "The Dead." "The
special odor of corruption which, I hope, floats over my stories" is the
true scent by which life is to be tracked to its last authenticity. It is not
without reason that Samuel Beckett is often said to have represented
Joyce in the Hamm of *Endgame,* the terrible blind storyteller who presides over the quietus of Nature, himself on the verge of extinction but
grimly cherishing and ordering what little life remains, setting against
the ever-encroaching void, which he himself has helped bring about, an
indomitable egoism that is itself an emptiness.

The power of Joyce's work derives, we must see, not only from the
impulse to resist nullity but also, and equally, from the impulse to make
nullity prevail. Something of the destructive force was remarked by T. S.
Eliot when, taking tea with Virginia Woolf and trying to convince his
hostess that *Ulysses* was not to be dismissed as the work of one or an-

other kind of "underbred" person, he characterized the author's achievement and the magnitude of his power by saying that he had "killed the 19th century." Eliot meant that Joyce by his radical innovations of style had made obsolete the styles of the earlier time, and also that, as a result of or in concomitance with the obsolescence that Joyce had effected, the concerns and sentiments to which the old styles were appropriate had lost their interest and authority. In 1922, the 19th cenutry was not in high repute and one might suppose that the report of its having been killed would make an occasion for hope: with the old concerns and sentiments out of the way, those of the new day might be expected to flourish. But Eliot expressed no such expectation. Although he took it to be part of the great achievement of *Ulysses* that it had shown up "the futility of all the English styles," he went on to say that Joyce had destroyed his own future, for now there was nothing left for him to write about. Nor for anyone else: Eliot later said that with *Ulysses* Joyce had brought to an end the genre of the novel.

If there is truth in Eliot's observation, a phrase of Walter Pater's helps us understand what concerns and sentiments of the 19th century Joyce may be said to have killed. In a famous paragraph of the Conclusion to *The Renaissance,* Pater spoke of "success in life." It doesn't matter that he was saying that success in life was the ability to burn with a hard gemlike flame, to make all experience into an object of aesthetic contemplation. The point is that, at the high moment of his exposition of a doctrine directed against crass practicality, Pater could use a phrase that to us now can seem only vulgar, a form of words which scarcely even stockbrokers, headmasters, and philistine parents would venture to use. In the 19th century a mind as exquisite and detached as Pater's could take it for granted that upon the life of an individual person a judgment of success or failure might be passed. And the 19th-century novel was in nothing so much a product of its time as in its assiduity in passing this judgment.

It was of course moral or spiritual success that the novel was concerned with, and this "true" success often—though not always—implied failure as the world knows it. But a characteristic assumption of the novel was that the true success brought as much gratification as conventional opinion attributed to worldly success, that it was just as real and nearly as tangible. The conception of moral or spiritual achievement was, we may say, sustained and controlled by the society from whose conventions the triumph was wrested. The houses, servants, carriages, plate, china, linen, cash, credit, position, honor, power that were the goods of the conventional world served to validate the goods of the moral or spiritual life. At the heart of the novel is the idea that the world, the worldly world, Henry James's "great round world itself," might have to be given up in the interests of integrity or even simple decency. What made this idea momentous was the assumption that the surrender is of something entirely real, and in some way, in the forcible way of common sense, much to be desired. Upon the valuation of what is given up depends much of the valuation of what is gotten in exchange. Poor Julien Sorel! Poor Pip! Poor Phineas Finn! It was a dull-spirited reader indeed who did not feel what a pity it was that the young man could not make a go of Things As They Are and at the same time possess his soul in honor and peace. But since the soul was one of the possible possessions, it was of course to be preferred to all others, the more because the price paid for it was thought real and high. In the degree that the novel gave credence to the world while withholding its assent, it established the reality of the moral or spiritual success that is defined by the rejection of the world's values.

Credence given, assent withheld; for a time this position of the novel *vis-à-vis* the world was of extraordinary interest. At a certain point in the novel's relatively short history, in the first quarter of this century, there burst upon our consciousness a realization of how great had been its accomplishment, how important its function. It was on all sides seen to be what Henry James in effect said it was, what D. H. Lawrence explicitly called it, "the book of life."

Yet no sooner had the novel come to this glory than it was said, not by Eliot alone, to have died. In all likelihood the report is true. The question of the viability of the novel today is probably to be answered in the spirit of the man who, when asked if he believed in baptism, replied that of course he did, he had seen it performed many times. Novels are still ceaselessly written, published, reviewed, and on occasion hailed, but the old sense of their spiritual efficacy is ever harder to come by. One thing is certain: to whatever purposes the novel now addresses itself, it has outgrown the activity which, in the 19th century and in the early days of the 20th, was characteristic of the genre, virtually definitive of it, the setting of the values of the moral and spiritual life over against the values of the world. This is a confrontation that no longer engages our interest. Which is by no means to say that getting and spending are not of great moment, or that moral and spiritual sensibility have declined. As to the latter, indeed, it flourishes in a way that is perhaps unprecedented—it may well be that never before have so many people undertaken to live enlightened lives, to see through the illusions that society imposes, doing this quite easily, without strain or struggle, having been led to the perception of righteousness by what literature has told them of the social life. Whatever we may *do* as persons in the world, however we behave as getters and spenders, in our other capacity, as readers, as persons of moral sensibility, we *know* that the values of the world do not deserve our interest. We know it: we do not discover it, as readers once did, with the pleasing excitement that the novel generated as it led toward understanding. It is a thing taken for granted. That the world is a cheat, its social arrangements a sham, its rewards a sell, was patent to us from our moral infancy, whose first spoken words were, "Take away that bauble."

So entirely, and, as it were, so naturally do we withhold our assent from the world that we give it scarcely any credence. As getters and spenders we take it to be actual and there; as readers our imagination repels it, or at most accepts it as an absurdity. What in the first instance is a moral judgment on the world intensifies and establishes itself as a habit of thought to the point where it transcends its moral origin and becomes a metaphysical judgment.

More and more the contemporary reader requires of literature that it have a metaphysical rather than a moral aspect. Having come to take nullity for granted, he wants to be enlightened and entertained by statements about the nature of nothing, what its size is, how it is furnished, what services the management provides, what sort of conversation and amusements can go on in it. The novel in some of its experimental and theoretical developments can gratify the new taste, but this is more easily accomplished by the theater, which on frequent occasions in its long tradition has shown its natural affinity for ultimate and metaphysical considerations. By means of the irony which it generates merely through turning a conscious eye on its traditional devices of illusion, the theater easily escapes from its servitude to morality into free and radical play with the nature of existence as morality assumes it to be. That life is a dream, that all the world's a stage, that right you are if you think you are—such propositions can be forcibly demonstrated by the theater, which, defined by its function of inducing us to accept appearance as reality, delights in discovering in itself the power of showing that reality is but appearance, in effect nothing.

At least at one point in his life, Joyce rated drama above all literary forms and made what he called the "dramatic emotion" the type of the "aesthetic emotion" in general. With the metaphysical potentialities of drama he was not concerned in an immediate way, but his famous account of the "dramatic emotion" has an obvious bearing upon the theater's ability to control, even to extirpate, the credence given to the worldly reality. Dedalus explains to Lynch that this emotion is "static," that it is brought into being by the "arrest" of the mind. "The feelings excited by improper art are kinetic, desire and loathing. Desire urges us to possess, to go to something; loathing urges us to abandon, to go from something. The arts which excite them, pornographical or didactic, are therefore improper arts. The aesthetic emotion (I use the general term) is therefore static. The mind is arrested and raised above desire and loathing."

Nothing, of course, could be further from the aesthetic of the novel in its classic phase. The novel was exactly, in Joyce's sense of the words, both pornographical and didactic, having the intention to generate de-

sire and loathing, to urge the possession of the good, the abandonment
of the bad. Assuming the prepotency of the will, the novel sought to
educate and direct it by discriminating among the objects to which it
might address itself. But Joyce characteristically represents the will in
entropy, in its movement through ambiguity and paralysis to extinction.
In *Ulysses*, for example, the objects of desire or intention of virtually
all the characters are either of no great moment as the world judges, or
they exist in unrealizable fantasy, or in the past.

There is one exception. The will of one person is represented as being, although momentarily in abeyance, on the point of becoming prepotent, and its object is represented as both capable of attainment and
worth attaining: Stephen Dedalus means to become a great writer and
we know, of course, that he does. The will of the artist is accepted in all
its legendary power and authority, fully licensed. And the worldly traits
of the particular artist Stephen Dedalus are entirely acknowledged—his
bitter intention of fame, his pride, his vanity, his claim to unique personal superiority, touched with class feeling, his need to be ascendant in
every situation. Yet the world to which these traits refer, that world to
which Yeats—the admirer of Balzac!—gave so lively a recognition, in
which the artist wins his prizes, has no existence in *Ulysses*. On the evidence that the book provides, there is nothing that can signalize the
artist's achievement of success in life. There is no person, let alone a
social agency, competent and empowered to judge his work and tell him
that he has triumphed with it, that he has imposed his will upon the
world and is now to be feared and loved. The honor he deserves cannot
be accorded him, since the traditional signs of honor are wanting—there
is no fine house to inhabit, no comfort or elegance that can gratify his
heroic spirit after strenuous days, no acclaim or deference appropriate
to his genius. His prepotent will lifts him above the primitive life, the
everlasting round of birth, copulation, and death, making him peerless:
his only possible peers are a certain few of the preeminent dead, among
whom God is one, on the whole the most congenial of the small company. It is chiefly in emulation of the work of this particular colleague
that Joyce undertakes his own creation, intending that his book shall be
read as men formerly "read" the "book of the universe." In his eyes a
thousand years are as but a day, or the other way around, and the fall
of the sparrow does not go unnoticed. The round of birth, copulation,
and death receives his sanction under the aspect of eternity and in the
awful silence of the infinite spaces, and his inscrutable but on the whole
affectionate irony is directed upon all that men contrive in their cities
for their survival, with a somewhat wryer glance toward what they contrive for their delight. Who that responds to the subtle power of his
work can ever again, as a reader, give serious thought to the appoint-
ments of the house, the ribbon in the buttonhole, the cash in the bank
and the stocks in the portfolio, the seemliness of the ordered life, the

claims of disinterested action (except as they refer to certain small dealings between one person and another, especially between father and child), the fate of the nation, the hope of the future? And however else we read *Finnegans Wake*, we cannot fail to understand that it is a *contra-Philosophie der Geschichte*, that its transcendent genial silliness is a spoof on those segments of the solemn 19th-century imagination—History, and World Historical Figures, and that wonderful Will of theirs which, Hegel tells us, keeps the world in its right course toward the developing epiphany of *Geist*.

But if Joyce did indeed kill the 19th century, he was the better able to do so because the concerns and sentiments he destroyed made so considerable a part of the fabric of his being. To read his letters as we now have them is to be confirmed in our sense of his denial of the world, but it is also to become aware that what is denied was once affirmed with an extraordinary intensity. It is to understand how entirely Joyce was a man of the century in which he was born, how thoroughgoing was his commitment to its concerns and sentiments, how deeply rooted he was in its ethos and its mythos, its beliefs and its fantasies, its greedy desires, its dream of entering into the fair courts of life.

In 1957 Stuart Gilbert brought out a volume called *Letters of James Joyce*,[1] which gave us most, though not all, of the letters that were available at the time. Taken as a whole, the collection proved disappointing. It included relatively few letters of the early years, always likely to be the most interesting period of a writer's correspondence; by far the greater number date from the years of maturity, beginning at a time when, although not yet famous, Joyce was already a figure, and of these a great many are devoted to business in the unremitting and often trifling detail in which Joyce carried it on. Nothing that bears upon Joyce's life can fail to command attention, but there is not much in Mr. Gilbert's collection that goes beyond the well-known public aspects of the career to make the appeal of intimacy.

It is true that some reviewers remarked on a quality of warmth and gaiety that they found in the letters and on how much more "human" this showed Joyce to be than had hitherto been supposed. By his middle years Joyce had developed a talent, if not for friendship, then at least for friendliness; whatever else his friends may have been to him, they were his aides, adjutants, and ambassadors, and in the letters in which he did business with them and through them, there sounds a note of geniality, often of a whimsical kind, which, as the reviewers noted, is at variance with what is often reported of his forbidding reserve. But it is possible to feel that the genial air is rather *voulu,* even contrived,[2] and at least

---

[1] [New York: The Viking Press.—Ed.]
[2] The letters to Frank Budgen are exceptional in suggesting Joyce's actual enjoyment of a relationship with another person.

one reviewer put the matter of the "humanness" in a qualified way—
Philip Toynbee said no more than that the letters "reveal a far less in-
human man than the myth had led us to believe." They may be thought
to reveal a man who, out of his sense of what is seemly, or perhaps for
reasons of policy, wished to conceal the full extent of his "inhumanness,"
of his detachment from the affections. On the evidence of the first published letters, only one event of his middle age seems ever actually to have
reached Joyce, his daughter's extreme mental illness. Even here the *apa-
theia* is to some degree in force, in part through the self-deception as to
the true state of affairs that Joyce practiced, although we are in no doubt
about the bitterness of his grief.[3] For the rest, the personal life seems to
have been burned out, calcined. The difficulties of the once obsessing
marriage appear to have been settled one way or another and no new
erotic interests are to be discerned. The dialectic of temperament has
come to an end—there are scarcely any indications of an interplay between the self and the life around it, the existence of which is recognized
only as the world rejects or accepts Joyce's art.

Immediately after the appearance of Mr. Gilbert's collection there
came to light a great trove of Joyce's letters, preserved through many
vicissitudes. They were available to Richard Ellmann in the research for
his definitive life of Joyce, and Professor Ellmann has edited them with
the erudition and intelligence that make his biography the superlative
work it is. The two collections have been conjoined to make a new *Letters of James Joyce* in three volumes,[4] of which Mr. Gilbert's is now
Volume I, Professor Ellmann's Volumes II and III. The arrangement is
anomalous and of course awkward, since the collections cover the same
span of time although in different degrees of completeness. But the practical nuisance should not be exaggerated. The Joyce scholars are inured
to worse difficulties than those to which the arrangement subjects them.
And the general reader will inevitably conclude that Volumes II and III
make the corpus of the *Letters* to which Volume I serves as a supplement.
His conclusion will be based not merely on the greater scope of the later
volumes but on the extent of their interest, which is beyond comparison
with that of their predecessor.

The letters of the mature years that are given in Professor Ellmann's
collection do not change in any decisive way the impression made by
those of Volume I, although they do modify it in some respects. It turns
out not to be true, for example, that there are no moments of crisis in
the marriage after the removal to Paris. In 1922 Nora Joyce went off to

---

[3] Joyce's long refusal to recognize the seriousness of Lucia's condition was abetted
by the doctors, who, whether out of ignorance or compunction, seem never to have
offered a firm diagnosis.
[4] [New York: The Viking Press.—Ed.]

Ireland with the children, threatening that she would not return. Joyce writes in desperate appeal to "my darling, my love, my queen," telling her that the check for her fur is on the way, that he will live anywhere with her so long as he can be "alone with her dear self without family and without friends. Either this must occur or we must part for ever, though it will break my heart." He goes on to report in detail his "fainting fit in Miss Beach's shop," and concludes: "O my dearest, if you would only turn to me even now and read that terrible book which has now broken the heart in my breast[5] and take me to yourself alone to do with me what you will!"

The substance of the marital correspondence at forty is not different from that of the twenties: the same belief in the importance of gifts, especially of fur; the extravagant demand for devotion made through the avowal of infantile weakness; the plea to be dealt with ruthlessly in his total and pathetic dependence. But as compared with the earlier letters of similar import that we now have, the energy of this one seems but dutiful, almost perfunctory. It appears early in Volume III and is the last expression not only of erotic feeling but of strong personal emotion of any kind.

From here on, the new letters of the later years are at one with those of the 1957 collection in suggesting that, however powerful Joyce's creative will continued to be, his affective will had been outlived. *"Only disconnect!"* had long been an avowed principle of his life, but not until now had it been put fully in force. It is true that the paternal tenderness and solicitude do not abate, that the form of courteous geniality is maintained, that an enterprise of helpfulness is not precluded, such as involved Joyce with the career of the tenor Sullivan, and we must suppose that some other magnetism in addition to that of his genius drew many people to his service. But nothing in the ordinary way of "humanness" contradicts our sense that the letters of the years of fame were written by a being who had departed this life as it is generally known and had become such a ghost as Henry James and Yeats imagined, a sentient soul that has passed from temporal existence into nullity yet still has a burden of energy to discharge, a destiny still to be worked out.

We are tempted to deal with the uncanny condition by bringing it into the comfortable circle of morality. Joyce's disconnection from the world, we may want to say, is the ground of his indomitable courage, before which we stand in awed admiration. The man who had ventured and won so much with *Ulysses* now pushes on with *Finnegans Wake* under the encroaching shadow of blindness and to the disapproval of his patron and virtually all his supporters: how else save by a disconnection amounting to "inhumanness" can he pursue the enterprise? Or our mor-

---

[5] Even two years later, Nora had not yet consented to read *Ulysses.*

alizing takes the adversary tack and notes the occasions when the disconnection issues in an ugly coarseness of behavior in regard to others. Joyce, who concerned himself with every detail of the promotion of his own books and enlisted everyone he could in the enterprise, when asked to support one of the posthumous novels of Italo Svevo, whose work he admired, not only refuses the request but sneers at the very idea of literary publicity. When his daughter-in-law, Giorgio's first wife, suffers an extreme mental collapse, he writes of the disaster in anger and describes the deranged conduct with contemptuous bitterness.

Eventually, however, we come to feel that no moral judgment can really be to the point of Joyce's state of being in his latter years. And psychology seems as limited in its pertinence as morality. It is inevitable that psychological speculation will be attracted to the often strange and extreme emotional phenomena that the new letters record, especially to what the early ones tell us of the extravagant energy of affective will that was to devolve into the disconnection from the world, the existence in nullity. Neither Joyce's representation of himself as Dedalus, nor Professor Ellmann's detailed account of his youthful temperament, nor yet the two taken together quite prepare us for the intimacy and violence of Joyce's early relation to the world, the urgency with which he sought to requisition the world's goods. And certainly the devolution (if that is the word) from this early egotism of the world to the later egotism of nullity is a biographical event that asks for explanation. But however brilliant and even true may be the insights into the disposition of the internal forces that brought it about, they will fail to do justice to its significance, which is finally not personal but cultural. The process recorded by the letters proposes itself as a paradigm of the 19th-century will *in extremis*. It leads us to reflect less on what transpired in the life of James Joyce than on what could formerly happen and cannot happen again—never in our time will a young man focus this much power of love and hate into so sustained a rage of effectual intention as Joyce was capable of, so ferocious an ambition, so nearly absolute a commitment of himself to himself.

Joyce was of course not exceptional in being a continuator of the titanism of the 19th-century artistic personality. The literary culture of the first quarter of the 20th century is differentiated from that of our own time by nothing so much as the grandiosity, both in purpose and in achievement, of its preeminent figures. In this respect their sense of life is alien from ours and is not uncommonly felt to alienate them from us. In one point of temperament, in the unremitting energy of their inner-direction, they have a closer affinity with their 19th-century predecessors than with their successors. But as compared with Joyce, none of the great modern chieftains of art put himself so directly and, as one might say, so *naively*, in the line of the powerful personalities of the age before his own. None so cherished the purpose of imposing himself upon the world, of being a king and riding in triumph through Persepolis.

If Joyce did indeed derive the impetus to his achievement from his acceptance of the ethos and mythos of the 19th century, a first salient example is his response to an idea that we take to be characteristic of the ideology of the period, the idea of the nation. One of the best-known things about Joyce is his ambivalence toward Ireland, of which the hatred was as relentless as the love was unfailing. With this passionate relationship his lust for preeminence and fame is bound up, and the more so because his erotic life is intricately involved with it. He is twenty-seven and on his first visit to Dublin after his exile and he is writing to Nora, telling her of the part she plays in his inspiration. "My darling," he says, "tonight I was in the Gresham Hotel and was introduced to about twenty people and to all of them the same story was told: that I was going to be the great writer of the future in my country. All the noise and flattery around me hardly moved me. I thought I heard my country calling to me or her eyes were turned toward me expectantly." He goes on to tell Nora that she is more important to him than the world and that everything comes from her. But in his thought of fame he cannot separate her from the nation, the "race": "O take me into your soul of souls and then I will indeed become the poet of my race." And among the things he has loved in her—"the image of the beauty of the world, the mystery and beauty of life itself . . . the images of spiritual purity and pity which I believed in as a boy"—there are "the beauty and doom of the race of whom I am a child." He calls her "my love, my life, my star, my little strange-eyed Ireland!"

And yet, of course, "I loathe Ireland and the Irish. They themselves stare at me in the street though I was born among them. Perhaps they read my hatred in my eyes." The hatred was of the essence of his ambition quite as much as the love. Three years later he is again in Dublin and he writes: "The Abbey Theater will be open and they will give plays of Yeats and Synge. You have a right to be there because you are my bride and I am one of the writers of this generation who are perhaps creating at last a conscience in the soul of this wretched race."

Some considerable part of Joyce's ambition consisted of what the 19th century called aspiration and conceived to be a mode of feeling peculiarly appropriate to generous minds, artists perhaps especially but also soldiers, statesmen, engineers, industrialists. Aspiration was the desire for fame through notable and arduous achievement. The end in view which defined it was the realization of one's own powers. That in order to reach this end one might be involved in competition with others, seeking to surpass and overcome them, was a frequent but accidental circumstance of aspiration which was not thought to qualify its noble disinterestedness.

That this is a reasonable way of looking at the matter is suggested by the astonishing letter the nineteen-year-old Joyce addressed to Ibsen. He makes a full and grandiose communication of his admiration and then goes on to say to the sick old man, "Your work on earth draws to a close and you are near the silence. It is growing dark for you." But there is a comfort that he can offer, the assurance that One—an unnamed but unmistakable One—comes after to carry on the great work. It is in all conscience a crueller letter than the young writer chose to know, yet the competition with the Father, the Old King, is sanctioned not only by tradition but by the very nature of life, and Joyce invests it with an absurd but genuine nobility by which the Master Builder, after a wince or two, might well have been grimly pleased.

But Joyce's competitiveness, which was extreme, was not always, not characteristically, in the grand style; as it showed itself in his relations with his age-mates it was often vindictive and coarse. Through all the early years in Trieste and Rome, Joyce lived in bitter jealous hatred of his former friends and companions in Dublin. He cannot mention them and their little successes without an expression of disgust: "Their writings and their lives nauseate [me] to the point of vomiting." The new letters make clear to how great an extent Joyce in his youth conceived of his art as a weapon to be used in personal antagonism, especially in vengeance. "Give me for Christ' sake a pen and an ink-bottle and some peace of mind and then, by the crucified Jaysus, if I don't sharpen that little pen and dip it into fermented ink and write tiny little sentences about the people who betrayed me send me to hell." The chief object of his bitterness, of course, was Gogarty, from whom, after the quarrel, he would accept no tender of reconciliation. It was his belief that the man who had so terribly offended him sought to make peace out of fear of how he would be delineated—the belief finds expression in the first chapter of *Ulysses:* "He fears the lancet of my art as I fear that of his. Cold steelpen."—and as early as 1905 it was assumed by Joyce's Dublin friends that a great revenge was in train; the form it would take was already known. "[Elwood] says," writes Stanislaus Joyce, "he would not like to be Gogarty when you come to the Tower episode. Thanks be to God he never kicked your arse or anything." Gogarty himself had every expectation that revenge would be duly taken, and Joyce coolly confirmed him in this; he reports that in refusing Gogarty's attempt to renew the friendship, he had said: "I bear you no ill will. I believe you have some points of good nature. You and I of 6 years ago are both dead. But I must write as I have felt!" To which Gogarty replied, "I don't care a damn what you say of me so long as it is literature." [6]

[6] In the event this proved not to be true—Gogarty cared many a damn when *Ulysses* appeared. As well he might, if only because Joyce led all the world to believe forever that he and not Gogarty-Mulligan was the rightful tenant of the tower and that the famous key was his: any statement of the fact of the matter, that the opposite

The unremitting bitterness with which Joyce remembered and commemorated his relation with Gogarty serves to remind us of the great authority that the ideal of male friendship formerly had. In this, as in so many other respects, the 19th century maintained its connection with the courtly cultures of earlier epochs. Out of the dream of the true friend arose the possibility of the false friend, and it is an element of the *Heldenleben,* as the 19th century understood the genre, that the hero is beset by treacherous comrades envious of his powers and eager to subvert them. Had these dwarfish natures been lacking in the actuality of his life, Joyce would have been quick to supply the want. His genius throve upon his paranoia, which was capable of anything—it is quite in his style to say in an early letter to Lady Gregory that the college authorities were determined that he should not study medicine, "wishing I dare say to prevent me from securing any position of ease from which I might speak out my heart." A belief in a hostile environment, in persecution and personal betrayal, was necessary to his mission. But in point of fact the false friends and the malice of their envy were real enough; they were fostered by Dublin life before they were cherished by Joyce as a condition of his art and the testimony of his being a dedicated spirit, singled out. Long before Joyce had anything like a career, his promise of genius was taken for granted by those who knew him, and Stanislaus's diary records the envy with which he was regarded by his contemporaries. In his early days of exile, when his thoughts turned homeward, it was to inquire what these lesser impotent beings said of his courage, his freedom, his unconventional marriage, and, as time passed, his approach to success. Their mischievous impulses in relation to him came fully to light in the strange episode of his friend Cosgrove telling him, falsely and seemingly out of the gratuitous impulse to play Iago to this Othello, that before the elopement Nora had been unfaithful to him, a communication that for a time had all its intended effect of making chaos come again.

The social life of late 19th-century Dublin as Joyce's class situation permitted him to know it was obviously in most respects quite elementary, but it was certainly not wanting in concern with social status, in judging who was "better" and stood higher than whom, and to such questions the young Joyce gave the most solemn attention. It was surely an important circumstance of the last interview with Gogarty that it took place in Gogarty's elaborate house and that the former friend, now set up in

---

was the case, will always be received with surprise and incredulity and soon forgotten. Such is the power of the literary imagination in the service of self-justification. Partisans of simple justice—alas, there are virtually none of Gogarty—may find some encouragement in the display of the actual lease in the tower; that a signboard calls the tower James Joyce's should not dismay them: the rights of the ultimate possession are now absolute.

medical practice, well-to-do and well married, should have invited Joyce
to come with him in his motorcar to have lunch in his country home.
The social advantages that Gogarty had previously enjoyed, perhaps especially his having gone to Oxford, were of the greatest moment to
Joyce, who was at constant pains to enforce the idea that, when it came
to social establishment, Stephen Dedalus, if the truth were seen, was the
superior of anyone.[7] Joyce was in nothing so much a man of the 19th
century as in the sensitivity of his class feelings. No less than Dickens
he was concerned to be a *gentleman* and he was as little shy as Dickens
about using the word, the Victorian force of which maintained itself for
at least two of the Joyces in the face of the family's rapid downward
mobility. In the midst of an expression of disgust with his situation at
Rome, James remarks to Stanislaus, "I feel somehow that I am what
Pappie said I wasn't [,] a gentleman." [8] He was at the time working in a
bank as a correspondence clerk; he lived with his wife and infant son
in a single small room; often his wages did not meet his weekly expenses
and the letters of the period are chiefly to Stanislaus in Trieste, their
whole burden being that money must be sent at once. The conversation
of his fellow clerks, as he describes it, is simian; he has no ordinarily
decent social intercourse with anyone, yet he finds it in his heart to describe his circumstances not as unfit for a human being but as unfit for
a gentleman.

His feeling for the social forms could be strict, often in a genteel,
lower-middle-class way. Although in 1910 black-edged writing paper was
still used by proper people in a period of mourning, the faintly barbaric
custom was not universally observed, but Joyce, at the death of his uncle
John Murray, thought it necessary to his sense of how things should be
done.[9] When he was virtually starving during his first sojourn in Paris,
he regretted that he could not attend the Irish Ball because he had no
dress suit. He is still working as a Berlitz teacher in Trieste and the

---

[7] In the tower scene Mulligan tells Stephen. "You know, Dedalus, you have the real
Oxford manner." And he speculates that this is why Haines, the Englishman who is
staying with them, can't make Stephen out. Haines is rich and himself an Oxford
man and Mulligan twice remarks that he thinks Stephen isn't a gentleman.

[8] The occasion of the judgment was John Joyce's reading *Gas from a Burner*.
Stanislaus seems not to have shared the social feelings of his father and elder brother.
Perhaps it was his puritanical rationalism that led him to adopt a rather plebeian
stance. The youngest surviving Joyce brother, Charles, apparently laid no continuing
claim to being a gentleman; when last we hear of him he is a postal clerk in London.
The idea of social status was part of the fabric of the Joyce family life—it is well
known how preoccupied John Joyce was with the superiority of his own family to
his wife's, which of course had some bearing on James's choice of a wife whose pretensions to breeding were notably less than his own.

[9] Joyce took account in *Ulysses* of his response to the claims of funeral pomps. "He
can't wear them," Mulligan says when his offer of a pair of gray trousers has been
refused by Dedalus because he is in mourning for his mother. "Etiquette is etiquette.
He kills his mother but he can't wear gray trousers."

family in Dublin is on the verge of destitution, but he directs his father to arrange to sit for his portrait. The family crest was his treasured possession.

At the present time, feelings about class in their old form are in at least literary abeyance and it is hard to remember the force they once had and the extent to which they defined the character and aspirations of the artist.[10] In an age when the middle classes seemed to be imposing their stamp upon the world, a young writer was led to set store by what he imagined to be the aristocratic qualities of grace, freedom, and indifference to public opinion, and the aristocratic mode of life seemed the model for what all men's lives should be. It was the rare writer who did not think himself to be "well born" in some sense of the phrase, and if he had any reason to think that he was actually of distinguished blood, he was pretty sure to find the circumstance of value. George Moore said no more than the simple truth when he remarked that "Yeats's belief in his lineal descent from the great Duke of Ormonde was part of his poetic equipment." Writing in admiration of Tolstoy, Joyce associates his genius with his class position and his ability to remember "the Christian name of his great-great-grandfather." And the young man who felt himself excluded from the patrician literary circle of Dublin and expressed his resentment in rude mockery of its members shared Yeats's dream of the culture—the word is Joyce's own—of the great houses and the ancient families. Writing to Nora, who had been a chambermaid in a Dublin hotel when he had first met her and whose lack of grammar he was not above mocking to his brother, he explains to her the inspiration of *Chamber Music:* "You were not in a sense the girl for whom I had dreamed and written the verses you now find so enchanting. She was perhaps (as I saw her in my imagination) a girl fashioned into a curious grave beauty by the culture of generations before her, the woman for whom I wrote poems like 'Gentle Lady' or 'Thou leanest to the shell of night.'" He goes on, surely in entire sincerity: "But then I saw that the beauty of your soul outshone that of my verses. There was something in you higher than anything I had put into them. And so for this reason the book of verses is for you. It holds the desire of my youth, and you, darling, were the fulfillment of that desire." Yet the discrepancy between the robust, barely literate chambermaid who had to be told not to copy her love-letters out of a letter-book and the girl fashioned into a curious grave beauty by her lineage was often a pain to Joyce, and much as he needed Nora's earthy strength, he flinched at the rudeness—so he called it—that

---

[10] A few years ago I had occasion to remark in an essay that my students, no matter what their social origins, were not prevented by Yeats's snobbery from responding to his poetry. One reviewer took me sternly to task for obscuring the transcendent achievement of the great poet by speaking of him as a snob. What made especially interesting the view of life and letters implied by the rebuke was that the reviewer was Leon Edel, the biographer of Henry James.

went with it. It was certain that he was a gentleman, but whatever else
Nora was, she was, alas, no lady.

That Joyce's preoccupation with his social status should go along with
an avowed interest in subverting the society in which he held his valued
rank does not make a contradiction. It was quite common in the 19th
century for gifted men to find sanction for their subversive intentions
toward society in such aristocracy or gentility as they could claim.[11] But
that Joyce should ever have been political at all will for most of his
readers make an occasion for surprise. For a few years of his young manhood, between the ages of twenty-two and twenty-five, Joyce called himself a socialist. Again and again in his letters to Stanislaus he insists on
the importance to the artist of a radical political position: "I believe that
Ibsen and Hauptmann separate from the herd of writers because of their
political aptitude—eh?" "It is a mistake for you to imagine that my
political opinions are those of a universal lover: but they are those of a
socialistic artist." He scolds Stanislaus for not sharing his "detestation
of the stupid, dishonest, tyrannical and cowardly burgher class." He explains the opposition of the Church to "the quite unheretical theory of
socialism" as being an expression of the belief that a socialist government
would expropriate ecclesiastical "landed estates . . . and invested mon-
eys." His cogent objection to the Irish nationalist movement is that it
takes no account of economic realities and is not aware that "if the Irish
question exists, it exists for the Irish proletariat chiefly." And it is a
further black mark against Gogarty that his political views exclude economic considerations. "Gogarty would jump into the Liffey to save a
man's life but he seems to have little hesitation in condemning generations to servitude." [12]
     Joyce never committed himself to political action or association, and
although he had a knowledgeable interest in the Italian radical parties,
he seems never to have put himself to the study of socialist theory; the
only reference to Karl Marx occurs in the course of an excited and rather
confused account of the apocalyptic Jewish imagination derived from
Ferrero's *Young Europe*. By 1907 his socialism had evaporated, leaving as
its only trace the sweet disposition of Leopold Bloom's mind to imagine
the possibility of rational and benevolent social behavior and the broth-
erhood of man. This, however, is a residue of some importance in the
history of literature: it makes *Ulysses* unique among modern classics for
its sympathy with progressive social ideas.
     In one of his early poems Yeats speaks of the places where men meet
"to talk of love and politics." To us at our remove in time, the conjunction of the two topics of conversation seems quaint, for of course by love

[11] This was especially true of the anarchists in Russia, France, and Italy.
[12] Joyce's disgust with Gogarty on political grounds was made the more intense by
Gogarty's anti-Semitism.

Yeats did not mean the rather touching interfusion of *eros* and *agape* that young people have lately come to use as a ground of social and political dissidence: he meant a love much more personal and egotistic, that ultimate relation between a man and a woman the conception of which had descended from courtly love, the "gay science" of the late Middle Ages, to become one of the powerful myths of the 19th century. Its old force has greatly diminished, perhaps to the point of extinction. No matter how gravely and idealistically we may use our contemporary names for the relation between a man and a woman, "sex" and "marriage," and even the phrase that is a vestige of the old name, "in love with," do not suggest, as "love" did for an age in whose sensibility *Tristan and Isolde* occupied a central position, the idea of life realized and transfigured by the erotic connection, fulfilled by its beauty, sustained by the energy and fidelity that constituted its ethos.[13] In the 19th century, politics was a new activity of free spirits and it naturally found affinity with a conception of love that made large promises of perceptivity, liberty, and happiness. Love was understood to be art's true source and best subject, and those who lived for love and art did harm to no one, lived the right life of humanity: so Tosca in a passion that reaches B-flat informs the tyrant Scarpia. The operatic example is much in point, for opera was the genre in which love and political virtue joined hands to make a lyric affirmation of life. The contemptuous indifference in which opera is held by our intellectual culture is not qualified by recognition of its political tendency. For Joyce, as everyone knows, opera was a passion. With a most engaging simplicity he gave the genre the response it asked for; he found it, as people used to say, ravishing. He would have been astonished and dismayed by the contemporary snootiness to Puccini; he held *Madame Butterfly* to be a work of transcendent beauty and power, most especially the aria *"Un bel di"* which at one period seems to have woven itself into the very fabric of his emotional life; when Butterfly sang the "romance of her hope" of what would come to her over the sea, his soul (as he wrote bitterly to Nora, who was not similarly moved) "sway[ed] with languor and longing": in the face of the harshness of circumstance, life is affirmed in erotic ecstasy, as when, in *A Portrait of the Artist,* Stephen has sight of the girl on the strand, gazing out to sea. For Joyce, as still for many men of the time in which he was young, human existence was justified by the rapture—lost archaic word!—of love.

Perhaps nothing in Joyce's life is more poignant and more indicative of the extent to which his imagination was shaped by the mythos of his time than the episode, on the threshold of his middle age, in which the famous vision of the lovely girl standing with high-kilted skirts at the water's edge, the most grandiose of the epiphanies, seemed to have pre-

[13] For an account of what *Tristan and Isolde* meant to the epoch, see Elliot Zuckermann's admirable *The First Hundred Years of Wagner's Tristan*, Columbia University Press, 1964.

sented itself as an attainable actuality. Martha Fleischmann was a young woman, seemingly Jewish, though not so in fact, beautiful, provocative but apparently not disposed to go beyond elaborate flirtation, whom Joyce came to know in Zurich in the autumn of 1918. As Martha recalled their meeting nearly a quarter of a century later, the scene stands all ready for the librettist. She was coming home "one evening at dusk" when a passerby stopped and looked at her "with an expression of such wonder on his face that she hesitated for just a moment before entering the house." The stranger spoke, explaining his astonishment by saying that she reminded him of a girl he had once seen "standing on the beach of his home country." [14] Martha's erotic temperament was ambiguous to a degree. She had a devoted "guardian," as she called him, and he expressed jealousy of her relation with Joyce, but there is some question as to whether her connection with this man was sexual in any ordinary sense of the word. On one occasion Joyce addressed her as "Nausikaa," signing himself "Odysseus," [15] and it would seem that the Gerty Mac-Dowell of the "Nausikaa" episode of *Ulysses* commemorates her genteel narcissism and sentimentality. Joyce's own erotic disposition at this time was scarcely of a more direct kind. His lust, like Mr. Bloom's, was chiefly of the eye and the mind. What seems to have been the climactic assignation of these two fantasts of love took place in Frank Budgen's studio on February 2, which was Joyce's birthday and the feast of Candlemas, and Joyce borrowed from a Jewish friend a *menorah* so that he might gaze on Martha's beauty by candlelight, perhaps the sole intention of the meeting.[16] With the passage of years the exquisite virgin, *La Princesse lointaine,* came to be represented in the great "Nausikaa" episode as nothing more than the sad, silly figment of ladies' magazines, and the dream of love-and-beauty as an occasion of masturbation. But at the

---

[14] The quoted passages are from Professor Straumann's account of his interview with Martha when, in Zurich in 1941, she called to inquire about selling the four letters and the postcard that Joyce had written to her. Professor Straumann did not make the purchase on that occasion, but he did so at a later time, in 1943, when, Martha being ill, her affairs were in the charge of her sister—at least he bought the letters; the postcard had vanished. Professor Straumann's account of the relationship of Martha and Joyce appears as a preface to the letters as given in Volume II, pp. 426–436; it is less full and circumstantial than Professor Ellmann's earlier account in his biography.

[15] The salutation and the subscription were, Professor Straumann says, the whole message of the lost postcard.

[16] Candlemas commemorates the purification of the Virgin Mary and the presentation of Christ in the Temple. "The blessing of candles is now the distinctive rite of this day. . . . Beeswax candles, which are blessed, distributed, and lit whilst the Nunc Dimittis is sung, are carried in a procession commemorating the entrance of Christ, the 'True Light (cf. Jn. 1.9) into the Temple."—*The Oxford Dictionary of the Christian Church.* In his second letter to Martha, remarking on his impression that she was a Jewess, Joyce says, "If I am wrong, you must not be offended. Jesus Christ put on his human body: in the womb of a Jewish woman."

time his feelings for Martha seemed to Joyce to challenge comparison with Dante's for Beatrice and Shakespeare's for the Dark Lady; at least he meant them to. "And through the night of the bitterness of my soul," he wrote in the last of his letters to Martha, "the kisses of your lips fell on my heart, soft as rosepetals gentle as dew," and concludes, "O rosa mistica [*sic*], ora pro me."

One of the four letters is mutilated—we are told that Martha "tore off the lower right-hand edge of the second sheet . . . because it contained what she considered an indelicate expression." The judgment on the offending word or phrase cannot be set aside out of hand as one of Martha's neurotic gentilities. The chances are that Joyce did actually write an indelicacy, even an obscenity, for his concern that the erotic object and situation be of an extreme refinement and beauty went together with a no less exigent desire for all that is commonly thought to sully, besmirch, and degrade the erotic activity, and he derived a special pleasure from expressing this desire in writing.

The dialectic between the essential innocence and the essential shamefulness of the sexual act has in our time lost much of its old force, at least overtly. If nowadays we obey the command of Blake's Los to "Consider Sexual Organization," it does not seem naturally to follow, as the demiurge thought it would, that we "hide . . . in the dust" for shame. Crazy Jane's observation that love has pitched his mansion in the place of excrement is received as an interesting reminder of the actual state of affairs rather than as the expression of a distressing (or exciting) thought in the forefront of consciousness. The words of Yeats's poem echo those of another divine utterance in *Jerusalem:* "For I will make their places of love and joy excrementitious," but the circumstance as Yeats refers to it is not conceived to be a curse: we understand Yeats to be remarking on an anomaly that makes human existence more complex and difficult than his long celebration of the *Rosa Mystica* would suggest, or more "ironic," or more "tragic," but for that reason more substantive and the more interesting. His sense of the shameful arrangements of the erotic life stands midway between the neutralizing view of them that our contemporary educated consciousness seems determined to take and the eager response to them made by Joyce, for whom shame was a chief condition of sexual fulfilment.

In the course of the two visits he made to Ireland in 1909, Joyce in his letters to Nora ran through the whole gamut of his erotic emotions and in full voice. Within a week of his first arrival in Dublin, Cosgrove imparted the news of Nora's double dealing in the betrothal time, and although the false friend spoke only of kisses, Joyce of course imagined more and questioned whether Nora had actually come to him a virgin —"I remember that there was very little blood that night. . . ."—and whether Giorgio is in truth his son. He is shattered by the dreadful revelation—"I shall cry for days"—but a fortnight has not passed before he can report blandly that everything has been cleared up by Byrne's having said that Cosgrove's tale is "all a 'blasted lie' "; and after having called himself a "worthless fellow," he vows to be "Worthy of your love, dearest," and goes on to speak of a shipment of cocoa he has sent, that same cocoa that he later urges Nora to drink a good deal of so that she will increase the size of "certain parts" of her body, pleasing him by becoming more truly womanly. His marital resentments are bitter and explicit: Nora, whose great fault is her rudeness, had called him an imbecile, had disagreed with his expressed opinion that priests are disgusting, had been indifferent to *"Un bel di"*; his apologies, when his recriminations have proved offensive, are abject. He is much given to expressions of tender and poetic regard and is engagingly proud of the courtly ingenuity of a gift of jewelry he has designed and had executed, a necklace of gold links, five cubes of old ivory and an ivory plaque bearing in ancient lettering words from one of his poems, which is to symbolize the lovers' years together and their sadness and suffering when they are divided; his Christmas present is *Chamber Music* copied out in his own hand on parchment, bound with his family crest, on the cover the lovers' interlaced initials. But his lively imagination of the elegances of love goes along with fantasies and solicitations that, as he says, make him the object of his own disgust and, he insists on supposing, of Nora's.

Professor Ellmann has not found it possible to carry out his intention of publishing in its entirety the group of obscene love-letters from Dublin preserved in the Cornell Library. What he is able to publish does indeed, as he says, suggest the tenor of these extraordinary documents (the adjective is Joyce's) but not the force and the strange dignity that they seemed to me to have when I read them at Cornell some years ago. It may be, of course, that my memory plays me false, but I recall the letters read in the completeness of the holograph as making the effect of having been written under a more driving compulsion, a more exigent possession, than appears in the curtailed printed version. Perhaps it was the holograph itself that contributed to the impressiveness, enforcing the situation in something like the awesomeness that Joyce himself felt it to have: the man who may well be the greatest literary genius of his age submits to the necessity of taking in hand his sacred cold steel pen and with it to sully sheet after virgin sheet of paper with the filthy words that express all that he feels in the way of delight at the dirtiness of his exalted nature. The words themselves have for him a terrifying potency. One of his letters has induced Nora in her reply to use what he can refer to in no other way than as "a certain word." The sight of it, he says, excites him terribly—"There is something obscene and lecherous in the very look of the letters. The sound of it too is like the act itself, brief, brutal, irresistible and devilish."

His longed-for perversities and depravities—we had best call them that without permissive apologies, since he thought of them so and we ought not deny the ground of his pleasure—were not of an especially esoteric kind. He expresses the wish to be flogged and not merely in show but fiercely, to the end of his feeling real pain; he blames himself for writing "filth" and instructs Nora, if she is insulted by it, to bring him to his senses "with the lash, as you have done before." Nora is an "angel" and a "saint" who guides him to his great destiny, and he longs to "nestle" in her womb, and he seeks to "degrade" and "deprave" her, he wants her to be insolent and cruel and obscene. Perhaps the controlling and to him most puzzling and most significant component of his polymorphous perversity is his delight in the excrementitiousness of the places of love and joy, what he called his "wild beast-like craving . . . for every secret and shameful part" of his wife's body, "for every odor and act of it." "Are you offended because I said I loved to look at the brown stain that comes behind on your girlish white drawers? I suppose you think me a filthy wretch."

No one, I think, will be so armored in objectivity as not to be taken aback by the letters. But their shocking interest fades as we become habituated to them, or to the idea of them. In the way of all drastic personal facts, especially in our time, they cease to be dismaying or amazing soon after they are brought into the light of common day and permitted to assume their institutional status—one might say their prestige—as biographical data. What does not fade, however, is the interest of the literary use to which Joyce put the erotic tendencies that the letters disclose and indulge.

To a reader of *Ulysses* nothing in the substance of the letters comes as a surprise. All the fantasies are familiar to us through our having made acquaintance with them in the mind of Leopold Bloom. But what exists in the mind of Mr. Bloom is of a quite different import from the apparently identical thing as it exists in the mind of James Joyce or might exist in the mind of his surrogate Stephen Dedalus. The reader of the letters will not fail to conclude that it required a considerable courage for Joyce to write them. His doing so went against the grain of a decisive and cherished part of his nature, his austere, almost priestly propriety. "As you know, dearest," he writes in one of the letters, "I never use obscene phrases in speaking. You have never heard me, have you, utter an unfit word before others. When men tell in my presence here filthy or lecherous stories I hardly smile." Yet he put on paper and sent through the mail what was not to be countenanced and, although he urged Nora to be watchful in guarding the secrecy of the letters, since he did not destroy them when he might have done so, he must be thought to have wished that they be preserved. One thing, however, he would not—could not—do: attribute the fantasies of the letters to the mind of Stephen Dedalus.

By assigning them to Mr. Bloom, he of course quite changes their character. As elements of Mr. Bloom's psyche, they become comic, which is to say morally neutral. Our laughter, which is gentle, cognizant, forgiving, affectionate, has the effect of firmly distancing them and at the same time of bringing them within the circle of innocence and acceptability. We understand that nothing very terrible is here, nothing awesome, or devilish, or wild-beast-like—only what we call, with a relishing, domesticating chuckle, *human.* And the chuckle comes the more easily because we recognize in Mr. Bloom, as we are intended to, the essential innocence of the child; his polymorphous perversity is appropriate to his infantile state. This innocence, it would appear, is part of Joyce's conception of Jews in general, who, he seems to have felt, through some natural grace were exempt from the complexities of the moral life as it was sustained by Christians. Writing to Stanislaus of his son having been born early, with nothing prepared, he says, "However, our landlady is a Jewess and gave us everything we wanted." The implication is that a Christian might or might not have provided the necessary things; Christian kindness would result from the making of a choice between doing the good deed and not doing it, and would therefore, by the Aristotelian definition, be moral; but a Jewish good deed was a matter of instinct, natural rather than moral. It is in natural goodness rather than in morality that Mr. Bloom has his being, and in the ambience of his mind the perverse fantasies have nothing of the fearsome significance they had for Joyce when he entertained them.

It is possible to say that the translation of the fantasies as they existed in the mind of James Joyce, and might have existed in the mind of Stephen Dedalus, into what they become in the mind of Leopold Bloom is a derogation of Joyce's courage as an artist. A Stephen Dedalus whose rigorous moral being is assailed and torn by sinful desires is readily received as a heroic figure so long as the desires can be supposed sinful in a received way. But a polymorphous-perverse hero would make a difficulty, would be thought a contradiction in terms. For Joyce the Aristotelian categories of tragedy and comedy, the one showing men as "better," i.e., more dignified, than they really are, the other showing men as "worse," i.e., more ignoble, than they really are, had an authority that, at the time of *Ulysses,* was not to be controverted.

It is also possible to say that Joyce's refusal to assign the perverse fantasies to Stephen is a derogation of personal courage. A polymorphous-perverse Leopold Bloom stands as testimony to his author's astonishing powers of imagination, of sympathetic insight into the secret places of nature at the furthest remove from his own. But a polymorphous-perverse Stephen Dedalus must advertise the polymorphous perversity of the author whose fictive surrogate he is inevitably understood to be. To this personal disclosure Joyce could not consent.

His fictional disposition of the polymorphous perversity must make a salient question in any attempt to understand the mind of James Joyce. What I have called—with, I should make plain, no pejorative force— a derogation of courage is an answer that has a kind of provisional cogency. But a comment on the obscene letters made by Professor Ellmann in his Introduction seems to me to initiate an explanation that goes deeper. Professor Ellmann says of the letters that they have an "ulterior purpose," that Joyce, in writing them, had an intention beyond immediate sexual gratification. One thing he intended was "to anatomize and reconstitute and crystallize the emotion of love." And, Professor Ellmann says, "he goes further still; like Richard Rowan in *Exiles*, he wishes to possess his wife's soul, and have her possess his, in nakedness. To know someone else in love and hate, beyond vanity and remorse, *beyond human possibility almost* [my italics], is his extravagant desire."

If this is so, as I think it is, it brings the obscene letters into accord with what I have proposed as the controlling tendency of Joyce's genius —to move through the fullest realization of the human, the all-too-human, to that which transcends and denies the human. It was a progress he was committed to make, yet he made it with some degree of reluctance. Had the obscene fantasies been assigned to Stephen Dedalus, they would have implied the import that Professor Ellmann supposes they had for Joyce himself. But Joyce, we may believe, did not want, not yet, so Hyperborean a hero as he then would have had. The ethos and mythos of the 19th century could still command from him some degree of assent. The merely human still engaged him, he was not wholly ready to go beyond it. The fair courts of life still beckoned invitation and seemed to await his entrance. He was to conclude that their walls and gates enclosed nothing. His genius is defined by his having concluded this rather than taking it for granted, as many of the generation that came after him have found it possible to do.

The Bent Knife Blade:
Joyce in the 1960's

by Robert Martin Adams

The critic who undertakes to reexamine and revaluate James Joyce in the light of the modern tradition obviously implies that he has a pretty precise sense of that tradition, of what the *Zeitgeist* is and where it's headed; my first step will have to be a vigorous disclaimer on that score. Professors of literature don't direct the *Zeitgeist* and have no special claim to an insider's understanding of it—or if some do, I'm not one of them. Yet it is scarcely possible for even a backward academic to avoid recognizing that Joyce in the sixties is not by any means the same force he was in the twenties. His books have changed, for one thing, by standing still in the stream of time; they have changed in the mere process of becoming classics, and so a part of the recognized cultural atmosphere; they have changed as a result of changes in our cultural and intellectual weather. All this quite apart from the more or less conscious changes brought about by exegetes and commentators. Defining a few of these gradual changes, which have crept over Joyce and us, may accentuate new aspects of his relevance, and irrelevance.

At least in America, we are no longer obliged to defend Joyce's morals. There is something of a relief in this development, for moral controversy about a work of art usually resolves itself into repetition and denial of the axiom that the artist can treat any subject he wants; and Joyce's subject is not exactly the most edifying thing about him. Bloom on his jakes, Stephen in the whorehouse, and Molly Bloom in bed—these are elements which we find it a good deal easier to digest than the genteel tradition possibly could. We have digested them, without ill effects of any obvious sort; and so, rather gratified by our exercise of broadmindedness, we may well have carried the hygienic view of Joyce further than the facts will sustain it. A few recent apologists have gone far toward maintaining that Joyce was a kind of Irish Homer Lane—morally and socially therapeutic, intellectually farsighted as well as consistent, a kind of moral surgeon plying his steely art upon the conscience of the western world. The facts as

"The Bent Knife Blade: Joyce in the 1960's," by Robert Martin Adams. Reprinted from *Partisan Review* (Fall 1962), pp. 507–18, by permission of the publisher and the author. Copyright © 1962 by *Partisan Review*.

we are coming to see them appear rather more complex and less dramatic. Like Swift, Joyce was a prurient author, as a result of both his temperament and his background. Dirty words and fecal images had a powerful inflammatory influence on his mind; he didn't generally use them (any more than Swift did) for therapeutic or cathartic effect. (Whether they can possibly have such an effect, I leave to the sexologists.) With his vigorous sense of obscenity and filth he combined a characteristically late-nineteenth-century worship of woman as the great redemptive force of modern life. Joyce found in sex a fearful and rapturous experience, the more dramatic because of all the taboos and cosmic rewards he grafted onto it. This combination of extreme attitudes on the subject of sex seems to me rather remote from any attitudes I recognize as widespread in the educated sixties. It is remote from healthy-minded "realism," from romantic promiscuity, or from the impersonal, empty mechanism which is the characteristic form of most modern literary sex. Joyce found in woman a doorway to heaven and/or hell; I think historical distance is making it easier to understand this view and less necessary to react for or against it.

Joyce's view of sex—no longer a revelation from Erebus or Olympus—is starting to be recognizable as a set of dramatic properties supplied by his social circumstances and personal temperament; much the same thing can be said of his politics, his "philosophy," his esthetics. I don't mean to sound condescending or triumphant here—as if at last, after all these years, we were starting to see around old Joyce. I mean only that, having been distracted all too long by questions about whether Joyce is bad or good for the young, or for Ireland, for the recognition of the truth, or the freedom of the psyche, we are finally coming to judge him as an artist, whose work is a structure of impressions. In building that structure, he came about as close to producing a durable scheme of philosophically impregnable positions as artists usually do. As a matter of fact, he had scruples all his life (honorable but probably quite unnecessary scruples) about his own power to create impressions, and thought himself a forger and a fraud precisely by virtue of his art. That he was a verbal prestidigitator is not the final truth about Joyce, nor is it even true of him in the same degree as of Eliot—whose flats and contrivances I take to be, by now, almost scandalously visible. But it is a real and inevitable part of the Joyce of the sixties, that the things he was able to hang people up on in the twenties—like the theory of epiphany, the bit about Dedalus the maze-maker, and the great Earth-mother image—are starting to look a little threadbare. This fact, which inevitably involves loss as well as gain, still frees us to recognize some interesting things about his art.

Though it is an important element in the working of Joyce's books and necessarily absorbs a good deal of the exegete's energy, the sort of intellectual and mythical scaffolding that he erected has remained largely idiosyncratic. During the twenties the use of classical myth as a principle of structure and order seemed an outstanding innovation of *Ulysses*; so no doubt it was, but this is not the feature which subsequent novelists have seen fit to use, any more than they have been inspired by the Viconian cycles of *Finnegans Wake*. The fact is that for a work of anything less than epic proportions, the mythical parallel is better used as adornment, as allusion, as passing commentary, than as structural principle. Joyce found it particularly handy as a groundwork for verbal and thematic embroidery; but Joyce's habit of mind was peculiar, indeed unique, in its passion for involuted decoration. He may well have inherited this trait, as he liked to think, from progenitors who had produced the Book of Kells; one may also feel that his intricate arabesques serve as a gigantic, complicated trap in which to involve and defeat the reader's conscious mind, in preparation for an appeal to deeper and darker levels of response. But neither rationale is capable of very general application. Whatever its function, whatever its origins, the crustacean, exoskeletal quality of Joyce's patterning has not been accepted as viable by other novelists, and seems likely to remain a personal oddity.

Much more interesting to people who are not professional Joyceans is Joyce's use of language. Here one has a considerable span of performance to deal with, from the stripped and polished subtleties of *Dubliners* to the dark oddities of *Finnegans Wake*. The first thing to say is that Joyce helped clean English fiction of its thick crust of nineteenth-century gingerbread, and made it impossible to write as badly as was commonplace before him. Of course many others took part with him in this cleaning of the stables, and it is impossible to sort out his specific contribution. But anyone who has prowled the jungle of late-nineteenth-century fiction, fiction written not by abysmal incompetents but by intelligent and often perceptive men, will testify to the stifling quality of the conventions which Joyce and his contemporaries inherited. Puffy and overstuffed language, a flat style, and a general disdain of literary effects—from Gissing to Galsworthy, and not excluding Hardy, these qualities were the rule. Now that the conventions are safely surmounted, it is easy to underestimate the considerable energy which was necessary to overcome them. But this is still only a historical reason for remembering Joyce, and he has better claims on our attention.

When one says that Joyce enriched the speech of English fiction, there is a natural tendency to think of the various taboos he violated, the various censorships he knocked down. The matter is more considerable than this. One has only to look at the first chapter of *Ulysses,* less than twenty pages of prose, to sense the dramatic richness, flexibility, and complexity of the language. The scene moves with elegance and under its own power; the hand of the novelist does not have to tug it along. Symbols are pervasive, vivid yet undemanding. The tonality of the chapter is sunlit, yet under the surface one senses the sulky, resentful power of Stephen's mind, cuddling its enmity. A complex of energies is effortlessly set moving in these pages; the economy of means and richness of achievement mark a genuine imaginative achievement. In the diction of a passage like this, Joyce worked to standards of subtlety, economy, and exactness by which English novels will be measured for years to come; his ability to do so was quite independent of technical innovations—stream of consciousness, mythic parallels, multilingual puns, and so forth.

As it was not Joyce's invention, the "stream-of-consciousness" device which he did so much to popularize can not be laid at his personal doorstep. Historically viewed, it actually does not seem to have been any one individual's contribution, and literary historians of the future will no doubt see it as simply one episode in a process by which the action of the modern novel was interiorized, its definition of reality changed from social to psychological. Seen simply as a shift in representational conventions, it is less than startling. Experience is caught at an earlier and less complete stage of digestion, but the artifice of expressing it is just as apparent as in the fully formed, grammatically articulated sentences of Jane Austen and Walter Scott. If the novelist had to go into the pre-articulate stages of his characters' existence, and stay there permanently, it is not clear that the device would be justified; used intermittently, it adds extraordinary mobility to the novelist's repertoire of effects, enabling him to move from inner fantasy to outward reality and back again, with a minimum of explanation. What he finds under the surface, too, can be expressed poetically without the implication that his character is a frightfully arty chap. A character like John Updike's Rabbit Angstrom displays, alongside an appallingly nebulous blank of mind and almost no verbal subtlety, an intricate gift of feeling conveyed in complex poetic metaphors. His brains are buried some where in his nerves, deeper than words, deeper even than neuroses, in his perceptions themselves; and I think it was Joyce, as much as anyone, who encouraged Updike to see them there. Flaubert said with a sneer that the debris of a poet is to be found in the corner of every notary's heart; Joyce makes good the observation without the sneer.

Of the prose of *Finnegans Wake* it is less easy to speak. If it was an experiment, it was given the most splendid and exhaustive tryout of any on record, and has left a whole generation of writers with no experiments to make which don't look puny by comparison. But the word "experiment" represents a weak evasion here; *Finnegans Wake* is a rigorously rational adaptation of language to the expression of the irrational. There is nothing tentative about it, and one has no sense that Joyce is trying to see what can be done with a technique. Joyce saw the history of a culture and a personality under the image of an immense litter-pile, its clutter arranged in vague layers and suggesting dim but complicated patterns. The manner of *Finnegans Wake* is a direct outcome of a mode of vision. Considered as a complete style of writing (not just a ragbag of occasional tricks), this manner is of relatively slight value independent of the insight it implies. The chief writers who seem inclined to share Joyce's point of view, nowadays, are the absurd-theatre fellows, who are barred from using *Finnegans Wake* prose by their medium. One wouldn't anticipate that a technique so exacting could supplant the conventional English of prose fiction (which is rather more a business these days than an art form), and so it hasn't. But the exploration of *Finnegans Wake* by a gallant band of enthusiasts continues with unslackened vigor, even though the book's broader influence remains mostly peripheral. If Joyce's last novel is to make its way, there seems no doubt now that it will have to do so as a unit—linguistic oddities, world view, structural principles, and all. As I shall argue presently, there are some signs that it may do just that; but at the moment, society is moving up on the book, not vice versa.

The Joyce we have had up to now was Daedalian—that is, he exercised over many minds the authority of a puzzle, which has to be solved on its own given terms and which promises, tacitly but nonetheless distinctly, that it has a final solution. It is truly amazing how many solutions, of remarkably different sorts, have been found for Joyce's remarkably various problems; it is also amazing how widely they are distributed across the surface of Joyce's work. Henry James' criticism centers perceptibly around the old *Turn of the Screw* problem, with secondary clusters around *The Ambassadors* and *The Portrait of a Lady;* Conrad's critics show a notable affinity for *Heart of Darkness* and *Lord Jim.* But of Joyce's major (and even minor) work, only *Exiles* has failed to attract a vigorous swatch of detailed exegesis. Whatever reservations one has about its solidity, almost all of this work has been resourceful, inventive, flexible, learned, and practically indefatigable. Outside the great epic poets, I don't suppose any author (much less any novelist) has accumulated so much exegesis; not even the epic poets accumulated their masses of commentary in less than half a century. Joyce, in short, has had an unprecedented amount of critical and biographical attention. Now, of course, nobody can tell with complete assurance that these researches will not someday yield the complete coherent pattern of symbolic relationships which their creators tacitly or explicitly envisage. (A few of the more visionary have announced it as a fact—every element in Joyce's entire canon is part of a single controlled composition; but most seem to hold it out as a hope or an ideal for criticism to work toward.) But by this time, I think we are in a position to say that the pattern very probably won't work out. Joyce is not, like Dante, a rigorous and utterly consistent systematizer. The more rigorously you read him, the more loose ends you uncover. The more intricately you explain one set of details, the less chance there is that this explanation can be made to dovetail with anything else in the book or the career. The more ingenious your explanations, the more explanation they seem to need themselves. At the moment, we are under no immediate compulsion to give up on the big-pervasive-pattern presumption—but it seems like a terribly apt time to start looking for alternatives. The reason is not simply that evidence on hand fails to establish the existence of such a pattern; it is that almost all the new evidence which keeps turning up works directly against it. There comes a time in the history of certain projects when someone has to say "We're never going to get a concert violin out of this thing, no matter *how many* toothpicks we use in it."

What, then, is the shape of the new Joyce? I think we must look for him in the figure of a visionary vulgarist, a man whose extraordinary view of life grew out of a defeat for, and disillusion with, the conscious, rational mind. The narrow young man whom Joyce calls Stephen Dedalus exemplifies one terminus of the conscious mind, when he tells prudent, flabbergasted Bloom that "Ireland must be important because it belongs to me." The sort of impressionism he has learned from Walter Pater (see the famous conclusion to *The Renaissance*) culminates in this near-solipsism. On another level, and within the same book, the long dry catechism of "Ithaca" contracts itself into that famous round black dot (which the Random House edition shamefully omits), and disappears into permanent darkness. Having tied itself in tighter and tighter knots throughout the book, rationality blacks out altogether, and the book culminates, not with the achievement of a symbolic pattern, but with the absorption of all thought in the endless spinning motion of the blindly appetitive lifeforce. Common as dirt, majestic, luminous, and all-embracing, the sensual life of Molly Bloom is, imaginatively, the beginning and end of us all. From the dark of "Penelope," Joyce passed to the deeper darkness of *Finnegans Wake,* and found there such rewards as, after rationality is defeated, remain to a great artist—a religion of man which he could scarcely formulate without deriding it; occult and pantheist notions which he took only half-seriously; a kind of know-nothing indifference to all ideas and causes, an indifference which he associated with Mr. Dooley; an immense and intricate structure of history which he borrowed from Vico as a frame to hang his artistic patterns on; language-games, macaronic puns, and lists. These materials are contemptible neither in themselves nor as the elements of great art (artists are traditionally, and properly, indifferent to the inherent nobility, if any, of their materials); but their very nature is evidence of the fact that Joyce in the last years of his life surrendered structural control over his materials to certain sorts of accident. There are stories from the biography which illustrate this trend. For instance, Samuel Beckett reports that one day when Joyce was dictating *Finnegans Wake* to him, they were interrupted by a knock at the door. Joyce said "Come in," Beckett incorporated the phrase in the manuscript, and there Joyce, despite the protests of his amanuensis, insisted on keeping it. Even more telling evidence of accident in the composition of *Finnegans Wake* is found in the collection of manuscripts at the University of Buffalo. Among them are various worksheets made by Joyce and his helpers in preparation for the version of *Finnegans Wake*

which was published as "Work in Progress." A few of these papers have
been edited under the title of *Scribbledehobble*. But this edition was
savaged because the unhappy editor, caught between Joyce's deliberate,
significant distortions and those due to his bad handwriting, was altogether without a clear rule for his text. No doubt he copied blindly at
best, inaccurately at worst. Yet there is every reason to believe that he was
better equipped for deciphering the scrawls in front of him than Joyce,
whose eyes were very bad, or many of Joyce's amanuenses, for whom English was not a native language. And the *Scribbledehobble* manuscripts
are at least all by Joyce. There are other worksheets in the collection, by
the amanuenses, which are disfigured by errors of primitive simplicity
and staggering grossness. The problem isn't that the manuscript is illegi-
ble; more often than not, one knows what the writer it trying to say, but
is appalled by inaccuracies which have not the slightest claim to significance. They are the obvious result of someone listening with a French ear
to an Irish mumble on an incomprehensibly private topic and trying to
write down the result. There is no evidence that anyone, at any stage of
the proceedings, tried to straighten out any of this confusion; or if Joyce
himself tried to do so, it seems inevitable that thousands of adventitious
errors got past him. There are plenty of them in *Ulysses* (errors of tran-
scription, errors of usage, errors of inconsistency and unintentional in-
accuracy), where for the most part Joyce had the conventions of English
speech and spelling to help him; whether one thinks they matter or not
—whether, in fact, they are all discoverable or not—there are unquestion-
ably even more in *Finnegans Wake*. And it is part of the argument for a
"bent" Joyce that in the last part of his life he was writing in such a way
that one cannot distinguish significant and purposeful from insignificant
and accidental elements of his writing.

His nickname in youth, bestowed by Gogarty, was "Kinch the knife-
blade"; and he pursued the metaphor with relish, describing his brother
Stanislaus and various other acolytes on whom he used to sharpen his
mind as his "whetstones." That the mind so assiduously sharpened
buckled in mid-career, and surrendered to accident, to whim, or to circumstance a great part of its control over its own materials may imply a
sort of defeat on Joyce's part. This isn't a point to be lightly conceded,
and there's not much doubt that Joyce would deserve well of any critic
who showed us a feasible way around it. At the moment, one would have
to describe informed opinion as regretfully sceptical that such a way will
ever appear.

Yet how much occasion for regret do we (as readers of the 1960's) really
have? Joyce was not a consistent, inclusive, or coherent philosopher, any
more than he possessed the power of transmuting metals; but he would
not be a man of our times if he had these powers, or believed that he did.
The medieval synthesis, out of which Dante wrote so firm and controlled
a world-poem, has long since been shattered; there is even doubt now

that it was ever as firm as it has since seemed to the eye of nostalgia. Neither Joyce nor any modern writer can count upon that framework of arching, intricate logic which entitles Dante to inscribe, without irony, over Hell-gate:

FECEMI LA DIVINA POTESTATE
LA SOMMA SAPIENZA E IL PRIMO AMORE.

Power, wisdom, and love, here invoked as coordinate forces without the slightest hesitation that they can be shown to work together, simply did not work together for Joyce—as they don't for our world, generally. There is nothing idiosyncratic about Joyce's "bending"; he took it, perhaps, harder than most because the early sense of unusual power and discipline engendered in him the conviction of a special intellectual destiny. No man who sets before him, as Joyce did in youth, the austere and rigorous example of Dante, can fail to be disappointed when he discovers that it is just not possible to write like Dante any more. An early review speaks with lofty contempt of "a young generation which has cast away belief and thrown precision after it, for which Balzac is a great intellect and every sampler who chooses to wander amid his own shapeless hells and heavens a Dante without the unfortunate prejudices of Dante." Except for admiring Balzac, the elder Joyce might be thought to exemplify precisely these terms of disdain formulated by his younger self.

In a famous essay of the twenties much hacked over lately, T. S. Eliot spoke of the "dissociation of sensibility" characteristic of our times as distinguished from the seventeenth century. Whether our sensibility is more dissociated now than it was then may be debated; what causes led to this dissociation (whenever we suppose it to have begun) may provide further subject of speculation. But the fact, simply as a fact, is scarcely open to question. The division between scientific knowledge and human feeling is not, however, the only "dissociation" we have to contend with; rifts and schisms in the world of the mind are so many and so deep that the modern sensibility can't be called simply "dissociated"—it is fractured, splintered, Balkanized. For good or evil, the characteristic arts of our age are unstructured; the invertebrate, episodic novel, music improvised or only loosely patterned, maze-like painting, these are our characteristic products. Not only this, but our social life seems to me more and more unstructured. We are in the age of the independent voter, responsive not to the principles but to moods, in the age of the wildcat strike, directed against union bureaucracy as much as against management. Distinctions between cultures, classes, even levels of mental organization are breaking down; witness, for instance, the peculiar ambivalence taken on by a word like "primitive." I even hear rumors of places where the distinction between the sexes is getting ambiguous.

To such a world, the very ideal of a monolithic structure of compelling belief is irrelevant. Setting aside the nostalgia of my conservative prejudices as unprofitable, I take Joyce as a type of the artist who is willing to live in and write for the future. The world he chose or was forced to choose, seemingly against the very nature of his gift, is the one we now inhabit. Having passed through the latter stages of *Ulysses,* we are entering upon the first pages of *Finnegans Wake,* a murky passage of confused time enlivened only by the incidental jokes of the indifferent. Joyce found not only the available structures of ideas and beliefs, but the very texture of language corrupted; and so undertook, not to build anew, but to write in a way that needed neither conventional ideas nor conventional language. His problem was one which it may not seem too pretentious to describe as a general problem of our time—how to wash clean in dirty water, how to do worthwhile work with bent, second-hand tools. *Finnegans Wake* may be perceived very handsomely as a game of billiards played

> *On a cloth untrue*
> *With a twisted cue*
> *And elliptical billiard balls.*

In its pages, Joyce has successfully performed the reduction of the arts to philology, and so far as is possible reenacted the creation of the cosmos (a new and private cosmos) within the proscenium of his peculiar gift. That he was able to do this using only the junk and litter of the original cosmos is a splendid achievement; but its splendor need not blind us to its perversity, and its perversity cannot be judged independently of the age to which it is a response. Thus we circle back to the *Zeitgeist,* about which it seems we must have opinions.

What Joyce saw (and it is an inevitable part of my argument that he saw truly) was an age of bind and smudge; of consciousness and above all of self-consciousness almost infinite in extent but foggy and unformulated in its topography. A peculiarity of modern feeling, as evident in Franz Kafka and Jackson Pollock as in *Finnegans Wake,* is loss of horizon, obliteration of perspective. Experience flickers through the darkroom of our consciousness like a film projected immensely too fast—out of control, altogether. With straining eyes and anxious small gestures we try to follow the flicker or even react to it; but our best postures are hollow and irrelevant. The language itself is *vermoulu;* the wells of thought and feeling have been fouled. The art of the later Joyce lies in extracting a kind of bubbling gaiety, a verbal vaudeville, from the desolation of this landscape. The old controversy roused by *Ulysses* over Joyce's alleged pessimism or optimism thus fades, for the 1960's, into a mere matter of emphasis. In particular, the view of Joyce as an intricate, unwearying cosmic ironist (a view which leads Hugh Kenner, for example, to see the *Portrait* as primarily an extended assault on Stephen and *Ulysses* as primarily an extended assault on Bloom) seems bound to fade. Joyce did not seek or make a desolation, he found it as in the air we breathe, and extracted from it the juice of a small and flickering joy. He is not the greatest modern ironist, he is the only great modern humorist.

One last speculation. The less we see Joyce's work as an intricate, logically arranged machinery of glittering, sterile edges, and the more we emphasize the commonness of his materials, the more we are likely to think his art itself a work of magic—one which touches, through intuitive insight, the chords of secret, irrational sympathies. These are not fashionable concepts in modern criticism, any more than in modern psychology; but modern criticism and psychology may well be obsolete before *Ulysses* is. In any event, Joyce (following Baudelaire and Mallarmé) himself accepted and made use of substantially this view of his art. An age more impressed than our own by its inability to understand its own reactions may well revert to a view of Joyce as verbal necromancer, if only because the fact of his impact is there, and the available ways of accounting for it are patently inadequate. The middle ages, Bloomishly fond of adapting antique temples into habitable hovels, reworked Apuleius and Virgil into the semblance of warlocks; very probably, in a century or so, the same process will be under way with Joyce. The new age will find, though, that Joyce has been beforehand with them—having not only constructed his own inimitable architectures, but himself pulled some of them down to make shanties and outhouses.

Chronology of Important Dates

1882	James Joyce born February 2 in Rathgar, Dublin. Eldest son in the large family of John Stanislaus Joyce, improvident rate collector and "praiser of his own past," and of Mary Jane ("Mae") Joyce.
1888	Joyce sent to Clongowes Wood College, a Jesuit school, remaining there until 1891.
1891	Death of Charles Stewart Parnell, "the uncrowned King of Ireland," on October 6. Joyce composed his first printed work, *Et Tu, Healy,* which praised the dead leader and attacked his chief political enemy.
1893–1898	Joyce's family in financial decline. Joyce sent to Belvedere College, another Jesuit school.
1899–1902	Joyce at University College, Dublin.
1900	Joyce read his paper "Drama and Life" before the Literary and Historical Society; his essay "Ibsen's New Drama" was published in the *Fortnightly Review.*
1901	His pamphlet attacking the Irish Literary Theatre, "The Day of the Rabblement," was composed.
1902–1903	Joyce left for Paris. Intending to be a medical student, he instead read, studied, wrote reviews, and lived on little food. In April he received a telegram: "MOTHER DYING COME HOME FATHER." He returned and watched her slow death.
1904	First draft of *Stephen Hero.* In June, Joyce met Nora Barnacle and fell in love with her. Together they left Dublin for Zurich, where Joyce expected to teach at the Berlitz School. The Zurich position was not open; they left for Pola, where one was. This year saw the publication, for the first time, of some of his poems and stories.
1905	Joyce was transferred to the Berlitz school in Trieste. His son Giorgio was born. Publishing difficulties with respect to *Dubliners,* not resolved until 1914, began.
1907	*Chamber Music* published. "The Dead" written. His daughter Lucia Anna was born.
1912	Joyce's last trip to Dublin.

1913   Joyce met Ezra Pound, who was able to interest *the Egoist* in the manuscript of *A Portrait of the Artist as a Young Man.*

1914   *Annus mirabilis. Dubliners* published by Grant Richards. Serial publication of *A Portrait* begun in *the Egoist. Ulysses* begun, but put aside for work on *Exiles.*

1915   Joyce departed Trieste for Zurich. After letters from Pound and Yeats, the Royal Literary Fund awarded him a small amount of money.

1916–1917   Publication of *A Portrait* in New York and London, successively. Joyce's eye troubles, not to end in his lifetime, began.

1918   *The Little Review* (New York) began to serialize *Ulysses. Exiles* published in London and New York.

1919   The subsidy of one of his benefactors withdrawn, Joyce took up teaching English at a commercial school in Trieste. His work on *Ulysses* continued.

1920   Pound persuaded Joyce to move to Paris. In New York, publication of *Ulysses* in the *Little Review* was discontinued after a complaint from the Society for the Suppression of Vice.

1922   *Ulysses* published on Joyce's birthday. His eye troubles worsened.

1923   The first pages of *Finnegans Wake* (known until 1939 only as *Work in Progress*) were composed.

1924   The first fragment of *Wake* published in the *Transatlantic Review* (Paris). Most of the book was thereafter to be published in fragments, later to be reworked.

1931   Joyce and Nora Barnacle were married, in London, "for testamentary reasons." Joyce's father died at age 82.

1932   A grandson, Stephen, was born. Lucia Joyce suffered a mental breakdown from which she was never to recover.

1933   In New York, Judge John M. Woolsey decided that *Ulysses* was not pornographic and that its American publication could be permitted.

1934   Lucia's mental health continued to deteriorate, as did Joyce's eyes.

1936   *Collected Poems* published.

1937   The last separate fragment of the *Wake* was published.

1939   Joyce was able to show the first bound copy of the *Wake* on his birthday. Official publication came later in the year.

1940   Joyce and Nora entered Switzerland after a hurried flight from France.

1941   James Joyce died January 13 of a perforated ulcer, in the Schwesterhaus vom Roten Kreuz in Zurich.

Notes on the Editor and Contributors

WILLIAM M. CHACE, the editor of this volume, is Assistant Professor of English at Stanford University. He is the author of *The Political Identities of Ezra Pound and T. S. Eliot* and articles on those two figures.

HÉLÈNE CIXOUS is Professor of English Literature, Université de Paris, Vincennes, and editor of *Poétique*. Her novel *Dedans* was awarded the Prix Medicis in 1969.

RICHARD ELLMANN is Goldsmiths' Professor of English Literature in the University of Oxford. He has also taught at Yale, Northwestern, and Harvard. Among his many publications are *Yeats: The Man and the Masks; The Identity of Yeats; James Joyce;* and *Eminent Domain: Yeats Among Wilde, Joyce, Pound, Eliot and Auden,* and *Ulysses on the Liffey. Golden Codgers: Biographical Speculations* is his most recent book.

HUGH KENNER is Professor of English at Johns Hopkins University; he has also taught at the University of California at Santa Barbara and the University of Virginia. The author of books on Wyndham Lewis, Eliot, Pound, Joyce, and Samuel Beckett, Professor Kenner has most recently published *The Pound Era* and *Bucky: A Guided Tour of Buckminster Fuller.*

EDMUND WILSON, the most widely accomplished and authoritative American man of letters in the last several decades, was, among other things, an early and brilliant student of the Joycean world..

S. L. GOLDBERG is Robert Wallace Professor of English Literature at the University of Melbourne and has also taught at the University of Sydney. He is editor of *The Critical Review: Melbourne-Sydney*. He has published two books on Joyce.

ANTHONY CRONIN, poet, novelist, playwright, critic, and editor, has recently published his *Collected Poems 1950–1973*. His play *The Shame of It* was presented in 1973 by the Abbey Company at the Peacock Theatre, Dublin. A prose narrative, *Dead As Doornails: A Chronicle of Life,* is forthcoming.

HARRY LEVIN is the Irving Babbitt Professor of Comparative Literature at Harvard University. He is the author of myriad books and articles, among them studies of Christopher Marlowe; of Hawthorne, Poe, and Melville; of *Hamlet;* and he has written extensively on general problems of literary criticism.

CLIVE HART is Professor of Literature at the University of Essex. He has written or edited several books on Joyce, including *A Concordance to "Finnegans Wake"* and *James Joyce's "Ulysses";* one on acronautics and one on kites; and he is co-editor of the *Wake Newslitter.*

LIONEL TRILLING, until his retirement the George Edward Woodberry Professor of Literature and Criticism at Columbia University, and now University Professor there, is the author of *Matthew Arnold, The Liberal Imagination, The Opposing Self, Beyond Culture,* and lately, *Sincerity and Authenticity.*

ROBERT MARTIN ADAMS is Professor of English at the University of California at Los Angeles. Among his extensive and wide-ranging publications are books on Milton and the critics, on Stendhal, and on Joyce. His most recent books are *Nil: Episodes in the Literary Conquest of Void During the Nineteenth Century; Proteus: His Lies, His Truths;* and *The Roman Stamp.*

Selected Bibliography

The Texts

Collected Poems. New York: The Viking Press, Inc., 1937. Compass Books, 1957.

Critical Writings of James Joyce. Edited by Richard Ellmann and Ellsworth Mason. New York: The Viking Press, Inc., 1959.

Dubliners: Text, Criticism, and Notes. Edited by Robert Scholes and A. Walton Litz. Viking Critical Library. New York: The Viking Press, Inc., 1969.

Exiles: A Play in Three Acts, Including Hitherto Unpublished Notes by the Author, Discovered after His Death, and an Introduction by Padraic Colum. New York: The Viking Press, Inc., 1951. Compass Books, 1961.

Finnegans Wake. New York: The Viking Press, Inc., 1939.

A First-Draft Version of Finnegans Wake. Edited and annotated by David Hayman. Austin: University of Texas Press, 1963.

Giacomo Joyce. Edited by Richard Ellmann. New York: The Viking Press, Inc., 1968.

The Letters of James Joyce. Vol. 1. Edited by Stuart Gilbert. New York: The Viking Press, Inc.., 1957. New ed. with corrections, 1966. Vols. 2 and 3. Edited by Richard Ellmann. New York: The Viking Press, Inc., 1966.

A Portrait of the Artist as a Young Man: Text, Criticism, and Notes. Edited by Chester G. Anderson. Viking Critical Library. New York: The Viking Press, Inc., 1968.

Stephen Hero. Edited by Theodore Spencer. New ed. with additional material, edited by John J. Slocum and Herbert Cahoon. New York: New Directions Publishing Corporation, 1963.

Ulysses. New York: Random House, Inc., 1934. Rev. ed., 1961.

Bibliographies

Beebe, Maurice, Phillip F. Herring, and Walton Litz. "Criticism of James Joyce: A Selected Checklist." *Modern Fiction Studies,* 15 (Spring 1969), pp. 105–82.

Deming, Robert H. *A Bibliography of James Joyce Studies.* Lawrence: University of Kansas Libraries, 1964.

Slocum, John J., and Herbert Cahoon. *A Bibliography of James Joyce, 1882–1941.* New Haven: Yale University Press, 1953.

Journals

James Joyce Quarterly. Thomas F. Staley, editor. Vol. 1, no. 1 (Fall 1963) to the present.

James Joyce Review. Edmund J. Epstein, editor. Vol. 1, no. 1 (February 2, 1957); ended publication with Vol. 3, no. 1/2 (1959).

Wake Newslitter. Clive Hart and Fritz Senn, editors. No. 1 (March 1962) to no. 18 (December 1963); New Series, Vol. 1, no. 1 (February 1964) to the present.

Biography

Ellmann, Richard. *James Joyce.* New York: Oxford University Press, 1959.

General Criticism and Scholarship

Adams, Robert Martin. *James Joyce: Common Sense and Beyond.* New York: Random House, Inc., 1967.

Burgess, Anthony. *Re Joyce.* New York: W. W. Norton & Company, Inc., 1965. Ballantine Books, Inc., 1966.

Cixous, Hélène. *The Exile of James Joyce.* New York: David Lewis, Inc., 1972.

Givens, Seon, ed. *James Joyce: Two Decades of Criticism.* New York: Vanguard Press, Inc., 1948. Augmented ed., 1963.

Goldberg, S. L. *James Joyce.* New York: Grove Press, Inc., 1962. Capricorn Books, 1972.

Goldman, Arnold. *The Joyce Paradox: Form and Freedom in his Fiction.* Evanston: Northwestern University Press, 1966.

Gross, John. *James Joyce.* New York: The Viking Press, Inc., 1970.

Kenner, Hugh. *Dublin's Joyce.* Bloomington: Indiana University Press, 1956. Beacon Paperbacks, 1962.

Levin, Harry. *James Joyce: A Critical Introduction.* New York: New Directions Publishing Corporation, 1941. Rev. ed., 1960.

Lewis, Wyndham. "An Analysis of the Mind of James Joyce." In *Time and Western Man,* pp. 75–113. New York: Harcourt Brace Jovanovich, Inc., 1928.

Litz, Walton. *The Art of James Joyce: Method and Design in "Ulysses" and "Finnegans Wake."* New York: Oxford University Press, 1961. Galaxy Books, 1964.

Magalaner, Marvin, and Richard M. Kain. *Joyce, the Man, the Work, the Reputation.* New York: New York University Press, 1956.

Noon, William T., S.J. *Joyce and Aquinas.* New Haven: Yale University Press, 1957.

Pound, Ezra. *Pound/Joyce: The Letters of Ezra Pound to James Joyce, with Pound's Essays on Joyce.* Edited by Forrest Read. New York: New Directions Publishing Corporation, 1967.

Tindall, William York. *James Joyce: His Way of Interpreting the Modern World.* New York: Charles Scribner's Sons, 1950.

————. *A Reader's Guide to James Joyce.* New York: Farrar, Straus & Giroux, Inc., The Noonday Press, 1959.

Wilson, Edmund. "James Joyce." In *Axel's Castle: A Study in the Imaginative Literature of 1870–1930*, pp. 191–239. New York: Charles Scribner's Sons, 1931.

Dubliners

Garrett, Peter K. *Twentieth Century Interpretations of "Dubliners": A Collection of Critical Essays.* Englewood Cliffs, N.J.: Prentice-Hall, Inc., 1968.

Gifford, Don. *Notes for Joyce.* New York: E. P. Dutton & Co., Inc., 1967.

Hart, Clive, ed. *James Joyce's "Dubliners": Critical Essays.* London: Faber & Faber, 1969.

Magalaner, Marvin. *Time of Apprenticeship: The Fiction of Young James Joyce.* New York: Abelard-Schuman Limited, 1959.

A Portrait of the Artist as a Young Man

Connolly, Thomas E., ed. *Joyce's "Portrait": Criticisms and Critiques.* New York: Appleton-Century-Crofts, 1962.

Gifford, Don. (See entry under *Dubliners*.)

Morris, William E., and Clifford A. Nault, Jr., eds. *Portraits of an Artist: A Casebook on James Joyce's "A Portrait of the Artist as a Young Man."* New York: Odyssey Press, 1962.

Scholes, Robert E., and Richard M. Kain. *The Workshop of Daedalus: James Joyce and the Raw Materials for "A Portrait of the Artist as a Young Man."* Evanston: Northwestern University Press, 1965.

Schutte, William M., ed. *Twentieth Century Interpretations of "A Portrait of the Artist as a Young Man": A Collection of Critical Essays.* Englewood Cliffs, N.J.: Prentice-Hall, Inc., 1968.

Ulysses

Adams, Robert M. *Surface and Symbol: The Consistency of James Joyce's "Ulysses."* New York: Oxford University Press, 1962.

Blamires, Harry. *The Bloomsday Book: A Guide Through Joyce's "Ulysses."* New York: Barnes & Noble Books, 1966.

Cronin, Anthony. "The Advent of Bloom." In *A Question of Modernity*, pp. 58–96. London: Secker and Warburg, 1966.

Eliot, T. S. "*Ulysses*, Order and Myth." *The Dial*, 75 (November 1923), 480–83.

Ellmann, Richard. *Ulysses on the Liffey.* New York: Oxford University Press, 1972.

Empson, William. "The Theme of *Ulysses*." *Kenyon Review*, 18 (Winter 1956), 26–52.

Gilbert, Stuart. *James Joyce's "Ulysses."* 2d rev. ed. New York: Alfred A. Knopf, Inc., 1952.

Goldberg, S. L. *The Classical Temper: A Study of James Joyce's "Ulysses."* London: Chatto and Windus, 1961.

Hart, Clive. *James Joyce's "Ulysses."* Sydney, Australia: Sydney University Press, 1968.

Jung, C. C. *"Ulysses:* A Monologue." Translated by W. Stanley Dell. *Nimbus,* 2 (June–August 1953), pp. 7–20.

Kain, Richard M. *Fabulous Voyager: James Joyce's "Ulysses."* Chicago: University of Chicago Press, 1947.

Schutte, William M. *Joyce and Shakespeare: A Study in the Meaning of "Ulysses."* New Haven: Yale University Press, 1957.

Shechner, Mark. *Joyce in Nighttown: A Psychoanalytic Inquiry into "Ulysses."* Berkeley: University of California Press, 1974.

Sultan, Stanley. *The Argument of "Ulysses."* Columbus: Ohio State University Press, 1964.

Thornton, Weldon. *Allusions in "Ulysses": An Annotated List.* Chapel Hill: University of North Carolina Press, 1968.

West, Alick. "James Joyce: *Ulysses.*" In *Crisis and Criticism,* pp. 143–80. London: Lawrence and Wishart, 1937.

Finnegans Wake

Atherton, James S. *The Books at the Wake: A Study of Literary Allusions in James Joyce's "Finnegans Wake."* New York: The Viking Press, Inc., 1960.

Beckett, Samuel, et al. *James Joyce—"Finnegans Wake": A Symposium.* Original title: *Our Exagmination Round his Factification for Incamination of "Work in Progress."* New York: New Directions Publishing Corporation, 1942.

Benstock, Bernard. *Joyce-Again's Wake.* Seattle: University of Washington Press, 1965.

Campbell, Joseph, and Henry Morton Robinson. *A Skeleton Key to "Finnegans Wake."* New York: Harcourt Brace Jovanovich, Inc., 1944. Compass Books, 1961.

Dalton, Jack P., and Clive Hart, eds. *Twelve and a Tilly: Essays on the Occasion of the 25th Anniversary of "Finnegans Wake."* Evanston: Northwestern University Press, 1965.

Glasheen, Adaline. *A Census of "Finnegans Wake."* Evanston: Northwestern University Press, 1956.

———. *A Second Census of "Finnegans Wake."* Evanston: Northwestern University Press, 1963.

Hart, Clive. *Structure and Motif in "Finnegans Wake."* Evanston: Northwestern University Press, 1962.

———, and Fritz Senn, eds.. *A "Wake" Digest.* Sydney, Australia: Sydney University Press, 1968.

Tindall, William York. *A Reader's Guide to "Finnegans Wake."* New York: Farrar, Straus & Giroux, Inc., 1969.

Wilson, Edmund. "The Dream of H. C. Earwicker." In *The Wound and the Bow,* pp. 243–71. New York: Oxford University Press, 1947.